KINK

KINK

AN AUTOBIOGRAPHY
KINK
DAVE DAVIES

HYPERION
NEW YORK

First published in Great Britain in 1996 by
Boxtree Limited, Broadwall House, 21 Broadwall, London SE1 9PL

Library of Congress Cataloging-in-Publication Data
Davies, Dave, 1947–
    Kink : an autobiography / Dave Davies.
        p.   cm.
    Includes discography and index.
    ISBN 0-7868-6149-5
    1. Kinks (Musical group) 2. Davies, Dave, 1947–   . 3. Rock
        musicians—England—Biography.   I. Title.
    ML421.K56D38   1997
    782.42166'092'2—dc20
    [B]   96-24545
            CIP
            MN

FIRST HYPERION EDITION
10 9 8 7 6 5 4 3 2 1

To the memory of my dear mother and father.
To my family.
To Nancy for her understanding and love.
To all my children,
who are a constant source of love and inspiration.

ACKNOWLEDGEMENTS
Special thanks to B. J. Robbins for her editorial assistance, enthusiasm and help, my sister Joyce, Doug Hinman, Doris, Sarah Lockwood, Jeremy Wakefield, Gordon Scott Wise.

YEARS FRAGMENTED

*Years fragmented, heroes and villains. The victors and
vanquished all now but bit part players in sweating dreams.
Brandy, cocaine, beer and laughter, curly-haired groupies
with big tits, angels and whores, the innocent and lost, the
users, the used . . .
The gay, the fray, the tattered and torn pull at my thoughts
pleading not to be forgotten, overlooked.
Roadies with aching backs, shifting gear, dreaming of
blow-jobs, drinking everything in sight, fucking anything
that comes near . . .
Balding record company executives, road crew, sluts and
fans, all end up in the noisy room party at the end of the
hall, the same as always, as if planned.
Grinning and drinking, partying long into the night.
Everyone looking for something so special yet never quite
getting it right . . .
A false sense of awareness stabs you awake, the sun shines
through the window, revealing the debris, what a state.
Morning smells of pizza, toothpaste and shit, of beer,
stagnant air, grass and wine.
The bathroom a shambles, Oh my God, my head, what happened,
is this room really mine? . . .
Next to you a beautiful stranger who talked through the
night, who tried so hard . . . putting the world to right.
Can't remember a word, or even her name. Where am I? TV
cackles to itself in the corner spewing out the absurd and inane . . .
Paranoia calls, distorted voices tease, tormenting my mind.
Hey, hang on, whose clothes are these?
The mirror stares back, holding its secrets yet telling
no lies. Six thousand miles from home, a million miles from
sanity . . .
Through the open door I see opposite, a Puerto Rican room
service waiter sniffing for tips.
Large big-arsed maids with puzzled expressions looking for
the bed, dismantled in shreds . . .
Holiday Inns, vodkas, gins, old roadies with golden memories
to share down the pub when the money runs thin.
Tarmac and airports, limos and tour buses, virgins and
hookers, young girls trying so hard not to give in . . .*

*A greedy sloth shakes the hand of the giver, the serpent
smokes a joint with the saint, a world so full of expression
trying so hard to be what it ain't . . .
Fragmented years, countless fears, cynical pressmen with
treacherous grins.
Kiss arsing, back stage passing, always ready to pounce,
he'll sell your soul if he could get it, make you a star
for an ounce . . .
Amplifiers full on, outrageous battered old Queens, at their
age still trying it on.
Dressing-room tantrums, guitars that won't tune, drums and
spotlights, ecstasy, misery, and boredom . . .
The pain and the strain all those beautiful days, the souls who
passed and who coloured my life.
A circus for the lost and alone to come, stand out of the
rain, under one sheltered roof, I pray that they all made it
home all right . . .
Merchandise sold, equipment trucks drive, another town
beckons, long-distance calls to the wife.
Yes I do, no I haven't, what, of course I'm not drunk, I
wish!
I close my eyes and smile and thank God that I'm still here
and that there's nothing I have missed . . .*

1

When my brother Ray and I formed the Kinks in the early 1960s, I never imagined that more than thirty years later we'd still be recording and performing all over the world. That we'd still be playing rock 'n' roll. I was a teenager when we had our first hit, 'You Really Got Me', in 1964, a wild and angry kid who suddenly had more money than I'd ever seen before, and an abundance of women and drugs at my disposal. I was sure that the party would end at any moment, and I wanted to live it up while I could. I never planned for the future. Who would have guessed that the Kinks would survive? Everything seemed effortless in those early days, with hit after hit and fans in every country, but as the years wore on the struggles became greater, the battles more brutal, the mind games more intense, weirder, and the lows much lower. It got to the point where it seemed that nothing good ever happened without a fight of some kind; with band members, management, record companies and, of course, my brother. My battles with Ray are notorious in the rock world, and as I reflect back on this crazy life I'm still trying to figure out what happened between us then and what continues to go on between us now. Maybe I'll never know. But one thread that's remained constant throughout these years is my love of music – and it's music, really, that has made it all happen. A great and powerful motivating force in my life.

When I was sixteen, I discovered how to make my guitar scream. It was an exciting and, as it turned out, an extremely dangerous moment. It happened in the front room of my parents' house in Muswell Hill, a small suburb of north London. The year was 1963 and what I had on my mind mostly that year, besides girls and football, was guitars.

I bought a small 10-watt amplifier called an Elpico from a local radio shop for about £6. It had a seven-inch speaker, and two controls, one for volume and one for tone. I always loved to mess around with amplifiers. One rainy afternoon, I decided to experiment with all the amplifiers I could get my hands on. There was an old 60-watt Linear amp, bought from an *Exchange & Mart* magazine; an old radiogram; my little Elpico amp; and my much prized Vox AC 30. Knowing very little about the possible consequences, I managed to plug each amp into the other. My guitar was plugged first into the Elpico. I took two wires from bare speaker terminals that were exposed at the back, put jack-plugs on the ends of them, then plugged them into the input of the Linear amp. I repeated the exercise with the radiogram. Finally I plugged the last lead into the AC 30. I turned on the mains and momentarily got the most crackling, distorted sound I had ever heard.

Suddenly, in less than the time it took to think about, I found myself on the other side of the room, thrown, landing in a heap with an almighty thud. One of the speaker wires had somehow got inadvertently crossed with a transformer on the back of the Linear amp – a very cheap, unsafe product in the best of situations. The shock passed right through me. My mum came running into the room and stared at me lying there on the floor. She was startled and confused, as I had evidently fused all the lights in the house.

This near fatal but, luckily, only minor setback turned out to be a useful experiment in the long run. I was determined to figure out what went wrong. The next time, I plugged the Elpico loudspeaker's output leads into the input of the AC 30, in effect using the smaller amp as kind of a pre-amp. It sounded great, but I wasn't satisfied. The crowning glory of my simple yet effective experiment was to slash the speaker cone of the Elpico with a razor blade so that the material, although now shredded, still remained intact with the outer side of the cone. As it vibrated it produced a distorted and jagged roar. In fact, the original set-up was so crude that the main amp's hum was almost as loud as the sound I had created. A sound was born, but I didn't know it at the time. Immediately I started using my set-up in live shows that I performed with Ray and our band, in the time leading up to the creation of the Kinks. Ironically, it was that sound, which we used on 'You Really Got Me,' that got the Kinks our first hit.

One afternoon in March 1964, Ray and I were fooling around in my parents' front room, the same room where I had previously flown through the air. Ray was playing jazz riffs on the piano while I was working on refining my guitar sound, bashing out heavy three-fingered bar chords that were by then becoming an important part of my playing style. We had recently seen a film called *Jazz on a Hot Summer's Day*. It was memorable for two reasons: it was the first time we'd seen Chuck Berry perform live and the first time we ever saw Jimmy Giuffre performing the tune 'The Train and the River'. Ray and I were mesmerized by Jimmy Giuffre's tenor sax riffs. Chuck Berry was fantastic; he was in at the very beginning of something that was going to change the face of popular music and it seemed as if he knew it. His back-up musicians were old jazzers and it seemed like they were taking the piss out of him behind his back. They didn't understand what was really going on, looking smug and almost condescending in the background. They just didn't get it. But Ray and I did.

Ray called me over to the piano to listen to a riff he was playing. It was, of course, the 'You Really Got Me' riff. He was playing it with just two fingers. F G G F G. I wondered what it would sound like as bar chords on my guitar with my new amp sound. So I tried it. It was as if something magical had descended upon us in that modest little room. Ray shifted the riff a tone. G A A G A. Then he repeated the same riff in D. I blared out the chords on my guitar. It was wonderful, instinctual. Ray went away and a day or so later came back with some lyrics. *Girl, you really got me going, you got me so I don't know what I'm doing.* Listening to that was so pure, so inexplicably pure and exhilarating. I would use the feelings I experienced that first time Ray and I played 'You Really Got Me' as a barometer in later years as a way of judging many other songs and music we'd compose, record and perform.

If those feelings were a high, they were only a sample of what was to come. That front room in Muswell Hill would prove to be fertile ground for some very creative times ahead. I flew for the first time in that room. After that I used a heavy dose of determination and a sense of purpose to develop the means to stay aloft.

Ray and I were the seventh and eighth of eight children of Annie Florence and Frederick George Davies, and the only boys. My sisters – Rose, Dolly, Joyce, Peg (Kathleen), Rene (Irene), and Gwen – and their husbands, not to mention my uncle Frank, my mother's brother, were always in our house in Muswell Hill. It was a small end-terrace house, not really big enough for a large family which grew to include grandkids and extended families, but somehow we managed. It was always fun and exciting there, and I have very great memories of parties every Saturday night in that house.

My mum and dad never had much money, but at Christmas and at birthdays we never went without. I knew that sometimes things were difficult, and it must have been hard for them to meet the needs of such a large family, juggling everyone's wants with such limited resources. I understood this at a young age, which only increased my desire to help them.

My mum's dad, Albert Wilmore, was evidently an only child, the product of very wealthy parents and the subject of a great family legend. As a young man he was put into the army but he didn't like it, so his parents bought out his commission. He met his wife soon after. My mum's mum, Katherine Emily Bowden, was known to us as Big Granny. She was born in 1878 and had quite a dramatic entrance into the world. She was a foundling, left on a doorstep because her parents (her father, she learned later, was a hansom cab driver) wanted a son. The doorstep they left her on belonged to a spinster relative named Aunt Anne. When Albert's family found out that he was marrying beneath him – to an orphan – they disinherited him. It was a long fall from grace for him, from great wealth to sudden poverty.

The only thing young, disenfranchised Albert knew about was horses, so he became a horse and cart driver for the railway. I guess not having siblings had a profound effect on both Albert and Big Granny because they had twenty-one children, including my mum, Annie. Mum always used to tell me about how she and her siblings had to sleep five to a bed, with three at the bottom and two at the top, and just one blanket between them. I can only imagine the kind of chaos that ensued in that household.

Little Granny was my dad's mum. Her name was Amy Kelly and, being one of a large family in Ireland, she was sent to

England to work as a servant. She later married my grandfather, Harry Davies, who came from the Rhondda Valley in Wales. He had probably been a miner at one point, but eventually came to be a slaughterman and trained our dad to be the same.

As a young woman my mum worked in a bronzing factory but was fired after she fell asleep on the job. She found another job at a coffee shop near the cattle market at the back of King's Cross. One evening a bloke who worked in the cattle market came in and asked her out and she ended up marrying him. It was the old man, of course.

When they first married, Mum and Dad lived in an awful place called Beaconsfield Buildings, near Farringdon Street. They moved several times before landing in Cumming Street, King's Cross. Cumming Street was where most of our sisters came into the world: Rosie, in 1924, Rene, 1926; Dolly, 1928; Joyce, 1930; and Peggy, 1932. Nevertheless, Joyce remembers the house as 'a terrible place' – especially because it was there that Peggy, as a little girl, was in a terrible accident.

There were railings outside the house and Peggy, who was not yet two, was leaning against them while playing with some other children. All of a sudden a lorry came careering down the road that had evidently been stolen from St Pancras station. It took the bend badly, and smashed into the children and into the railings. All the children were hurt, but Peggy came off the worst. One arm was permanently damaged, and she also lost some of her hearing. She spent a great deal of time in and out of hospital. It's ironic, when I think about it. In the end, it would be Rene who would suffer the greatest tragedy of all the sisters. Peggy, although badly injured, would survive to tell her story.

The family moved around the corner to Rodney Place in 1933 and stayed there until 1939. In 1938 Gwenny was born, the year, Joyce recalls, of 'the Crisis'. Children were being evacuated from London to the country because of the impending war. Mum had got all the children ready to go, from Rosie, who had just left school, to baby Gwen, but at the last minute she couldn't do it. She just couldn't send her children away. So in the autumn of 1939 she moved the family to a house in Huntingdon Road, East Finchley, just outside London.

Unfortunately, most of the children in Huntingdon Road had already been evacuated. This left a neighbourhood of a lot of older people who were not interested in seeing Annie and Frederick's brood of girls. They were a noisy lot, and it didn't help that Little Granny lived with them along with her daughter, my dad's sister Rosie. It was a big house, but there were constant complaints from the retired neighbours. After six months, the experiment had truly not worked. Mum, ever plucky, got the message and moved the whole gang once more, to Denmark Terrace in Fortis Green.

It was January 1940. The Fortis Green house, where I was eventually to grow up, was smaller than the one on Huntingdon Road. The only positive development was that it had a lower rent, so it was no longer necessary for Little Granny to chip in. Her daughter, my aunt Rosie, got married and moved away. Eventually Little Granny went to live with her and her husband in south London.

The war was now fully under way. Dad was working as a slaughterman, as his own father had, which in those days was termed a 'Reserved Occupation'. This meant that men like him were not sent to war because they were needed to produce food at home. The family, meanwhile, grew and grew. In 1943, the year before Ray was born, my sister Rosie got married to Arthur. Ray was born in 1944. Rosie and Arthur had their son, Terry, in 1945. I was born in 1947. The story goes that my mum was so embarrassed to be having another child at forty-two that she didn't tell anyone she was pregnant. She was a large woman, so she didn't think anyone would notice. Even her own mother didn't know. All of a sudden I appeared on the scene, to everyone's surprise.

The house on Denmark Terrace was already quite full by the time I arrived. Dolly and her husband Joe got married at the same time as Joyce and her husband Ken and they all lived there. Dolly had the upstairs front room; Joyce had the upstairs back. Mum and Dad would sleep downstairs in the middle room. Peggy and Gwenny slept upstairs in the middle room. And, of course, there was Ray and me! When I was very small I slept with Mum and Dad, and then when I was a little older Ray and I shared a bed. In 1950, when I was three, Joyce and Ken had a baby girl, Irene, which only added to the confusion. Joyce and Ken eventually moved next door when it became vacant. They later had a son called Phillip.

Around that time Peg, who was a bit of a loner, would often go out dancing in the West End. She met a black guy and before she knew it she was pregnant. It was unthinkable to have an illegitimate baby at that time, so Peg and the fellow made plans to get married. But he was in the country illegally and was deported to France (he was from French West Africa). Peg gave birth to a little girl named Jacqueline Michelle, whom we called Jackie. It was considered a terrible scandal for a white English-woman to have a black child, and while Ray and I thought nothing of it and treated her like a sister, Jackie suffered terribly when she went to school. Children were horribly cruel – and adults as well. I always felt very protective of that sweet, happy little girl, as did my mum, who was more a mother to her than Peg. One day Mum found out that Jackie had been abused by her kindergarten teacher. 'The fat old cow', as Mum called her, had been locking Jackie in a darkened cupboard. She went round to the teacher's house and nearly pulled the woman's hair out. I remember hearing her say, 'Did I give 'er what for!' Mum was tough, but she had to be. She had a sad and hard life.

Life was never dull in the Davies household, not with so many of us around. Age differences played a big part in our house, as they would with any big family. After all, our sisters had children who were close to both Ray and me in age. We certainly thought of them as siblings. My sister Dolly's son, Michael Warwick, was three years younger than me but more like a brother to me than Ray. Luckily Dolly and her husband Joe lived in my parents' house and so Michael and I became very close. Even after they moved into their own place in Highgate, I spent a great deal of time with them. Joe, who worked as a truck driver and then a bus driver, was very protective of me. He made me feel like Mike's older brother and as much a part of their family as of my own. They never had any money but Dolly was very resourceful and there was always enough food. Dolly loved the music of Hank Williams and Slim Whitman. She particularly liked Fats Domino, Les Paul and Mary Ford. Dolly was also a sexy dancer. I loved to watch her at parties. Joe always reminded me of a taller version of James Cagney, rugged, confident and cool. Dolly and Joe had three other children besides Michael. June was the eldest, then Mike, followed by Coral and Paul. Mike, though, was special to me, a sensitive and loyal friend.

When I was a little boy I was quite mischievous. Mum had to be the disciplinarian; she would hit me with a broomstick if she was lucky enough to catch me, or pull me by the hair whenever I got caught doing something naughty, which was often. Of course this wasn't considered abusive in those days, but simply typical working-class behaviour. Often it was more 'threat' than anything unsavoury. Dad was usually in the pub when he wasn't working and was quite a womanizer, I found out later. He was always after some floozie or other, and while my deep love for him hasn't diminished over the years, I do feel badly that Mum had to suffer in silence. Divorce was virtually unheard of in working-class families at the time. As Mum would have said, 'You've made yer bed . . .'

Having so many older sisters afforded me great opportunities to learn about the ways of women, and as a young boy I loved to sneak a peek at my sisters dressing and undressing. They all had such lovely flowing hair and such wonderful figures, sexy and beautiful breasts. Peggy looked like Marilyn Monroe, with her long wavy hair dyed blonde, and with a figure to match. She was beautiful and fashion-conscious. In fact they all were. They all wanted to look glamorous.

My sisters would often go ballroom dancing, which was all the rage when they were growing up in the forties and fifties, before 'trad' and jive. They danced to the music of Victor Sylvester, the foxtrot and the quickstep – all strict tempo dancing. Joyce was a member of a dance club in Finchley Central called the Arcadia. She sometimes went there five or six times a week. Many years later these memories would become the inspiration for the Kinks hit 'Come Dancing' in 1982.

Music filled our house all the time. The most important piece of furniture in the front room, before television took hold, was the piano. All my sisters played; Rene was the best, although Joyce and Gwen eventually became quite accomplished as well. The girls also had a 78 rpm wind-up gramophone on which they played records Rosie had bought. She brought Judy Garland and Gene Kelly into the house with songs like 'For Me and My Girl' and 'When You Wore A Ribbon'.

However, records were not as popular then as they later became. The big thing directly after the war was going to the cinema. Joyce worked as an usherette in a local theatre and there was constant talk in the house about this latest film or that. The whole family would go to the cinema at least once a week. We'd queue up outside the theatre, children and all.

But our greatest form of entertainment was the parties at our house every Saturday night. The whole family would come, including Uncle Frankie, Mum's brother, and all the aunties; and Dad's mates and cronies from the pub. The men would go to the pub, buy a few bottles of spirits and crates of ale, and come back and the piano would be opened. Dad used to dance and play the banjo. Then Mum would be down in the kitchen, where she always managed to whip up a plate of sandwiches. The music went on until two or three in the morning, music-hall stuff, songs from the thirties. 'Bye, Bye Blackbird', 'If You Were the Only Girl in the World', 'My Old Man Said Follow the Van'. Everyone had a special song. Dad's was an old song by the Victorian music-hall entertainer Gus Ealing, about the warnings and pitfalls of marriage. I think it was called 'Underneath the Thumb'.

*It's a great big shame and if she belonged to me, I'd let her know
   who's who
Naggin' at a fella who is six foot four and her only four feet two
Well they hadn't been married for a month or more when
   underneath the thumb goes Jim
Oh isn't it a pity that the likes of her should put upon the likes of
   him.*

But of all our sisters it was Rene who surprised us and changed our closely knit world. She was fragile, born with heart disease. Rheumatic fever, which she had had as a child, left her with a hole in her heart. Nevertheless, she got married in 1945 to a Canadian Army soldier, and moved to Canada as a war bride soon after. Her husband was known as Big Bob, but not in any affectionate way. My mother and sisters knew that he neglected Rene, who was sick much of the time, and their child. Joyce remembers him as a drunken bully who did not mind taking a crack at his ailing wife from time to time.

I met my sister Rene for the first time in 1952. I was five and Ray was eight, I guess. She was with her son, Bobby, who was around my age. She had left Bob and had taken a job at an optician's in the High Road, East Finchley, while little Bobby went to school temporarily.

Many years later I read some of the letters Rene had sent to Mum from Canada, secretly kept and squirrelled away. They were airmail letters treasured with great love and affection, but with words that in part must have wrenched bitterly at my Mum's heart:

'Mum, I've got a surprise for you. Me and Bobby are coming home. It should be soon . . . I'll send a telegram when I know for sure. I shall be getting my Army allowance as usual. I'm really looking forward to seeing you all so much. The doctors say it should be all right to travel soon . . . Bob seems to find his friends a lot better company than us these days. He stays out quite a lot, but as long as he doesn't get nasty with us, I don't ask him about his affairs. So we don't have many arguments . . .'

But after about a year she was lured back to Canada to meet with a specialist who was pioneering a new operation on heart valves. She wanted that operation so desperately. I remember being mesmerized by a story Rene related to the family around the kitchen table in Denmark Terrace shortly after she returned to England after her operation.

'I was lying on the operating table,' she said. 'But I started to float up to the ceiling. As I looked down I could see my body below. It was such an incredible feeling. I felt light as a feather. As I looked ahead I saw these two colours coming at me from opposite sides. One was red. One was green. I instinctively knew that I had to somehow keep these colours apart. Somehow I knew if they met, I would die. I had to use all the power of my will to keep them apart.'

Rene had been a great inspiration to Ray. Often she would sit with him patiently at the piano, showing him chords and notes. She knew that his talent needed nurturing and knew how to do it. She had been a teacher in Canada and knew how to deal with difficult children.

Rene lent my mother the money to buy Ray his first guitar, which was to be given to him on his thirteenth birthday. But sadly and tragically 21 June 1957 was to prove an awful date for the Davies family, for that was the day that Rene died. She was thirty-one. Mum always maintained that even though Rene had been ill, Big Bob put her in an early grave.

She knew the night before that it was the end, so Mum told me many years later. But she went out dancing anyway, at the

Lyceum Ballroom in the Strand. It was a favourite haunt of hers and she collapsed and died in the arms of a stranger on the dance floor. Doing what she loved to do the best. Dancing. What dreadful mixed feelings my brother must have experienced on that following morning. For months he had been on and on about that bloody guitar in the window of Les Aldrich in Muswell Hill and now at last his wish was to come true. But he was sadly denied the joy of receiving it, having to come to terms suddenly with the shock of Rene's death. Not only had we lost our sister, but Ray had also lost a mentor and source of inspiration.

There was a movie out at the time about a man who develops a strange paralysis and is admitted to the hospital. After much observation and examination he is finally declared dead. The voice-over in the movie is that of the poor man, despairing and anguished to the point of utter terror, knowing that he is alive but totally paralysed. He is unable to communicate the slightest movement to the outside world, even to move his eyelashes. Even his heart has stopped. He is certified clinically dead.

As he is wheeled out of the hospital and into the morgue, a nurse notices a tear fall from his cheek. He is not as dead as he looks. The memory of that movie is stuck in my mind alongside Rene's death. Being buried alive was a recurring phobia of hers. Mum told me Rene had requested that if anything ever happened to her she was to be cremated, her fear was so great. And so she was.

After his mother died, little Bobby – my nephew – grew up as a brother to me. We were very close. Some years later Bobby traced his father to a hospital in Canada where he was being treated for pernicious dementia brought about by alcohol abuse. He could barely sign his name, but got one of the hospital staff to help him write a letter to his son. I remember Bobby telling me it was a letter full of loneliness and remorse.

Just as I had somehow drifted to one of our satellite families, so did Ray. He spent much of his early adolescence with our sister Rose and her husband, Arthur. (Arthur later became a recurring character in our music, and we were to name an album after him.) Ray developed a relationship early on with their son, Terry, and in the same way that I was close to my nephews Michael and

Bobby, Terry and Ray were probably more brother-like in their relationship than Ray and I.

Of all our sisters, Rosie was the most strict and disciplined. I always felt it was she who truly understood Ray. Rosie could somehow reach inside him and get at the source of what was bothering him. He never got away with anything with her. I, on the other hand, got away with murder.

As a boy, Ray always seemed like an outsider. He was withdrawn, quiet, and reticent at joining in with other kids. We didn't play together much, but I do remember a time when we created an unusual bond. Ray was thirteen and I was about ten and we had just seen a strange French film about a man named 'Lion' who had escaped from an insane asylum. He stood in doorways talking to himself and had a full mane of long hair, hence his name. This odd character had become a social outcast. He never understood or came to terms with the world and preferred to live in one of his own. As a way of protecting himself from the onslaught of a vicious, spiteful world, he developed his own language which nobody could understand. Ray and I thought this strange character hilarious. Ray would often draw little cartoons depicting him, and we invented our own little 'mad' language. The words were gibberish, but we spoke them as if they had great meaning and would crack ourselves up laughing. Although it seems awfully silly now, this was one of the closest times I can remember sharing with Ray while growing up. And this sharing of a similar sense of humour would help greatly to sustain us in difficult situations that were to come, although it would never be enough, sadly, to repair all our differences.

When Ray was about eleven or twelve Mum would take him 'up the clinic', as she used to say, for counselling with a psychologist because he seemed unusually depressed and quiet for such a young boy. Of course, seeking psychiatric help was not openly discussed in our house because in those days, especially in provincial Muswell Hill, psychiatry was frowned upon. People were not very tolerant about mental therapy: if you went to a psychiatrist, you were considered a loony! Nevertheless, Mum was smart enough to know that Ray was troubled in a way the rest of us had not been. At least not noticeably. She was looking, however much in vain, for some answers.

I remember on one occasion, when I was around nine or ten,

Dad told me he was concerned about Raymond, as he had such soft, tender hands. I would be all right, he went on to say, because mine were firm and tough.

Ray sleepwalked quite often and one night it was particularly disturbing. I awoke at one or two in the morning to see Ray standing bolt upright with his eyes large and glazed, staring into open space at the edge of the bed. I slowly got up to approach him and as I did, he began shouting incoherently and ran out of the room. He was no longer sleepwalking: he was sleep*running*! I yelled for Mum and we chased after him as he sped, trancelike, down the stairs. How he didn't fall or bump into something was a miracle. By this time the whole household was awake.

Ray ran out into the garden with me calling out to him, 'What's the matter, what's the matter?' He was in full sprint and charging through the underbrush at the foot of the garden. 'Help, help,' he shouted, 'it's that tiger, he's chasing me.' I was very scared by this time.

Mum finally grabbed him and shook him awake, while Dad looked on in his usual calm, amused and nonchalant manner. Ray soon woke up and scanned our faces with much surprise. He genuinely did not know what had happened. I realized that night even though I was the younger brother, I would somehow have to fulfil the role of the older one and keep a look-out for him. Shit. I was worried that life was becoming more serious.

Much has been said over the years about the rivalry between Ray and me, and I believe a lot of the difficulties we've had as adults were planted as seeds when we were very young. My sister Joyce recalls that when Ray was a toddler he would often try to sing out loud before he could talk – particularly at those family parties where there was lots of music and singing. He'd wave his arms and sing 'Temptation', to the amusement of everyone. But then I came along and stole a bit of his space in the limelight. As the baby of the family I was constantly being spoiled and adored by my mother, sisters, and other family members. Of course he was loved equally, but as the years went by he became more shy and withdrawn, and many hidden jealousies and resentments would surface, unleashing themselves in cruel and abusive ways.

In those early days I wasn't really aware that Ray and I had any real problems between us. We weren't close but we both gravitated towards music and the guitar. Ray learned to play guitar before me. Early on he developed a classical style of playing which was very impressive. Our sister Peg's husband, Mike, who was an electronics buff as well as a musician, gave him lessons and Ray took to them right away. Where my style of playing was rough and ready, self-taught, more natural, Ray had a better hook on remembering notation and reading music. Like many other rockers at that time, I would listen intently to records I liked and pick out the riffs. To me, music was a great awakening light, a voracious liberator of my feelings and a way to express my personality.

I was never much of a student, at least in the conventional sense. At the age of eleven I left St James Primary School after flunking an exam called the eleven-plus. It was an examination which was supposed to separate the so-called academics from the average students. Those who passed would go on to a grammar school; those who didn't, like Ray and myself, were condemned to life in the comprehensive school system. Of course our older sister Gwen, who was the most academic one in the family, had already passed the same exam with flying colours. Clever drawers. Before I even took that test, I knew I had failed. The continuous brow-beating by various teachers and by the school system had prepared me quite suitably for failure. The fear I felt walking into that room on the day of the eleven-plus is never far away. I was so nervous I couldn't remember one answer.

I would end up at the William Grimshaw School, where my troubles only became worse academically and better musically. Still, in my first few days I had to prove myself. As an initiation, or hazing, by the young thugs who ruled the school playground, a newcomer was stretched out along the wire mesh fence outside. Hands and arms were then pressed painfully against it until submission. Fortunately, because I knew many of the older boys – Ray, his friends, my older nephews – I was saved some of the humiliation and pain. At least temporarily, I was protected by them.

It was at the William Grimshaw School that I set out to impress a woman for the first time. She was Miss Joshua, my English and French teacher, and I had a terrible crush on her. I actually excelled for some time at both subjects.

Towards the end of that year, I had taken up boxing and was picked alongside others, including Ray, to represent the school in the Middlesex School Boxing Championships. Both Ray and I had had some practice with boxing. There were always boxing gloves and things in the house that belonged to my sister Dolly's husband Joe, whose brother had been an amateur boxer. One day Ray and I decided to have a boxing match in the front room. I was nine, he twelve. I caught him with a lucky punch. As he fell he hit the side of his head on the piano. I thought I had killed him. He was lying there with his eyes closed and I was bent over, shaking him. I said, 'Ray, Ray, whatsa matter, are you OK?' I was overcome with concern and panic.

I got really close to see if he was breathing. Suddenly he opened his eyes, and with a vicious and angry glare he raised his right arm and punched me full in the face.

On the day of the championships, I met my opponent outside the dressing-rooms. His friends were giving me a hard time, trying to psych me out by telling me what a great fighter he was. 'The last guy who fought him wound up in the hospital,' someone said, which made an impression on me no matter how I thought about it.

The time came for me to approach the ringside. I was terrified. What had I let myself in for? There was no turning back, especially since Miss Joshua was visible from where I stood. Through my fear I stepped up into the ring and glanced across to that kind and beautiful woman. Miss Joshua smiled affectionately back at me. I looked across at my opponent and then back to my teacher. And then at the floor. The bell rang out for the start of the first round. I shuffled hesitantly into the centre of the ring and closer to my much-feared opponent. Trembling, I lashed out at him with as much viciousness as I could possibly muster. Suddenly I became lost in the excitement of the moment. It was overwhelming. Several minutes seemed to pass before the referee stopped the fight. I'd won. I'd beaten the shit out of the other guy. The joy of victory was nothing compared to the look of approval and pleasure I received from Miss Joshua. I will never forget her shy smile. What a treasured moment that was; my soul had come alive.

Some time later that afternoon, long after receiving my small, yet coveted, prize of a silver medallion, I watched Ray's match.

Ray had been drawn against a young amateur champion from the district who was a boxer of some acclaim and of far greater experience than he. It was so painful to watch the fight; I flinched at every blow, winced at every punch. I was torn between my own joy over winning, and concern and worry for my brother. I was so relieved to hear the final bell. Ray had lost the bout, but had won much respect and admiration from the crowd for the courageous fight he'd put up against a more seasoned boxer. I burst with pride.

My boxing career did not last long. Even though my sports teacher thought I had potential, the following season I gave up boxing in favour of music, football, and girls. Just seeing the older boys with flattened noses and puffed-up ears made me decide to keep my looks.

What was also missing was Miss Joshua, who'd married and, sadly for me, left the school. With her went my optimism about academics; my previous resentments of school life flooded back. I viewed the teachers and the school with contempt. I even formed a gang with my friend George Harris, called the Black Hand Gang. Each member had to wear a black glove on the right hand. There was security in numbers; being in a gang was a means of survival.

It was around that time, when I was twelve, that I got my first guitar, a Harmony Meteor. I taught George how to play and we would often skip school and spend hours playing blues records at his house while his mother was at work. The guitar – and our love of music – was bringing me and Ray closer as well. At weekends my brother-in-law Mike introduced us to the music of everyone from Django Reinhardt to Earl Scruggs. Other important influences were Buddy Holly, Eddie Cochran, Little Richard, Johnny Cash and Lonnie Donegan. Peg was a big fan of Johnny Ray and Perry Como and would often sing songs like 'Volare' and 'Little Darling' accompanied by Mike on guitar. Mike was a really fine guitar player, and a big fan of jazz guitarist Diz Dizzly. One record we especially liked was the Hawaiian War Chant. We ended up making a Hawaiian guitar from scratch – one which I was to use later on a couple of Kinks songs: 'Holiday in Waikiki' and 'Creeping Jean'.

By the age of thirteen I had become increasingly disillusioned with school. I found home life and activities outside school much

HIRE PURCHASE PAYMENT CARD

Property of

SELMER MUSICAL INSTRUMENTS, LTD.

(TEMple Bar 0444)

114/116 Charing Cross Road

London · W.C.2   A/c. No. SM/12,446

Hirer ..... Mr. F. G. Davies,

Address ..... 6 Denmark Terrace,

..... Fortis Green,E.Finchley,
N.2.

Agreement dated ..... 4th December, 1959.

Total Amount of H.P. Agreement £29 :14 : 6

The Monthly Hire of £ 1 : 9 : 5 is due on

the ..... 23rd. ..... of each month commencing

23rd. December, 1959.

WHEN REMITTING

Always send this Card.

Cross Cheques and P.O.s $\begin{smallmatrix} d \\ \& \end{smallmatrix}$ and make payable

to Selmer Musical Instruments, Ltd.

Register Treasury Notes and Cash.

NOTE: The Company cannot accept any
responsibility for payments made other
than to their Office or Bank, nor for
payments lost or mislaid in the Post.

Dad's hire purchase card from Selmer's for my first guitar.
Eventually we paid it off!

more stimulating. Football and music were everything to me. They were all I lived for until I met Susan Denise Sheehan.

Sue was my first love. She was a year older than me and from a local girls' school in Golders Green called Henrietta Barnett. She was pretty, clever, tall, with large breasts and beautiful long legs. To me she seemed like the perfect woman, more sophisticated, I thought, than the other girls I had known. I must have been afraid of my feelings for her, because the first time I asked her around to the house, I wound up having Ray tell her I wasn't in. But I arranged to meet with her again.

After our first kiss, it was all over for me. My old life was over. All I wanted was Sue.

Sue was an only child who lived with her parents in Duke's Avenue in Muswell Hill. Her mum was a crabby old woman; her father was stern and required a walking-stick. Neither one of them approved of me. Nevertheless, they could not overcome our mutual attraction. It was inevitable that we would wind up losing our virginity to each other. Little could either one of us imagine the consequences.

One evening we came back to Sue's house after spending the evening with friends at the El Toro, a local coffee bar. Sue and I sat sipping tea in the kitchen, which was at the back of the house overlooking trees which surrounded an old abandoned railway station just beyond. Sue's mum came in and wished us goodnight as she was off to bed. Soon it was quiet. We pushed our chairs together and began to kiss, deep tender kisses. As the kitchen was quite small, Sue straddled herself across my lap after hitching up her delightfully pleated skirt and I entered her. It was a truly magical moment. After that, Sue and I made love at every opportunity: on park benches, on my mother's settee, in doorways, but our favourite place was the overgrown railway slope at the back of Highgate Woods. We were very much in love. We wanted to share all our time together. She would wait for me after school (her school ended before mine). We would often go back to my house, as Sue and my mum got on really well. I think Sue enjoyed my large family – so many people popping in and out, a stark difference to her own severely quiet home life.

In addition to my romance with Sue, Ray and I had become increasingly more absorbed in our music. It was by now the winter of 1961. Although I was all of fourteen, Ray and I performed instrumental duets regularly for family and friends and at Dad's local pub, the Clissold Arms. Chet Atkins, as well as the Ventures, were our main influences. Ray played the lead parts as I bashed out the rhythm. We knocked out such tunes as 'Sweet Sue' (which had special meaning for me), 'Sweet Georgia Brown', and a self-penned tune called 'South', a Chet Atkins-inspired instrumental piece which later became the basis of the song 'Tired of Waiting'. Ray and I later made it into a demo at Regent Sound in Denmark Street.

Peter Quaife was then a classmate of Ray's and a neighbour: he lived on the local Coldfall Housing Estate. Pete had a 'Futurama', a six-string copy of a Fender Strat, which was very impressive. It was considered very cool at the time to own one. After some jamming and loose rehearsals it was decided that Pete would team up with us. We drew lots to see who would play bass guitar and Pete lost. We would look for a drummer to make the group complete. The school's music teacher introduced us to a budding drummer named John Start. He lived near the school and his parents were quite well off. They had to be for him to own a 'whole' drum kit with cymbals and all. John was a sweet guy who had an awful stutter. His mum and dad were in the jewellery business and believed that drumming would be good therapy for him.

By late 1961 we were playing local halls and the seasonal school dances. Sue was now my constant companion. At one school dance she even got up and sang 'There's a Hole in my Bucket', a novelty folk song of the time.

Ray and I would often take turns singing, but we both felt uncomfortable doing it, so one day a neighbourhood friend, Peter Jones, whom we called Jonah, auditioned with us. (His mum owned the sweet shop down the street.) It didn't quite work out, but Jonah became one of our first roadies, helping us out with equipment and the like.

The band didn't possess a proper name yet. Sometimes it was the Ray Davies Quartet. By the beginning of 1962 we started to be known around town as RDQ. Ray was going through an unsettling time out of school, disillusioned by the boring routine of working in a draughtsman's office, and returned temporarily to William Grimshaw School to get his art and craft 'A' level exams so that he could enrol at the Hornsey College of Art. Later that year he got in.

It's strange to think back how sometimes seemingly small things can leave an indelible mark on a person. In retrospect, we were two years away from having our first hit, from our lives changing for ever. But in those two years so much happened. My dearest friend, George Harris, got expelled from school in early 1962 for constant truancy. He had a lot of problems after his father died. I was very angry at his expulsion. With him gone, there hardly seemed any point attending school at all.

My school days consisted then of a set of boring routines devoid of any real meaning or creative stimulation. All except art class. Every Thursday afternoon I looked forward to the art lessons, spurred on this time not by the subtle lure of a teacher but by my own enthusiasm. To me, art was a release, a way to express the many intangible feelings I had inside me.

I felt the same way about the guitar. Nothing gave me more pleasure, joy, and fulfilment than playing the guitar. I could vent all my emotions: love, anger, frustration, pain. Sue did not share my enthusiasm. She was terribly jealous of 'that guitar', the way I held it, the way I took care of it. She always thought I loved it more than her.

On a beautiful sunny June morning in 1962, Sue and I decided to skip school (yet again) and spend the day together. We walked and talked and walked some more, lost in each other's company. Kenwood is a large park in north London just east of Hampstead Heath. That time of the year the grass has usually grown high, so we decided to go there. We could make love unseen, or so we thought.

As we went through the gates to the park we took in the beautiful view of London and headed for the long grass. The brow of that hill is one of the highest points in London. But the long grass was gone, cut. Just our luck, I thought. We found a small cluster of trees and bushes and sat alongside them. There was no one in sight so we kissed and fondled each other. I undid the top of my trousers and she slid her hand into my pants. All of a sudden, two men in raincoats burst out from behind the bushes. Neither Sue nor I had much time to adjust our clothing while these men quizzed us. 'What are you doing here?' they demanded. 'Why aren't you in school?' I was ashamed and felt totally humiliated. For all my bravura, I was still only fifteen.

Sue was dreadfully embarrassed as well. We didn't learn until later that we'd been followed by truant officers. When their report was made, the authorities at both our schools acted swiftly. I remember waiting in the headmaster's office with Mum beside me, wondering what form of punishment he had in store for me. The bastard caned me three times hard across my open hand before telling me that I was expelled.

Mum cried as I slowly walked down the steps of William Grimshaw for the last time. She was so ashamed, but even though I felt awful about letting her down, I was actually quite relieved. 'Don't worry, everything will be all right from now on,' I told her, although I'm sure we were both interpreting that differently. Truth is, I hated regimes and the feeling of liberation was wonderful. Strangely, I felt truly free!

Sue had it worse than me. She'd been expelled as well and her parents were in a state of shock and panic. They refused to let her see me, but we saw each other anyway – it seemed as if nothing could keep us apart. She got a job at Selfridges department store in London's West End; I would meet her regularly after work and we'd take the tube to East Finchley together.

During the months that followed, Ray, Pete, John and I rehearsed and played. At home I was always urging Ray to sing. He was very good at impersonations and did Buddy Holly and the comedian Jerry Lewis especially well. I always dreamt of being able to sing like Little Richard, whose 'Good Golly Miss Molly' never failed to make the hairs stand up on the back of my neck. But I thought I had this horrible, high, screeching little voice.

Ray and Pete Quaife had both finished their courses at Hornsey College of Art, and Ray was now attending Croydon School of Art while Pete got a job at the *Outfitter*, a menswear magazine. John Start was working at his dad's jewellery shop and it was also time for me to get a job. Every morning poor Mum dragged me out of bed and sent me to the Labour Exchange, as the unemployment office was then called. At some job interviews I would deliberately act badly so they'd refuse to hire me. Some days Sue would come with me, and often we joked about how I took the piss out of my prospective employers. We had great fun walking around the City or the West End, taking in the sights.

One day I heard of a job at Selmer's music shop in Leicester Square. A chance to work with guitars! I got the job, but alas, I was not to work in the main shop. Instead, I would apprentice in the workshop at the back of the warehouse, repairing brass and woodwind instruments. This quickly turned from a novelty into boredom. One saving grace was that I met another young guy there who'd been working at Selmer's for about a year. His name was Derek Griffiths. Derek played the clarinet quite well and on our lunch breaks we would jam in the lathe room, where most of the brass-polishing went on. We would play songs like 'In the Mood', 'Stompin' at the Savoy', and other such standards. Derek liked Artie Shaw and Benny Goodman. During our sessions he was always joking around, and it came as no surprise to me when some years later he became a television personality as an actor-comedian.

Peter Quaife and I would sometimes meet at lunchtime or after work to venture round second-hand music and record shops. This was long before record store chains like Tower or Virgin or HMV. In the late fifties and early sixties, record stores were still very small-time. One of our favourites was called Dobell's, where we'd hear Ella Fitzgerald, Lionel Hampton, Diz Dizzly, and of course Django Reinhardt. This is the store where I first discovered Eddie Congdon. They also had many blues records which were refreshingly new to me – Big Bill Broonzy, Leadbelly, Sonny Boy Williamson, Sleepy John Estes.

I also hung out with a guy called Lou Lewis who played clarinet. His father, once a clarinettist with the Benny Goodman Orchestra, owned a pub in Highgate called the Victoria and we would often jam in the coal cellar. He had many pictures of big band jazz stars spreading along the walls of the pub. But it wasn't really jazz that excited me. It was the raunchiness and earthier flavour of the blues. Ray was also getting into the blues around this time. By late 1962 he was drawing a lot of blues influence from fellow musicians he'd met at art school. Blues-oriented jazz was very prominent at art-school parties at the time. (I never liked those parties very much. They always seemed phoney. I preferred local parties where rock 'n' roll was played.) Dixieland jazz had had its heyday and was on the wane; it wasn't emotional enough, deep enough, searching or soulful enough.

In August 1962, music and Sue took up my life. I was fifteen and had managed to escape school. What could be better? Then Sue hit me with some unexpected news: she was pregnant.

'I don't know what to do,' she said.

'Marry me,' I blurted out after a few nervous moments. We went to Oxford Street the very next day and bought an engagement ring that cost me £6.

Sue was terrified to tell her parents. We both felt that my mum would be more understanding. Brimming with joy and expectation, we went back to my house and I took Mum into the front room to hear what we thought would be regarded as wonderful news.

'Mum,' I stuttered, 'Mum, Sue and me, we want to get married.'

Sue raised her hand to show the engagement ring. My mother's jaw dropped.

'Oh, David,' she said solemnly. 'You can't do that. You're both too young.'

I looked into Mum's eyes and felt like a child again, being reprimanded for some silly misdeed. I thought to myself, 'What have I done this time?' Sue and I were happy and – strange as it may seem now – we really wanted to get married and raise our baby together. We were in love.

Mum took another look at Sue and blurted out, 'Oh my God, David, she's pregnant, isn't she?'

After that, everything took a turn for the worse. I assumed that after the initial shock wore off I would marry Sue and everything would be fine. But this was not to be.

Without any warning at all, Sue was out of my life. Mum told me that Sue didn't love me any more and didn't want to see me. It was over for good. 'You'll have to get used to it,' she said, 'because that's the way things are.'

All the dreams we had of raising our baby together disappeared for good. I was left with a horrible feeling of emptiness. I couldn't believe it. How could Sue love me one minute and then not love me the next? We had been together for over two years and I couldn't understand how she could reject me so heartlessly. I was completely devastated. I started out for her house to find out if all this was true, and instead sat quietly in the alleyway in the back of her garden. I hoped to catch a glimpse of her through the kitchen window. The light from the window shone brightly and tantalizingly across the murky darkness of the garden. I cried. I felt as though someone I'd loved had died – like the day my sister Rene had died, but worse. After a while, I fell asleep under the night sky. In the morning I walked home, and told my mother I'd stayed at my sister Dolly's flat in Highgate.

I wanted to visit Sue and once, while she was pregnant, I went to the front door of the Unmarried Mothers' Home (they actually called it that). But I wasn't allowed in. I wasn't aware of it at the time, but Mum was in contact with Sue and she told me when the baby was born. It was a little girl and Sue named her Tracey. I brought some flowers to the Home but the woman who ran it wouldn't let me see Sue or Tracey. I would not see Sue again for a very long time and the unresolved feelings I had for her, and my inability to express them to her, would haunt me for many years to come.

What I didn't know was that Sue's parents had conspired with mine to split us apart. While I thought Sue was rejecting me, in fact she was being told by her parents that *I* didn't want her any more. I would finally find this out, but it would be many years and nearly a lifetime later.

2

And so I was out of school, liberated at fifteen, and savouring the street life and nightlife of London. Anything could happen in those carefree days. It was the dawn of 1963, the beginning of an era of rock 'n' roll we could not have predicted.

Teenage boys swarmed London looking for action and I was one of them. Ray was, too. By January 1963 he was playing guitar quite regularly with the Dave Hunt Band, a kind of jazz-influenced pre-R & B group. They were an interesting blend of traditional blues with gutsy vocals. I would often go to see them play, particularly at the Piccadilly Club. One night Dave Hunt's opening band was a young rag-tag group called the Rolling Stones. I was really taken by them. They were rough and edgy-sounding; it was wonderful. After their set I could hear the older players in Dave Hunt's band slighting them and poking fun at them. I didn't understand their rancour – I thought they were great.

Ray soon formed a band with Hamilton King called the Blues Messengers. King was Dave Hunt's singer. This new band was earthier than Hunt's band. They were the genuine article, raw, authentic. I saw them play one night at a club in Gerrard Street called the Kaleidoscope. Mick Fleetwood – still several years away from starting Fleetwood Mac, but very much a blues enthusiast even then – was the drummer. I was very impressed with one tune Ray and Hamilton King had composed called 'Oh! Yeah', a heavy blues riff-based piece which was very hypnotic and repetitive. The Ray Davies Quartet, which was happening simultaneously, was still actively gigging around, although with a new name – the Ramrods – taken from Duane Eddy's instrumental hit of the same name. Eddy was a great influence on us.

25

Not every parent, meanwhile, was crazy about their young son heading off to London in a leather jacket with a guitar slung over his shoulder. By July 1963 John Start's parents had had enough and forced him to drop out of the band. They didn't see it going anywhere. So the Ramrods gained a new drummer called Mickey Willett. Mickey was a really good drummer but he was much older than we were, in his late twenties, downright ancient as far as we were concerned. But I think the group became more cohesive around that time, more focused. Ray and I started to sing, albeit hesitantly, as neither of us thought we could.

Those were the days when we thought we were invulnerable, and music meant everything to me – even if it meant risking life and limb. On one occasion it almost did. Knowing our obvious fascination with Duane Eddy, my brother-in-law Mike had bought us tickets to see him at the Finsbury Park Empire in North London. On the afternoon of the show I was messing around with my niece, Jackie, in the garden. We were sword-fighting with bamboo canes from my dad's garden. Jackie's cane was shredded at one end and during our fencing she accidentally caught me in the right eye. It was smarting and watering badly. Mum put a cold compress on it and insisted we go to the hospital. Although my eye was killing me and I couldn't see out of it properly, there was no way I was going to miss the Duane Eddy concert.

Mum and Dad pleaded with me to see a doctor, but I stubbornly refused. I made a deal with them: let me go to the show and Mike would take me to the hospital straight after. I sat through two opening acts holding a cloth to my eye. Duane Eddy eventually appeared on stage, and it was one of the most thrilling experiences of my life, despite my discomfort. The sound was amazing: he used a very small Gibson amp. He looked so cool, so nonchalant. Jim Horn on tenor sax was wonderful. (He later went on to appear on some Beatles records and played for many other top recording artists.) After the show, Mike took me to the hospital, as promised. Luckily the shredded bamboo had just missed my pupil and my eye would heal after all.

My devotion to Duane Eddy was not misplaced and in fact may have turned out to be something of a lucky charm for us, because using the name Ramrods seemed to do the trick. For the first time we got signed by an agent. His name was Danny

Haggerty and he started to get us work on US air bases in England and at private parties.

One steady gig we had was backing a black body-builder/ singer called Rick Wayne. He was a really funny guy, a nice bloke, but working as his back-up band felt like working in a circus act. We would play a few instrumental tunes, then Rick would arrive on stage and start grinning and flexing his muscles. He twisted his limbs into all kinds of weird poses while we bashed out 'Big Noise from Winnetka'. One night Haggerty booked us to play a US air base with Rick and a couple of over-the-hill strippers. As we walked on stage, we noticed right away that there was something different about the audience. Not only were there uniformed officers, but also their wives and children! Rick Wayne proudly and obliviously showed off his well-honed muscular body to the gaping crowd. But when the two old strippers got up and started peeling off their outfits like a couple of drunken Baby Janes, it was too much for the soldiers to bear. They stopped the show in disgust and ordered everyone to leave.

It was quite hysterical: officers' wives crying while escorting their children from the debauchery. The strippers were furious, of course, insulted and peeved because they couldn't finish their act. Rick Wayne, sweaty and muscle-bound, argued with a stern, crew-cut officer and got nowhere. It would be our last show with Rick and our last as the Ramrods. We changed our name to the Ravens, partly after a horror movie, *The Raven*, made in 1963, starring Boris Karloff, Vincent Price, Peter Lorre and a very young Jack Nicholson, which was a favourite of mine at the time, and also because the expressions 'It was a rave', and 'She's a raver' were becoming part of our everyday language. Later we changed our name again, to the Bo Weevils, after an Eddie Cochran B-side. Better luck this time, we hoped.

What we needed, Ray and I both knew, was management. We parted company with Danny Haggerty and found Robert Wace and Grenville Collins, two very tall young upper-class guys. Neither of them had much experience managing a pop group, but they were wealthy – at least in comparison to us – and above all, enthusiastic.

Robert was a bit of a rebel. His father wanted him to follow in the family business, but Robert resisted and wanted to make his own way in the world. He fancied himself a ladies' man and, strangely enough, a bit of a singer. As part of our deal, Robert wanted to sing with us and he asked the Bo Weevils to be his back-up band. We auditioned him at the Athenaeum ballroom in Muswell Hill. Ray, Pete and I thought it was quite a laugh because we were such an unlikely grouping: four scruffy R & B musicians with a tall, gangly, society dude who sang Buddy Holly songs in a strong upper-class accent while wearing £150 Savile Row suits. Robert really only wanted to sing to impress his upper-class friends, but the experience of playing with him did give us the chance to do some better-paying, if not unusual, gigs. It opened up a whole new world for us. We would play at society dos, parties thrown by wealthy aristocrats and posh friends of Robert's, billed as Robert Wace and the Bo Weevils. I remember one of Robert's friends – a smart, well-spoken playboy called Xavier – telling me that for a mere £200 he could get me a date with Princess Margaret. I'm sure he thought I was just an impressionable kid, but I believed him anyway. He was obviously more than well-connected with the royals. He also had contacts with the best and most expensive hookers who worked the society beat: Shepherd Market, Curzon Street, the Grosvenor House, and so on.

One particular private party for Robert's friends was at the Grocers' Hall in London. It was great fun and in total contrast to what we were used to. None of us took it or the people there very seriously. Mickey Willett was still our drummer but he didn't really like Robert or Grenville. I think he felt they were taking the piss a bit, taking advantage of a bunch of unsophisticated kids like Ray and me. But I loved those society parties; it was hilarious to drink champagne and chat up débutantes.

These parties gave Robert a chance to show off in front of his friends. He'd sing a little – his repertoire consisted of two or three old Buddy Holly songs. He didn't have a particularly bad voice, but his condescending manner and posh accent did not fit in with our rock 'n' roll sensibilities. It was a bit like Noel Coward singing 'Hound Dog'. It was just too ridiculous.

During one set at the Casanova Club in London, Robert came on stage and started to sing 'Rave On'. As we reached the first chorus, he accidentally smashed the mike into his mouth, removing both his top front teeth. He promptly left the stage and Ray took over singing. This was probably the first time Ray

Changing names: tickets Mum kept from our early gigs. Just three months apart, but enough time for the Ravens to become the Kinks.

fronted as a singer. I remember that it felt so natural and so right. After the show Grenville told Robert that he thought Robert's singing was atrocious and that the band sounded a lot better without him and with Ray singing. It was Grenville's enthusiasm that gave Ray the confidence to sing. Robert was forced to accept the idea of managing and not performing.

The latter part of 1963 seemed to move in fast-forward. By late October, Robert and Grenville had brought Brian Epstein, already famous as the Beatles' manager, to one of our rehearsals at the Camden Head pub in Islington, where we regularly rehearsed. Epstein was very polite, almost shy, as he sat through our set. He said he enjoyed it very much and that he would call Robert. But he never did.

So we continued to play the débutante balls and society parties. We did make some friends on that circuit, including a group called A Band of Angels. Really just a group of young socialites, their music was a bit limp and not particularly good. Years later their lead singer, Mike D'Abo, would replace Paul Jones in the Manfred Mann band, and be the voice for a classic pop song of the sixties, 'The Mighty Quinn'.

By November we had recorded some demos in Denmark Street. One of these was a song I had written called 'I Believed You', a Beatle-esque love song. The other was called 'I'm a Hog for You, Baby', written by Leiber and Stoller. Robert and Grenville began to make the rounds, shopping the demos to various publishers. Eventually we got some interest from Kassner Music.

Edward Kassner was a typical cigar-toting Austrian business-man who probably enjoyed the sound of coins dropping in the till rather than the raucous sound of rock 'n' roll. Kassner assigned Larry Page to take care of us. Larry, like Robert, was a failed pop singer. He had changed his name from Davis to Page so that he could use the phrase 'Larry Page, the Teenage Rage'. Even though he dyed his hair pink, his act did not catch on. Larry was very old school, still living in the world of Cliff Richard and Billy Fury. He did seem to have a feel for what we were doing, though, maybe because he came from a similar working-class background.

After we had done some more demo sessions at Regent Sound, Robert, Grenville, and Larry took the tapes to various record companies, with very little luck. By this time we were under contract to the three of them, paying each 10 per cent plus a commission on publishing royalties to Kassner, and we still didn't have a recording contract! When we complained about this to Larry one day in a pub, he said, 'Look, boys, at least you got a chance to make the right connections. After all, what did you have before? What's 100 per cent of nothing?'

Larry was a crafty and smooth sod, always talking out of the corner of his mouth nervously, moving his eyes from side to side in the hope that people might actually believe what he was saying. In the beginning he seemed to be on our side, but inside I felt that he was really a jealous guy underneath. He envied Ray's songwriting talent. I thought that with his help we could make the right contacts with a record company. He was helpful, to some degree, but later on, when things started to go wrong, I really felt he let us down. I can never forgive him for that. I thought he was a small-time operator from an older generation with outmoded ideas. He wanted to cash in on our music, our talent, and when we really needed his support he wasn't there.

Mickey Willett, our then drummer, soon left over a dis-agreement about money with Robert. Robert had confided in me that Mickey had been grumbling about commissions and other payments due to us. I think he knew more about the business than Robert liked.

When he left, Mickey issued a friendly warning to me: 'Dave, watch out for those guys. They're gonna steal from you.' They already were, but of course we were far too naïve, and too excited about our prospects, to pay much attention. Later on, we would pay a price for our naïveté.

Despite this, I really liked Robert. He also got on extremely well with my mother, and they would often sit nattering over tea and bread and dripping, a favourite snack of Robert's, at our house. I think he was much more sensitive than people gave him credit for at the time. He was smart and had a good heart; in the few years that followed I think he was a great influence on Ray, although there was an awful lot of bitchiness between them. I just rode it out. To me, I was on a great adventure, and I didn't want anything or anyone to ruin it. The three of us – Ray, Pete, and I – had a spirit and energy which I sensed was very special.

After being turned down by Decca, Phillips and other record

companies, our management got us a deal with Pye records. Two other important things happened to us that year: we met Shel Talmy, an American independent record producer who had connections with Pye. And we met Arthur Howes, our first serious booking agent. He had an air about him; to us he seemed big-time. We believed if we could go with his agency, things would really start to happen for us. Arthur was a great character, a short man with squinty eyes, a full generous face, a dark hedgehog hairstyle and a seductive laugh.

Robert had arranged for us to play at a New Year party that Arthur was attending in the Lotus House restaurant at Marble Arch, a popular place for music-business people at the time. After the show, Arthur told us how much he liked the band. I remember feeling that night that we were finally on our way. It was Arthur who suggested we change our name to the Kinks, because we wore 'kinky' leather jackets and capes. He thought the name was provocative. I thought the idea of being called the Kinks silly, but Arthur saw the potential in it, how it shocked and surprised people. It was a saucy name for the time. The Profumo affair was all over the news then – establishing the names of Christine Keeler and Mandy Rice-Davies – and phrases like 'kinky sex' were starting to appear in the tabloids. And so we changed our name yet again, and this time, of course, it would stick.

So now we had managers, an agent, a publisher and a record contract. We happily signed whatever agreements were placed in front of us, not wanting to jeopardize in any way the willingness of the publisher or the record company to work on our songs and recordings. We thought that if Larry or Robert said it was OK, then it was. Wasn't that what management was for?

It was unfortunate that we were so naïve in regard to the copyrights, the publishing and performing rights of our original material. We didn't understand the principles involved, as was the case with a lot of young performers/writers in those days, and indeed we never realized that we needed to negotiate for better terms. Obviously we were pretty green, and thrilled just to get a recording contract. After paying our agent Arthur Howes 10 per cent, our managers got 30 per cent, 10 per cent each to Larry, Robert and Grenville.

Robert and Grenville didn't understand the workings of the

business at first, although they soon caught on, but Larry did. Of course he was working for the publishers and they weren't about to do us any real favours. Our early publishing deals were based on a 50/50 split between publisher and writer and less when taking into account overseas income. Kassner owned the rights indefinitely.

Nowadays, depending on how much of an advance a writer gets from a publisher, the writer's royalty is usually split 40/60 or, more commonly, 30/70 to publisher and writer respectively. The publisher owns and takes charge of the copyright of the song on behalf of the writer for the duration of the contract and for a period thereafter which often can be for life of copyright, depending on what is negotiated up front. The duration of the contract can run from five to ten years, sometimes longer, or the time it takes to write three or four albums depending upon how the deal is structured.

Publishers will sub-publish with companies overseas. Normally the foreign publishers keep approximately 20–25 per cent of receipts before passing on the remaining monies to the publisher. In foreign territories, if the split is 30/70, the writer will receive in effect 70 per cent of the 75–80 per cent received by the UK publisher from a sub-publisher.

In the old days it was not uncommon for music publishers to set up companies abroad and take 50 per cent of the receipts before handing over the remaining 50 per cent to the UK publisher, which they also owned. These monies were broken down yet again into a 50/50 split between writer and publisher. In essence, the writer was only earning a 25 per cent royalty on foreign rights.

Nowadays, writer's mechanical royalties are based on 8½ per cent of the dealer price of the record. These writer's mechanicals are collected by the Mechanical-Copyright Protection Society (MCPS) and are in turn paid to the publisher, where they are split according to the writer/publisher deal. This mechanical royalty is a writer's royalty based on an agreed industry rate and is paid to all writers from record sales irrespective of who they are. This income is drawn mainly from record sales, although a smaller portion is paid from a variety of sources – video companies, music libraries, computer games, juke-box suppliers, etc.

When a song is registered with the Performing Rights Society

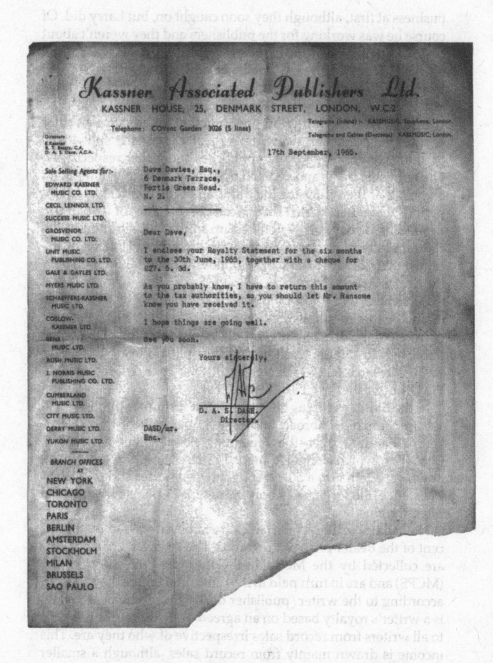

The letter from Ed Kassner's office that came with my royalty statement for the first part of 1965.

by the writer, they collect the royalties for the writer from radio air-play, TV, live performances, etc. These are paid directly to the publisher. (The PRS takes a small administrative fee, as do all collecting agencies.) The publisher's share is then divided up and split between writer and publisher as laid out in their original deal. The PRS was basically formed in 1914 to protect the composer, due to the changes in society at the time. Music was normally performed in the home from sheet music, then along came radio and the gramophone, which made it harder to keep tabs on what was being played and when and where.

It is the publisher's job to exploit the song or music, to 'get it placed', and to act as a collecting agency for the writer's royalties received on the sales of records or covers or whatever. These days it is common practice to have promotional staff in a music publishing company in order to follow up work done by a record company's promotional team. As back-up. Promotion and marketing are crucial aspects in the selling of albums, CDs or whatever. A good promotional team can help to break a record and help sustain sales. This can cover procuring air-play, TV and the like.

Separate from the writer's royalties are the artist's royalties, which are paid by the record company to the recording artists. The Kinks' original royalty rate with Pye was made at the shit end of the scale. They paid us 2 per cent and leased the tapes to Reprise in the US, where we got only a 1 per cent royalty rate. It was upgraded to 4 per cent UK, 3 per cent US and the rest of the world by 1965, and in 1966 to 8½ per cent UK and 5 per cent the rest of the world excluding the States, where it remained only 3 per cent. The Kinks still receive monies based on these rates. Pye owned the rights 'in perpetuity'. Which at sixteen I didn't know meant for ever. It still means the same today.

As is still common today, Pye deducted from the retail price a percentage to cover such items as 'container charges', a deduction for so-called 'free-goods' and 'returns'. In the end our royalties were based on only 85 per cent of actual sales.

Nowadays for a new act/artist it is normal practice for a record company to own the rights to ownership of the 'recorded tapes' in perpetuity. For more established artists it is obviously easier to negotiate for better terms. Ownership rights can last for five years, sometimes ten to fifteen years, often the duration of the contract, before the tapes revert back to their 'rightful' owner – in my view, that's the artist. At the time of writing, all the Kinks' Pye recordings are owned by Castle Communications, who bought them from PRT. They inherited the catalogue from the old Pye label.

Today, artist's recording royalties are negotiated by managers, lawyers and artists and are based on either retail or dealer price. This can vary from 10 per cent at the low end of the scale, to 15–20 per cent plus at the other end. Generally, singles royalties are about 2 per cent less than those for albums.

The record company's actual costs also have to be accounted for. These costs include a percentage for development and research, A & R and marketing, manufacturing and distribution costs, and general overheads.

As part of the overall negotiated deal with a record company the artist also receives a record performing royalty via Video Performance Limited (VPL) and Phonographic Performance Limited (PPL). These collecting agencies draw income from sources such as juke-box suppliers, shops, discos, etc.

An advance against overall record royalties is usually paid to the artist, which normally would also cover the expense of making and mixing the record plus whatever extra can be negotiated. This can range from £20,000 to millions. These advances are usually recoupable against record sales/royalties. A new act will get anything from £20,000 to £150,000, in some cases even more. Out of that they may spend anywhere from £20,000 to £100,000 on recording costs. It is also important when negotiating a recording contract to make adequate provision for suitable promotional costs, which are normally paid for by the record company.

Some Kinks compilation CDs of our earlier material have been badly packaged. They keep churning out these bloody things with twenty or so tracks on them and we are only receiving monies earned based on the old royalty rate, and have no control over the artwork, packaging, or whatever. It is a ruthless and greedy business. Of course a fan is going to be interested in buying a £12 CD with 20,000 songs on it. Never mind the quality, just give me as much as possible. This 'Jabba the Hut' mentality – wow! How many times can they milk out profit from rehashing yet again 'You Really Got Me' amongst others, throwing them together in some thoughtless and haphazard way just to make a buck, when we as artists are not getting what we should?

Rhino Records in the US leased from us our old RCA catalogue. In my view they got it too reasonably, but nonetheless they put some great packages together. The sound quality is great and the artwork is true to the original.

It is crucial for a new act these days to understand the basic principles involved, as it is easy in the excitement of it all, once the blood rushes to the head, to sign shitty deals and lose control over one's work. The Kinks over the years have been deprived of revenue that is ethically and morally ours because of bad deals that our management negotiated in those early days, and there's no way to recoup it. Obviously with our later deals with RCA, Arista, MCA and Columbia we received far better and fairer royalty rates, in keeping with more 'normal' business practice. Fortunately many have learned from our mistakes and from others like us. Young musicians and composers today are generally a lot more aware of the possible pitfalls than we were. Or if not, they should be. 'Inperpetuity? I can't find that word in the dictionary.' 'Oh, don't worry about that, it's just a legal term.' You're damn right it is.

Of course we didn't know any of this at the time, and to us, everything seemed to be clicking and going right. We were all committed to the group. I had long been sacked from my job at Selmer's for falling asleep on the job after gigging late the previous night. Pete had left his job at the *Outfitter* and Ray had left Croydon. But now we needed a drummer. For some reason there were hardly any drummers around at the time who had the right musical background. Most of them were still hovering in and out of the jazz field. It was very hard to find a drummer who could play a solid-based rock tempo. Most drummers were still 'thinking cymbals', thinking jazz. There were a lot of drummers who were jazz snobs. We auditioned many of them but it seemed like we would never find the right one.

There was one guy I really liked called Viv Prince. I had heard him on a session at one of the small recording studios in Denmark Street. But he missed the audition. I found out some time later, when Viv and I became friends, that he'd been stoned the night before the audition and no one could wake him.

Another drummer who missed his audition was Robert

Henrit, who was eventually to join us in the eighties and is still part of the Kinks today. He told me that he had been on tour at the time in Scotland with Adam Faith. He had planned to come to London for the audition on his day off and go back the same day. But Adam wouldn't let him go; he was too insecure.

When the Kinks started recording with a session guy called Bobby Graham, I realized what great rock drumming was all about. There were, in fact, English musicians with the right attitude. Graham would hit the drums so hard probably because otherwise the engineers couldn't record them properly – especially the bass drum. And did he hit them! He was a great inspirational drummer.

The search went on until one day Mick Avory appeared. When he arrived at the steps of the Camden Head, I wasn't very sure about him. He was short-haired, nervous, and wary of our campy appearance. He looked so different from us, like a navvy builder with his Sunday best on. He must have thought our leather jackets, PVC, and long hair a bit much, to say the least. Pete and I were always camping it up: hands on hips, pouting lips, you know. Mick thought our behaviour a little suspect at first, but after he joined the band he soon got the idea. He was very defensive and unsure of himself, a bit clumsy, but he was the right age and had played with Mick Jagger and Keith Richards in an early version of the Rolling Stones. Robert and Grenville suggested that once Mick let his hair grow out he'd fit in more. They were right.

Before Mick started playing with us, we started rehearsing for the studio with Shel Talmy, who seemed genuinely excited by our music. In January 1964 we went into Pye Studios and recorded our first proper session. The songs included 'You Do Something to Me', 'You Want Me', 'Long Tall Sally', and 'I Took My Baby Home'.

After Mick joined the band, we rehearsed frequently at the Camden Head and still performed at a couple of favourite local haunts to break Mick in before more serious sessions on ITV's *Ready Steady Go* – our first ever TV performance, on which Arthur Howes, together with Robert, had got us booked as the new 'flavour of the month'. I had never been on TV before and we were all very nervous, but then the adrenaline kicked in. It was probably one of the most thrilling experiences of my life. The show was a great success for us even though our song, 'Long Tall Sally', only charted at number 42 in *Melody Maker* and then disappeared from view.

It was now time for us to cut our teeth on the touring circuit of clubs and ballrooms throughout the UK. Initially, we played up north: mostly Manchester and Liverpool. Manchester had clubs like the Jungfrau, the Oasis, the Twisted Wheel. Liverpool had the Cavern. Other cities included Bradford, Sheffield, Leeds, Notthingham. On one show we were actually billed as the Kinks from Liverpool. We quickly built a respectable following not only among fans and critics, but among groupies. A lot of the girls I met were quite young, but very willing. Young girls were prepared to do anything to be with their adored stars. By March 1964 – when we went out on our first package tour with the Dave Clark Five – I was already quite experienced with women at the ripe age of seventeen.

These tours put us in front of larger audiences and took us to venues like the Odeon in Walthamstow, De Montfort Hall in Leicester, City Hall in Newcastle, and similar places all over the country. The shows were very much like the early American package tours, where you would have two main acts and three or four opening acts, which we were, and a comedian who doubled as an MC.

The Hollies, featuring Graham Nash, were on that tour and we became great friends, pretty much at the expense of the Dave Clark Five. None of us really liked the DC5, especially the Hollies' bass player, Eric Haydock; he no doubt thought that the Hollies should have been top of the bill instead.

Graham Nash and Eric took us under their wing, since we were a scruffy, inexperienced bunch of kids. The Hollies were older and more polished. Because our styles were so different they never considered us a threat. I loved the Hollies' harmonies and admired their slick arrangements. On the other hand, we all thought the DC5 was contrived and unoriginal, cashing in on the Beatles, who had just hit America. I did like Mike Smith, Dave Clark's singer, despite his sometimes embarrassingly cringing parody of John Lennon.

It was great fun travelling on the coach with the other acts, which included the Trebletones, Mary Wynter, and the Mojos. I tried to imagine what it must have been like on the legendary American package tours with people like Buddy Holly, Eddie Cochran (my hero), and Sam Cooke all travelling together. We had a really silly coach driver who used to talk about the old days. He was a very bitter guy, very envious of us younger musicians. He always talked about how many Germans he'd killed during the war and how he studied karate, but we laughed at him – we thought him a bit pathetic, really. I remember one day he was parking the coach and it was completely surrounded by young fans. It was an accident waiting to happen. Sure enough, as he angled into position, a girl got caught between the rear of the bus and a wall. Her pelvis was crushed. He showed little remorse. He said, 'She should have looked where she was going.' Maybe he'd driven through one too many crowds of screaming teenagers.

While we were on the Hollies–DC5 tour, Arthur Howes heard a rumour that our act wasn't shaping up. So he sent along a guy called Hal Carter to 'groom' us. Hal had worked with Billy Fury – by then a big star – and was considered an expert at image-making. I suppose Hal thought he was going to do something for us, but my main memory of Hal Carter is the pretentious way he dressed, with his collar up fifties style, polka-dot silk scarf around his neck and his turned-up nose looking down at us. He looked silly and smug, although I'm sure he thought he was quite cool. Maybe it was an omen, but the lasting picture I have in my mind is of him standing under an exit sign backstage.

Hal was a sweet, well-meaning bloke but his ideas were rather passé. He was always trying to improve our stage act – or so he thought. He told me things like, 'Look, during your guitar solo I want you to run across the stage, jump up on your amp, and wiggle your arse. C'mon, rave on your own.' It was embarrassing.

During one rehearsal he was shouting at us, bullying us into doing some kind of silly dance routine or the other. When I just couldn't take it any more, I turned round to him and said, 'I can't do this, Hal, it's bloody silly, we're not the Shadows. It's stupid, it's just not us.' Hal went on to lecture us all on how to perform in front of an audience and how great Billy Fury was, what a consummate professional he was.

Hal constantly rambled on about Fury. I finally said to him, 'If Fury is so great why don't you go back to him?' He just turned slowly, cocked his head to one side, lowered his eyelids in that daft condescending way of his, and said, 'Well, at least Billy is an artist.' Then he shouted at the top of his voice, 'And take that fucking polo neck jumper off.' He then smugly lowered his voice. 'You wouldn't see Billy wearing one of those.' We all burst out laughing.

During another rehearsal Graham Nash was watching from the wings. Even he couldn't stand it any longer. During a discussion about how Ray should spin round during a certain song, Graham walked on stage and told Hal exactly what he thought. 'Look, Hal,' he said, 'why don't you fuck off and leave them alone, they'll do fine on their own.' Graham was right, we did do all right and Hal in the end did fuck off. I'll always appreciate what Graham did; it made us realize that we didn't need any old-fashioned show-biz tricks to express ourselves or our music.

The release of 'You Really Got Me' in August of 1964 changed everything. I knew we had something special that day in the front room at Fortis Green, although the first time we recorded it with Shel Talmy it was a disaster. Shel thought himself another Phil Spector, whom he greatly admired. But that style of production – with lots of echo and overdubs – was totally wrong for the raunchy and gritty sound that we wanted. Shel's well-meaning attempt at recording it was awful. He really didn't get it at all. After we threatened to pack the whole thing in if they released it, Robert and Grenville lent us the money to go back into the studio and record it again. I think it cost £200. We used Bobby Graham again on drums and, for the first time, a piano player, Arthur Greenslade. If it hadn't been for Robert's support, the Kinks could have ended before they'd begun, then and there.

'You Really Got Me' exploded on to the charts. I remember the first time I heard it on the radio. I had just left our agent's office and got in a friend's car to drive back to north London when it came blasting out of the car radio. I was momentarily stunned with excitement and awe. It was as if it was somebody else performing it and I was simply listening in admiration. All of a sudden I knew that we had made it. It was a truly incredible feeling. It sounded and felt so real, so positive, so powerful, seductive and hypnotic. As if its earthiness could cut through walls.

It was fantastic to knock stars such as the Beatles, the Stones, Jim Reeves and the Honeycombs off the top of the charts. 'You Really Got Me' climbed the charts quite quickly and became number 1 within a few weeks. It all happened so fast it was like living in a dream come true.

We performed on *Ready Steady Go* and other TV shows. All of a sudden we were in demand by the press. Robert hired the services of publicist Brian Sommerville, who had worked with the Beatles. He was a strange guy. He reminded me of a slightly overfed politician, dressed in a smart pin-striped suit with an anxious sweaty brow and a kind of serious chin-up stance. I never felt he liked me very much; he always seemed a bit creepy, but what did I care? The Kinks were now firmly in the spotlight. All of a sudden our scruffy R & B outfit had become the latest pop sensation, spoken of in the same breath as the Beatles, with a record at the top of the charts.

1964 was quite a year. Mods and rockers, pill-popping and punch-ups at Southend and Brighton. Harold Wilson, leader of the Labour Party, became Prime Minister. Cassius Clay became world heavyweight champion.

We did countless interviews, cover stories in *Fab* and *NME*, *Jackie* and other music and fashion magazines. It was incredible doing interviews for the first time: you could say anything and people would think it interesting or at least newsworthy, and if you couldn't think of anything then you just made it up. It was all so naïvely spontaneous. It was an unparalleled thrill to see my picture in a magazine or a newspaper, especially alongside 'other' stars such as Michael Caine, Susannah York, Susan George, Roger Moore, David Hemmings, Terence Stamp, Twiggy, the Beatles, David Hockney, Honor Blackman and Cathy McGowan. Posing with top models, and chatting with Pete Murray, Brian Matthew, Jimmy Saville, Alan Freeman, Dusty Springfield, Eamonn Andrews and Petula Clark in the BBC bar was truly 'fab' man, 'super'.

I always thought Pete Murray was really cool. What a great bloke, a true 'gent'. I really liked him. Pet Clark was 'smashing'. I loved her, she always reminded me of my sister Dolly. A really nice lady, a genuine person. She had a very carefully concealed sexuality about her that I found quite alluring.

I loved to hang out backstage at the TV studios with Dionne

Warwick, Billy J. Kramer, Sandie Shaw, Cilla Black, the Searchers, Lulu, and the Mersey Beats. It was a 'scene' man. Really 'kinky', ya know. Cilla Black seemed to be everywhere and know everyone. Sandie Shaw was really nice and she looked great, she understood the timing of that 'fashion moment', a cool look hitting just at the right time. I was so boisterous but I was always careful not to tread on her feet. Lulu was great fun; she was always ready for a laugh. A cheeky little lassie, a lovely bubbling personality, just like one of the boys. The sound of her spoken voice was husky, throaty and really sexy. A bit of a turn-on.

Dionne Warwick had to be one of the quietest and most polite women I had ever met in those days. Strangely, we hit it off straight away. She was so open and friendly, a lovely woman. Very sensitive.

In the clubs, we listened to music by the Four Tops, Ben E. King, the Supremes, Wilson Pickett, James Brown, Martha and the Vandellas and, of course, the wonderful Otis Redding. It was becoming 'in' to play soul and R & B in all the night-spots alongside the hits of the time. I adored Otis Redding; I must have played his first album until the stylus skidded across the face of the record and it became unplayable. What an inspired singer and band. God bless Otis.

By the autumn of 1964, Ray and I were recognized everywhere we went. I spent most of my time in clubs. I had always found it easy to make friends, but it was astonishing how much easier it was now that we had gained an element of success. I was very much a show-off, a cocky young sod. I enjoyed the attention and lapped it up. If you acted confident people thought you knew something they didn't. In fact, I was just making it up as I went along.

I also was making more money than I'd ever thought possible. One of the first things I did with my new-found money during this time was to go to a fancy department store in the West End called Gamages. On the top floor they had on display a giant Scalextrix electric model motor car track complete with model houses, trees, and miniature people. As a boy I had always dreamed of owning one. I walked straight through the crowd and up to the attendant.

'I want to purchase the whole lot,' I said. 'Everything down to the last detail.' At first he was surprised, but when he realized that I was totally serious he was all over me. A few days later they delivered the track complete in every detail to my house in Muswell Hill. I had it set up in my bedroom and it just about fitted in the room with my bed. It was a childhood dream come true.

Another time I went to a shop in Muswell Hill and bumped into my old headmaster, Mr Loads. I smiled and thought to myself, 'That was the bastard who caned me, made my mum upset, and expelled me from school. Big man he thought he was.' I watched him out of the corner of my eye without him noticing me. After some time he eventually saw me and excitedly walked up to me with a false and insincere smile. He said cheerfully, 'Hello there, Davies, how you doing? I saw you on the telly the other night.' I shrugged my shoulders, smirked at him and looked away, saying nothing. Then I brushed past him, giving him the cold shoulder, and walked out of the shop. As I walked by him I realized that he wasn't such a big man after all; in fact, he appeared rather smaller than I remembered him. He collected himself and went about his shopping. Who would have imagined that such a terrible student would go out into the world and make something of himself? Surprise, surprise. It was truly a moment to treasure.

As the band started to take off, Robert and Grenville set up a management company called Boscobel Productions. They rented offices on Kingly Street, which runs parallel to Carnaby Street, soon to become famous around the world for its mix of fashion and drugs and sex. (A few years later, it seemed to me, the Carnaby Street scene would drift to San Francisco and launch Haight Ashbury, the Summer of Love, and hippies.) There were just a few boutiques open in Carnaby Street at that time, like John Stephens, but the proprietors were only too eager to accommodate the needs of a 'pop star', giving us outrageous discounts on clothes and sometimes freebies. In exchange they hoped to see their garments in fashion magazines or on *Ready Steady Go*. I was a bit of a fashion junkie, and particularly when I was stoned I would buy the silliest or most outrageous outfit possible. Anything to shock or embarrass.

It was probably the first time since the war that fashion and art were gradually coming into step with the times, with the youth of the day reflecting a truer picture of the feelings and expressions of a new generation. Generally the movies that were being made had a kind of fifties feel about them, but a few films did reflect a sense of the times. One in particular that really stood out for me was *Saturday Night and Sunday Morning*, made in 1960 with Albert Finney, Shirley Anne Field and Rachel Roberts. It really demonstrated a true working-class spirit, a real feel of a young man growing up in a harsh working-class environment, a rebel desperate to have some fun, to find self-expression in an otherwise mundane existence.

Robert Wace opened a boutique in Rupert Street in Soho around that time. It seemed the done thing to own a boutique. These shops were sprouting up all over the place because of the amazing success of the Carnaby Street stores. One morning Robert received an unexpected visitor at our Kingly Street office. A smartly dressed city type walked in and announced that he had some business to discuss with Robert that would be of mutually beneficial help. He knew that Robert had purchased a shop in the area and understood that many business owners had taken out special insurance against damage, fire and the like. He suggested that for a reasonable fee his company could provide such insurance coverage. Robert politely declined the offer, saying that he wasn't interested. As the gent got up to leave he placed his business card on the table, then said goodbye and left. The company he worked for was called Kray Enterprises.

Some weeks later, during a rehearsal, Robert came in and said that his shop had been smashed to pieces, the windows broken and the inside wrecked. Shortly afterwards, he sold the boutique before it had even had a chance to get off the ground.

In the eighties, long after the Kray twins had been put away for various crimes, including murder, the Kray family approached my sister Gwen in the hope of getting in touch with Ray and me. Apparently Ronnie and Reggie Kray were big fans of the Kinks, and during the early stages of a first draft screenplay about their lives they wanted me and Ray to play them in the film. Gwen told their representatives that we were away in the States touring. We didn't hear any more until some years later, when the film was finally coming together. Again we were approached to play the notorious brothers. After some thought I declined the more than interesting offer, thinking at the time that it wasn't right to be involved in a project that glamorized crime. Looking back, we should have done it. Peter Medak made a really good film and managed to capture the time really well. The Kemp brothers from Spandau Ballet gave very convincing performances, but on reflection I think Ray and I would have been better suited to the roles. I remember Chrissie Hynde often joked about Ray and me being the Krays of rock 'n' roll.

I first discovered drugs in those days during many visits to El Toro's, our local coffee bar in Muswell Hill. Ray and I also played there sometimes as a duo, doing instrumental stuff. 'Reefers', as marijuana or hashish cigarettes were called, were associated with the late fifties Beatnik period, and heroin was considered very old-fashioned, the drug of choice for an older generation – bums and jazzers – who had serious drug problems. There were a lot of jazzers in Soho taking heroin – it was part of their scene. Our drugs of choice in those days were amphetamines called 'Purple Hearts,' and hashish. They were considered 'fun' drugs and were easily obtained from the pubs and clubs in Soho and the West End. Previously, drugs hadn't been rife in working-class society. Drug usage had always been prevalent among musicians and show-biz people in general in earlier generations, but now it was becoming more common for the average person to obtain them.

The most popular pub in Carnaby Street was called the Shakespeare's Head. On a Friday night it was a great place to score Purple Hearts or hash. If I didn't have any luck there, I would go around the corner to the Blue Post. Some evenings I would meet my mate Mike Quinn there for an early evening 'drink' that would usually start with a glass of white Sauternes and Coca-Cola. We would wash down some Purple Hearts with a few of these concoctions before moving on to other pubs in the district. When the pubs closed we would go on to the nightclubs. In Soho I liked to go to the Whisky A Go Go or the Flamingo, where Georgie Fame and the Blue Flames would often be in residence. I got to know Georgie well; he was a nice guy who knew how to enjoy himself.

The Scotch of St James became a favourite haunt of mine and was a good place to pick up girls – models, aspiring actresses or just a visiting suburbanite looking for some excitement. Some nights I would be so out of it by the time I got there that I would arrive with an entourage of people whom I hardly knew at all.

The owners let me run a tab that sometimes would extend from one night into the next. I didn't have much money, but it was a considerable lot more than I was used to, and I was very generous with it, spending most of it on friends and partying. The Scotch of St James later became one of the trendy places for actors and rock stars to visit; the regulars included Paul McCartney and John Lennon, Brian Jones of the Rolling Stones and Eric Burdon and the Animals. Eric lived there, it seemed. I think he had a flat upstairs.

I really liked Lennon – he always seemed so cynical. He seemed to me as if he was in some kind of pain. I could relate to him. When I wasn't too stoned to know whether or not he was there, we managed to find our way into some disagreements. Once during a conversation he suddenly got up from the table and left. His parting words: 'You cynical bastard! You're probably one of the most obnoxious people I have ever met!' I suppose in retrospect I should have regarded those words as a compliment. Yes, I was arrogant and obnoxious, but I believe that it was the drink and drugs that made me behave so badly. Although I appeared very single-minded and stubborn on the outside, on the inside I was really quite shy.

My shyness, however, never extended to girls. They were everywhere. All the girls I came into contact with were into fashion, music, and drugs and ready to try anything. Wherever we played, we were followed by thousands of female fans who seemingly screamed their throats raw. Groupies were ubiquitous. After one gig in Sheffield, I pulled two girls who were waiting outside the stage door into the back of our van. One girl was an unusually attractive blonde named Rasa, whom Ray had his eye on; her friend was a pretty dark-haired girl named Eileen, whom I took back to my hotel.

Ray and Rasa began to spend a lot of time together and a few months later they would marry. Eileen hung around a lot but I wasn't interested in her as a constant companion. There were too many girls to see in other towns we visited.

I was still living with my parents in Fortis Green. I often smuggled girls in and out of the house, and my parents mostly tolerated my 'guests'. Often Mum would try to bash down the door to make sure there weren't any under-age girls. Of course there weren't . . . But on one occasion I was with a girl whose hymen was so difficult to break that for a moment I thought she still had her tights on. Eventually my lifestyle and insatiable sexual appetite became more than Mum could handle, especially after she caught me in bed with five girls. I decided to move out and rented a house in Connaught Gardens, Muswell Hill.

When Ray and Rasa decided to marry in late 1964 our publicist thought it would have an adverse effect on our record-buying public, so the wedding was a very hush-hush affair in Bradford. I was the best man and Eileen was the maid of honour. After the church ceremony we went back to Rasa's family's house for the reception. Rasa's full name was Rasa Emilija Halina Didzpetris; her family were Lithuanian refugees, extremely serious people with high moral values, polite, nice people with impeccable manners who were somewhat austere.

Eileen and I arrived at the house a bit before the reception was to begin and I invited her into one of the upstairs bedrooms, where we began making love. In the background we could hear the chatter of the arriving guests, but we didn't care. After a little while my sister Peggy poked her head around the bedroom door. Her initial frozen and shocked glance across the room at Eileen and me lying locked in sexual ecstasy melted nervously after some seconds. 'David,' she stuttered, 'what are you doing? You're supposed to be giving the wedding toast!' Eileen and I somehow managed to make our way downstairs, with Eileen propping up her lopsided bouffant hairstyle with one hand while she sat and awkwardly smiled at the other guests. We sat and ate and drank and as usual I drank more and more. By the time it came for me to give the speech, I was rather 'speechless', as it were. I spurted out some inane drivel like, 'I'm too fucking pissed to say anything . . . I hope everybody gets drunk and has a great time.' I winked at the vicar and kept calling him 'Vic', much to his annoyance. I don't remember much more that day, except that everyone burst out laughing, all except Rasa's family. Her parents were not at all pleased with my delicate announce-ment of good wishes for the bride and groom.

Ray and Rasa first moved into a flat near the crossroad of Fortis Green and Muswell Hill Broadway, and later bought their own house in Fortis Green, where their first daughter, Louisa, was born. I remember often having to wait ages for Ray to come out of his house in the early days of his marriage, as was the way with young newlyweds. They never wanted to be separated.

In those early days Mick often stayed at my sister Gwen's house (her husband Brian was our road manager) and Pete lived just ten minutes way. Pete, being the true 'mod' that he was, soon bought a Vespa scooter and would often use it to get to gigs, sometimes accompanied by his girlfriend Nicola. He would often arrive at the soundchecks with his face covered in dirt and grime from the roads or soot from the exhaust of lorries. Pete seemed to live in his bloody anorak, which I never liked because I thought it looked scruffy. My mum would wash and clean our stage clothes and she would comment regularly about Pete being a dirty little sod who obviously never took a wash, judging by the dirt marks on his shirt collars.

When Ray moved into that house in Fortis Green it was the beginning of an immensely creative period for the Kinks. Rasa was a great inspiration for Ray. She was a budding singer herself and had good natural instincts when it came to ideas and comments on our music. Rasa and I got on famously. She was cheeky, attractive, quick, and fun. At last there seemed to be someone outside my immediate family who could act as a perfect catalyst for Ray and myself.

We would often stand around the white upright piano that Ray had in his back room and work out vocal parts, go over sections of songs, work out arrangements, exchange ideas. Ray would call me up when he had some ideas and I would go around and offer my ideas and suggestions. It was a time full of unconditional creativity and love, a wonderful period where the music seemed to flow in and out of the house like the air.

Towards the end of September 1964 we recorded 'All Day and All of the Night'. It was a great record, full of aggression and natural, unashamed youthful abandonment. Pure unadulterated passion. We recorded it simply and quickly, without all the problems that had surrounded the 'You Really Got Me' sessions. We recorded it at Pye No.2, a compact little studio which gave us a sound we loved. All of a sudden it seemed that engineers, musicians, etc. had become very interested in my distorted and raunchy little sound. The frowns of derision and sarcastic scowls had now turned to smiles of approval and looks of admiration. During sound checks on the DC5 tour, musicians and technicians alike would often nose inquisitively around my amp set-up, wondering what the hell it was. Some joked in a mocking way, but I didn't care. Sometimes I felt as much like an inventor as a musician.

In October 1964 we joined the Billy J. Kramer tour of the UK to promote 'All Day'. It was a comparatively short tour, only two weeks. On the bill were Cliff Bennett, the Nashville Teens and the Yardbirds. I got on really well with the Yardbirds, all except Clapton, who was a very quiet, shy sort who always seemed to keep to himself. The Yardbirds were a lot like us, heavy blues-based music, rougher and more aggressive. There was a kind of friendly rivalry between us. After the shows Keith Relf, Paul Samuel Smith and the others were usually around for late drinks and a chat, but I only ever saw Clapton when he was performing.

Not long after Ray and Rasa's wedding, Eileen informed me that she was pregnant. It had been only two years since Sue had told me the same thing, but in those two years my life had changed dramatically. Eileen filed a paternity suit, and Robert and Grenville went berserk. They were so worried about this news ruining my career (I was just seventeen) that they hired the best lawyers they could.

Eileen brought in doctors and blood tests were taken. The lawyers for our side managed to persuade the doctors that I was definitely not the father and the case was dropped. It was amazing what 50 quid could buy in those days. But it was a terrible time; I felt badly about Eileen, who looked sad and alone in the courtroom. But I also felt manipulated, since I had only had sex with her three or four times and I knew that she was also hanging around with other rock bands at the same time. I guessed that she had been put up to it by her parents, who probably figured that as a well-known personality they could hit me up for a few bob. Unlike with Sue, Eileen and I never had a close, loving relationship. I wasn't entirely convinced that the baby was mine.

Recently I saw Eileen after a show in Halifax. She was tearful and showed me pictures of her son, who was married and had a young boy. He was living in Amsterdam and was doing very well. But I just didn't have any deeper feeling about it beyond my curiosity and natural concern. I didn't 'feel' like I was his father and he my son.

3

In 1964, Paris and London were the main music/fashion centres in Europe, and the nightlife was equally hot. The Kinks often went to Paris to do TV and live shows. The hottest club in Paris was called Castilles. It was an outrageous place where anything went and usually did. Forget about the stories you've heard about Studio 54 in New York in the 1970s. At Castilles, strange, painted night people danced with animals – pigs, chickens, and sheep! Sometimes even I found it a little too surreal. But the atmosphere was exciting and the people strangely warm and friendly. Parisians at the time usually had enormous respect for artists, however odd they seemed. In fact, the weirder the better.

After one drunken night at Castilles, I took my Paris girlfriend Su-Su back to my quaint little hotel room near the Moulin Rouge. We had met on one of my previous trips to Paris and had been lovers for a couple of months. We got undressed and made love as the dawn gradually stretched into the room. While we talked, Su-Su, who was remarkably experienced in the ways of lovemaking, blurted out in her sexy, charming, broken English that she had often bedded Brian Jones of the Stones when he was in Paris. To my surprise I was actually turned on by this news. We half joked about what would happen if both Brian and I happened to be in Paris at the same time. Although there always seemed to be plenty of women to choose from, I said to her that I had always kind of fancied Brian and that it would be fun for the three of us to get together, *ménage à trois*. She then added that she had recently told Brian about our affair and that Brian had expressed similar feelings to her about me. I thought I would have to bring this up in conversation when we next met. At times later when Brian and I did talk, the opportunity never arose for us to approach one another about it. The timing was never quite right. Maybe we were both too embarrassed; maybe we respected each other too much. Or maybe its titillation as a mutual fantasy was enough.

I always felt that Brian was the soul and centre of the Rolling Stones, their 'musical intuition'. I had got to know him fairly well during this early period. I remember him as being funny, sensitive, smart, with a slightly affected and fake upper-class accent, a little pretentious, and very camp. I liked Brian a lot.

I did, however, have rather more real encounters with men. I should make it clear that while I enjoyed experimenting sexually, I never really considered myself gay. It was fashionable at the time, especially in show-business, to be adventurous and try different things, and there was never any stigma attached to my interest in other young men. I've always felt that if you have a genuine respect and love for another person, who gives a shit if the partner is a boy or a girl? There's so much emphasis on sex and not enough on the fact that most of the time people simply want to be cared for.

I was into the club scene more than ever. The only London club that stayed open until 4 a.m. was the Cromwellian. Many nights I would stay there until closing time, sometimes sharing the company of Jeff Beck (another really obnoxious party-goer from the period), the Yardbirds, and the Searchers, Eric Burdon and the Animals, among many others. I think Chris Curtis from the Searchers only hung out until the end to catch the male staff before they went home. He had a fetish about what he called 'ugly waiters'.

Around the corner from the Cromwellian was a small private hotel called the Ashburn. It became a regular haunt of mine, a discreet place where I could take girls after the clubs had closed and nightlife had given way to day life. Unless we were on tour, I would normally stay there until the late afternoon before heading home or to a gig. The hotel manager was very discreet. Each night I would arrive on his doorstep with a different girl (and occasionally, boy) on my arm and ask for a room, and not once did he ever ask any questions. In fact he would only say something if he remembered the person from a previous night. 'Oh, how are you?' he might ask. 'Nice to see you again.'

Long John Baldry was a famous habitué of the Cromwellian and I enjoyed talking with him about Leadbelly, Muddy Waters, and music in general until the wee hours of the morning. One night, when I noticed that Long John had been drinking too much, I suggested he stay with me at the Ashburn. I didn't know that he was gay.

To save the hotel manager embarrassment, I asked for a room with two single beds. Nevertheless, once we got in the room we sat on one of the beds and kissed. It felt like a kiss of friendship rather than a kiss of lust or sexual intention. Long John and I sat talking, kissing, and holding hands. It was very beautiful. I always remembered that feeling of being close to another man, of being intimate in a respectful way. I think there is a tender side of a man-to-man relationship that is often sadly forgotten and definitely misunderstood.

I had many male friends, particularly during this period, whom I enjoyed being close and intimate with, and not necessarily in a sexual way. My sexual relationships with men were not nearly as satisfying to me as my liaisons with women. I was an angry, rebellious kid and I wanted to try everything, anything that was against the norm, whether it was getting high, or wearing outrageous clothes, or having sex with whomever I pleased.

Everyone around us was experimenting sexually. Ray and I had a friend who was a prominent writer/producer and TV personality and who is still a close friend. He has an Oscar Wilde type of intellectual wit, and used to throw parties in Chelsea in the sixties, many of which I attended. Sometimes there would be maybe ten different guys and women strategically placed around the room. Drinks would flow, and at about three in the morning he would put stuff in the drinks, like aphrodisiacs. My first night there I suddenly felt dizzy at about three and thought, God, what's in these drinks? I looked around and all the women had gone and there was a naked man sitting next to me touching my arms. Someone else eventually picked him up. But I met a designer called Allen and we had a sexual relationship for a while. He was quite a nice guy.

Ray was married to Rasa and was becoming involved in family life. He was always withdrawn and thoughtful, more of an observer, than I was. While I was out carousing and living it up, Ray was content to observe. I did the partying; he wrote about it.

I started to share my rented house in Connaught Gardens with

Mick Avory, who had left his family home in Molesey, south London. The house had a strange vibe about it and everyone thought it was haunted. But we had some riotous times there. There were always girls in the house; I often had two or three in bed with me at a time. Mick and I even named some of the bedrooms, tasteful names like 'Whore's Hovel' and 'Spunker's Squalor'.

A little while after moving into the house I began having a fully-fledged affair with Michael Aldred, a host on the TV show *Ready Steady Go*, whom I had met after our second appearance. I was very fond of Michael, who looked a little like a shorter version of a young Dirk Bogarde. He was dark, with deep brown eyes that seemed to possess a mystery, a secret, or so I thought. I really liked him, but I tried to avoid having sex with him because I never enjoyed it as much as I liked just sharing a relationship with him. I never really thought much of it, in fact; to me it was just perverse fun. I think he really did love me and I must have hurt his feelings, but I was young and arrogant and possessed too much of an insatiable hunger for women to be faithful to him.

After some time, Michael moved in with Mick and me and had his own room. He tried his best to come to terms with my passion for the opposite sex, but if he saw me with another man? God! How does the expression go? 'Hell hath no fury like a woman scorned.' One night I was out with my friend Mike Quinn, who owned a boutique in Carnaby Street. We'd been out on the town and in fact had got into a fight in an empty parking lot with two thugs who had tried to score some drugs from us. We managed to shake off our pursuers and wound up getting drunk in a club in Greek Street. It was about 1 a.m. when we finally headed back to Muswell Hill by cab – and it was then that I remembered that Michael had been making dinner for me at home. When we arrived, he stood in the doorway with his apron on. His hands were on his hips; a stern and angry look was on his face. He glared at me spitefully.

'Where the hell do you think you've been?' he said with the highest drama. 'And with *him*!' He glanced briefly at Mike Quinn with a jealous loathing. It was like a soap opera. 'Have you any idea what the time is? Tonight was supposed to be *our* night. Well, I'm not standing for it. I'm leaving.'

'Michael, hang on. Wait a minute,' I said. 'Mike and I only

went out for a drink. You know how all of a sudden it's late. Don't be silly.'

With that, he tore off the apron and flung it dismissively in my face. 'You bastard.' He rolled his eyes to the ceiling, holding his head in a pained yet dignified manner. 'Your beans and toast are in the oven.' And he stomped into the garden.

Mike Quinn smiled at me. He didn't care for Aldred and thought of him as a 'poof'. He put up with him because I liked him. Wisely now, Quinn made his exit.

I could not console Michael. He started to cry. 'You fucking bastard. You'd fuck anything, wouldn't you, you slut.' By now he was in a hysterical state. Then, screaming at the top of his lungs, he bellowed, 'And get rid of that fucking Quinn, I don't want him around here any more.' He pulled off his shoes and flung them viciously at me.

As I headed into the house, he pounced on me from behind and we started to fight. He tried to punch me. I parried and pushed him away. He threw another punch, which was really just a frustrating slap that caught the side of my head. Again, I pushed him away. He fell to the floor. 'Fuck you,' I said. 'I'm going to bed.' I walked quickly up the stairs but he chased me and grabbed me on the landing. This time he was hugging me and crying and saying he couldn't live without me.

For a moment he had me in a vice-like grip but I tried not to let him notice that I was intimidated by his strength. I had never seen him so uncontrollably angry before. We walked arm in arm into my bedroom and sat on the bed. He cried on my shoulder for a while. I was thinking to myself that the relationship was getting too out of hand for my liking. I asked Michael to go downstairs and fetch me a drink as we kissed and made up. While he was gone I double-locked the door so that he could not enter. He knocked and whined all night outside that door. It was very distressing for us both. The next day I decided that he must move out and that we should not see each other for a while. Of course we did see each other afterwards, but infrequently and only as friends. Eventually we drifted apart. But I must say I learned a lot from Michael. I'll always hold special feelings for him.

Recently someone asked me if I had ever been in love with any of the men I slept with. And the answer is I loved them but I was never in love with them, not like being in love with a woman. But from that incident the most important thing I learned is always to respect another man's feelings. I think it was a great lesson.

We continued touring throughout 1964. We also recorded and released our first album, *The Kinks*, which reached number 4 in the charts and stayed on them for twenty-three weeks. Pye's Louis Benjamin and his A & R department wanted to cash in on our astonishing and surprising success, so we recorded the album in a matter of days.

We had already rehearsed most of the material for that first album, so it was recorded quickly without much fuss. We had been performing 'Beautiful Delilah', 'Long Tall Shorty', 'Cadillac', and other blues-based songs live for a while. Shel Talmy did a good job this time, unlike his near disastrous contribution to 'You Really Got Me'. He understood what we wanted now, and allowed the music to come through more naturally. We knew what we wanted to sound like, and if he could bring something to the party without getting in the way of that sound then so much the better.

Robert wanted us to have a more sophisticated image, so we temporarily discarded our casual art student scruffy 'don't give a shit' dress in favour of Savile Row's hunting pink. These were the expensive riding jackets that aristocrats wore to go fox-hunting. I don't know why they were called 'pink' when they were actually red (maybe the material was supposed to match the blood of the animals they killed). We wore them with frilly shirts. The pictures from that first photo session were stunning, even though I thought Robert and Grenville only wanted us to dress 'posh' to impress their friends and society chicks. Robert's girlfriend at the time was a woman called Tiger, who was very into society parties. She was quite funny, very opinionated and outspoken. I think she must have been the one who put the idea in Robert's mind. Tiger was a bit of a raver beneath all her airs and graces, as were quite a few of the so-called 'ladies' that we met around that time.

On Grenville's advice we hired an accountant and formed our first company, Kinks Productions Ltd. Our business affairs were run through our management offices. The money started to flow in slowly, after our agency and management 'commissions' were paid. My first weekly wage was about £40 before tax. Everyone took advantage of us in those days. Even Shel got into the act in a minor way.

During the making of the album he suggested that we cover two songs by Odetta, a popular folk singer. One was called 'Bald Headed Woman' and the other 'I've Been Drivin' on Bald Mountain'. Only when the album was released did we notice that those two songs were not actually written by Odetta but were simply credited to someone called Trad.Folk.Arranged by Talmy. I found out that this was quite common. A producer would take an old folk song by an untraceable composer in the public domain, do an arrangement of it, and grab the writing credit – and the royalties. Curious, eh! But as so often happened, we found out when it was too late. A year later the Who fell for the same trick when they recorded their own version of 'Bald Headed Woman'. Produced by Shel, of course.

It seemed as if we were on the road the whole of 1964. But 1965 was to prove even crazier. We toured France, Australia, New Zealand, Hong Kong, Singapore, the USA, Scotland, Scandinavia, Ireland, Holland, Switzerland, Germany, and embarked on our first UK package tour as headliners, which ended in near disaster at Cardiff. At the beginning of the year we went on tour with Gerry and the Pacemakers, Gene Pitney, and Marianne Faithfull. Marianne, of course, was Mick Jagger's girlfriend when she wasn't Brian Jones's girlfriend. At the time she was having a hit with the Stones' song 'As Tears Go By'. Marianne was constantly 'prick-teasing' everyone. All the guys boasted about how they had had sex with her. She would sit in the coach with her lips puckered and her fake Sloane accent intact. I think she was really quite shy. It must have been tough for her being cast with such a bunch of seething loonies who were out to wreak havoc anywhere and any time.

Others on the bill were the Mike Cotton Sound, Bobby Shafto, and the Mannish Boys, who had a saxophone player named David Jones who would later find phenomenal success as David Bowie. But the most fun people were Gerry and his band, who had great success around the world with songs like 'Ferry 'Cross the Mersey' and 'How Do You Do It?' They were a great laugh, always playing practical jokes and fooling around. Gerry was mad and outrageous, silly and funny, ready for anything. I believe the word 'raver' really came into its own meaning on this tour.

To be a true raver meant to be a party animal primarily, but its real definition falls into the category of 'someone who is ready for anything, any time, any place. To fulfil all necessary requirements in order to comply with having a "thoroughly good time" and to enhance the spirit of fun and excess.' The mark of true ravers is that by their presence alone they can uplift the mood and atmosphere of others and push the fun barrier to the limit.

This definition, however, is not to be confused with 'raving loony'. There was a singer in England in the late sixties, David Sutch, or 'Screaming Lord Sutch', as he called himself. One night I saw him stab his saxophone player on stage during a concert. There was blood everywhere. This is not raving! That is 'raving lunatic'. David Sutch, by the way, is now a politician. Spokesman and leader of the Monster Raving Loony Party.

Raving sometimes gave way, however, to downright vandalism. There's been a lot of talk about rock stars trashing hotel rooms and a lot of waffling on about the histrionics attached to the act, who did what and where and why. But the truth is that most of these incidents were born out of frustration, anger, pure drunkenness, or even loneliness. I look back now and can't believe the kind of destruction that was perpetrated. All I can remember is feeling very angry and usually very homesick. Others I'm sure viewed my behaviour as antisocial, which I suppose it was, but to me at the time it was a way to vent my frustrations, whatever they happened to be. As a young kid on the road, hotel rooms seemed the perfect targets for my anger. I actually like staying in hotels now, if they're not too shabby. They have been such a necessary part of my life that I've finally got used to them – as with flying. For years, particularly during the late seventies to the mid-eighties, I was absolutely terrified of flying. But now I don't mind it.

Hotel rooms can also be the loneliest places on earth. During the US tours of '69 to '74, when we virtually had to rebuild our careers, we stayed in some dreadful ones, awful, soulless prisons with filthy plastic shag carpets and orange walls. Nightmare. Being away for weeks and months without the emotional support of family can be torture, especially when things aren't going well.

One of my more memorable hotel-bashing incidents occurred during that UK tour with Gerry and the Pacemakers. We were staying in the Grand Hotel in Taunton. There are two areas of major importance to remember if anyone out there is considering a future as an hotelier. Number one: do not refuse to serve late drinks to already-drunk rock musicians after the bar has been closed; and two, do not under any circumstances refuse entrance to any young lady or ladies accompanying them. If you remember these two 'crucial' points it could save an immense amount of trouble in the long run.

The staff at the hotel that night did not adhere to these simple rules. Not only did they refuse to serve me and Gerry, they wouldn't allow the two girls with us to stay. After some time spent brooding, Gerry and I decided to go downstairs and see if we could break into the bar. The lobby was quiet; only the night porter was around.

The bar's door was locked, but I mentioned to Gerry that I had seen some ornamental antiques on the wall of the lobby, including some swords and an axe. Gerry took the swords and I wielded the axe. By this time the night porter had disappeared. I swung the axe in the air to get a feel of it, and brought it down venomously on the reception desk, which was made of fine old oak. It made an almighty crunch as shafts and splinters of wood spat into the air. Gerry lashed his swords at furniture, curtains, and absolutely everything else within view. After noticing that my axe blows were causing far more damage than his blunt swords, he insisted we swap. It was now his turn to vent his anger on the reception area. Chunks of wood flew into the air. Out of the corner of my eye I saw the night porter approaching. We quickly smashed the only light and ran outside, where we hid like two skulking fugitives. After a while we re-entered the hotel via a rear door and went to our rooms. In the morning we acted as if we knew absolutely nothing about the incident and no one at the hotel said a word to us.

It was a memorable tour for other reasons as well. I took a girl back to my room after a show and while we were having sex I heard a loud snapping noise. At first I had no idea what it was, then I felt a pain in my crotch. I turned on the light and was shocked to see blood everywhere. The girl was smothered in it. The sheets were full of it. I examined my penis and blood was pouring from it. I had split the foreskin. It was quite painful, but fortunately the bleeding stopped after a short time. I was tempted to see a doctor but after a few days it had healed fairly well so I didn't bother. It wasn't long before I was back in action. But I did have a scare, to say the least.

Meanwhile, the girl was still in my room and I wasn't quite sure what to do with her. She was very apologetic, even though it wasn't her fault, simply an accident caused by over-zealous sex. I was a keen photographer in those days and often developed my own photos. I had her take off her remaining clothes and put on these thigh-high black suede boots that I wore constantly. Grenville always told me I looked like a musketeer in them. She posed for me in every position imaginable as I happily clicked away, gleaning at least some pleasure from what could have been a truly disastrous evening.

On that same tour I met a beautiful blonde girl named Vivien in Wigan. One night, when I was totally stoned on amphetamines and Scotch, I took her to my hotel room. At about six in the morning Vivien's father called from outside the window, looking for her. Evidently he was a bit of a disciplinarian. Vivien finally went to the window and explained that she had been taken ill and was staying with a friend, but her father ranted and raved and insisted she come down. She hurried out of the room. I got very angry and threw chairs around and turned over the bed. In those days not all hotels had televisions in the rooms, which was just as well really, especially for this hotel. I urinated in drawers and in the wardrobe and in my final act of crazed triumph I defecated in the hand-basin. To my manic delight and surprise it was a formidable-sized piece of excrement.

The following week our office received a bill from that hotel addressed to Dave Davies and requiring payment of 30 shillings. I assumed that it was for removal fees. God, I was so embarrassed.

Another member of this wild tour was Gene Pitney, a great interpreter of melodramatic numbers like 'Town Without Pity'. His keyboard player was Dave Rowberry, who later joined the Animals. After one show, Dave and I got into a silly argument over who could drink the most. So we decided to have a bet on it. I had with me a girl named Jill from Manchester. She was small, pretty, with dark hair and very quiet. She was so loyal that even when I went with other girls she would always wait for me afterwards. We played a lot up north but I liked Manchester the best. Manchester girls were always the prettiest.

The rules were simple: we both sat on stools at the bar and each would take turns ordering a round of drinks. Whoever's round it was would order whatever he liked and the other had to drink the same. Both drinkers of course could go to the toilet at any stage, but unassisted. The first person to fall off the stool or throw up would lose. Rowberry and I mounted the stools at the bar like a couple of gladiators. Jill watched patiently as the drinks were drunk, rounds went by, and the conversation began to border on babble. More brandy, more Cuervo, and when we moved to double whiskies in the next round the babble turned into incoherent waffle. But still our stubborn and mighty heroes clung to their stools, neither one wishing to give in to the other. As the room started to swirl around me, I realized that I had taken on a more than worthy opponent. But never say die.

More drinks followed. My stool teetered and I began to feel queasy. Just as I was about to throw in the towel, Rowberry's head stooped forward and he fell, crashing to the floor, stool and all. Victory was mine, but at what a price!

In the morning when I awoke alone, Jill having abandoned me at some point during the night (and who could blame her?) I was sick to my stomach. It wasn't the first time and certainly wouldn't be the last.

Back in those early days of the Kinks' conquering of London I also dated a lovely girl named Kim. She managed a store in Chelsea called Biba. It was one of the most fashionable women's clothes shops at the time. She was from Kensington and had a posh accent. I thought she was pretty but she had these slightly protruding bunny teeth which gave her a touch of a lisp. She was charming and really sweet and of course dressed in the height of fashion.

One night, after a drug and drinking binge yet again, I ended up for the last call at the Cromwellian. Stooped over the bar was Georgie Fame's then trumpet player, Eddie Thornton. Eddie was a great guy, a West Indian who was always laughing and happy. I think the latter was because he was usually able to score the best dope in town. When he was stoned he had such a strong accent that it was almost impossible to understand what he was saying

– that is, until you became just as stoned as he was and then everything he said made perfect sense.

As it was really late, Eddie invited Kim and me back to his little flat not far from the club. The three of us got in a cab and left. Eddie's place was really not much more than a glorified bedsit, or studio apartment, but it was comfortable. There was only one main room that had single beds, one for Eddie and the other for his vacationing room-mate.

Eddie insisted that we try some great new smoke which he had surreptitiously acquired. He put on a Chet Baker record, followed by some smooth jazz by Miles Davis, and began rolling really huge joints. Kim and I started undressing each other and sat on one of the beds kissing and caressing. Eddie lit a joint and handed it to me.

I took a long and deep drag, held my breath and exhaled slowly. I was already out of it from earlier on, but it somehow seemed natural just to keep going until you could go no more. I handed the joint to Kim. We listened to the music and smoked some more. After a while I became very dreamy and very sensitive. Kim and I kissed deeply. Eddie was lost in the music, only occasionally looking over at us. The stuff was strong. I smiled at Eddie with Chinese eyes and a Cheshire cat grin as Kim licked my chest and eased her tongue down on to my stomach and then on to my penis. She eased her mouth on to it so delicately. As she continued, I started to feel dizzy. Uncontrollably, and without warning, I was overcome with terrible nausea. Suddenly I threw up all over poor Kim, who was so far into her act that it was downright tragic. Eddie ran to get a cloth and Kim looked at me with disbelief and, of course, disgust. I dressed quickly and ordered a cab while Kim ran in to take a shower. Eddie was really sweet; he kept reassuring me that everything was all right. I remember being as white as the sheet used to be as he handed me a small bag that contained some more of the dope. 'Come back soon,' Eddie said.

Kim and I continued to see one another, although I was also dating a well-known English film and theatre actress, Adrienne Posta. Although I really liked Adrienne, when she came up with suggestions of marriage I fled like a rat up a drainpipe. Kim wanted to get married as well and the thought of it scared the hell out of me. I just froze emotionally every time the subject arose. I liked Kim, but I was enjoying my life too much to be tied down at that point. I wanted her and needed my freedom. I gradually saw less and less of her, but as it turned out it wouldn't be long before I met the woman who would change my mind about settling down.

4

Early 1965 was an intensely creative time for me and Ray. We were very focused in the studio in spite of our heavy schedule and the raving. We prepared some songs in Ray's front room at Fortis Green but a great deal was actually done on the spot in the studio. That's why a lot of our music had such a raw, spontaneous sound and feel. Ray was writing prolifically, and the songs came together with comparative ease because of the emotional and creative support we were then able to give one another. It was a time when Ray and I got along well.

Kinda Kinks, our second album, was recorded in just a few days in February 1965. It had been mutually decided by all concerned that 'Tired of Waiting' was to be our third single even though we actually recorded it before 'All Day'. But our management was concerned that it was too different from 'You Really Got Me' and would have been a risky follow-up.

The recording of 'Tired of Waiting' went well, but there was something missing on it and it was my raunchy guitar sound. Ray and I were worried at the time that putting that heavy-sounding guitar on top of a more ponderous song might ruin it. Luckily, however, it in fact enhanced the recording, giving it a more cutting emotional edge. 'Tired of Waiting' became a number one hit after only a few weeks of release. It was a pivotal record for the Kinks, even though we didn't have much opportunity to savour its success. In my opinion, 'Tired of Waiting' was the 'perfect pop record'. We were now holding our own with the Beatles and the Rolling Stones and in less than six months we had become one of the most consistent singles artists in the UK.

We toured Australia with Manfred Mann and the Honeycombs. An Australian singer named Tony Worsley, a macho surfer type, was also on the bill. The Manfred Mann band were a strange assortment of characters. Their guitar player was a wimpy, complaining schoolteacher type with a public-school accent, a most unlikely candidate for a rock star. Manfred and bass player Tom McGuinness, who later went on to found a fairly successful band in England called McGuinness Flint, used to provoke him into arguments. I think they did it for the amusement value, as a way to pass the time.

Manfred was a self-styled intellectual, cynical, grumpy, hyper-critical and very funny – at least to us. He was so complaining and miserable that he used to have us in stitches with his scathing comments, his sardonic and scornful sense of humour. He was a very entertaining person. One time we were watching the Honeycombs at the side of the stage. Manfred was staring in grim disbelief, sucking the inside of his mouth as if contemplating a carefully planned foray of intelligently phrased abuse. He shook his head from side to side and then his face became blank as if he were overwhelmed by an inexpressible sense of hopelessness. Suddenly he became animated and raced to a nearby piano. He started playing and singing 'Have I the Right' in the style of an old drunken pub pianist, banging the keys with his left hand in an aimless and clumsy way. I think he thought the Honeycombs were completely devoid of any musical talent and actually found them offensive. He was a terrible snob, really. All of them were except for the drummer, Mike Hugg, who was very cool. Quiet, dry, taking everything in his stride, with a kind of nonchalant air about him.

I wasn't too fond of Australia then. The young kids were much like us, but the older generations of Australians seemed to suffer from some kind of mass inferiority complex, sometimes over-compensating with clumsy and obnoxious remarks.

The tour was a continuous stream of dates, press parties and TV interviews. Following us around from city to city, or so it seemed, were the Stones. We would play a show one night and the Stones the next and so on. One night in a Brisbane hotel Pete Quaife and I were in Mick Jagger's room talking about music. Mick never really gave much away; he always seemed to be on his guard, preferring to make a joke rather than discuss anything in depth. There was an obvious rivalry between the Stones and the Kinks, and Mick especially appeared a bit wary of us.

Pete was a great exaggerator. Every time he told a story it

became more outlandish. For instance, he often went rock-climbing, but in his telling the rocks became mountains, and minor spills became near-fatal accidents. Taking a wrong turn to Pete became being lost for days, aimlessly wandering without food or water. I always found him amusing, but at times he could be irritating. During one of Pete's far-fetched stories, Jagger interrupted him, laughing in his inimitable way, and said, 'Quaife, you're just a fuckin' liar, aren't you?' Then he picked up a nearby acoustic guitar and did a very bad rendition of 'You Really Got Me'. Somehow it didn't really suit his voice. But it was funny.

After a long press party, I started talking to Tony Worsley and found out that before he had entered show business he had been a hypnotist. He demonstrated on a few people in the bar and I found it quite extraordinary. He could hypnotize people without them even knowing it. He showed me a few basic principles and techniques. So for the next day or two I practised on any willing person who came along.

One night there was a particularly beautiful woman in the hotel bar, a dancer at a nightclub next door. She had gorgeous black hair that hung down to the crack of her arse. After a while I managed to persuade her to become the subject of my hypnotic experiment. We went to my room and I asked her to sit on the end of the bed. After a brief explanation, I began. I held a silver coin right at eye level and told her to concentrate on the coin while I talked to her in a consistent monotone. I reassured her by telling her that at any time during the hypnosis, if I were to do or say anything to offend her or encroach upon her sense of moral conduct, she would wake up immediately. I had already been successful with other little experiments, such as making people's hands feel hot or freezing cold, or so heavy they couldn't be lifted, so I was confident that this would work.

After the preliminary steps had been taken I counted to three and she appeared to fall into a fairly deep trance. She said she felt warm and relaxed. I asked her to lie on the floor and spread her lovely hair flat across the floor behind her head. I asked her questions about her job and her family – some very personal – and she responded in a very direct way without any shyness or embarrassment. After a while I asked her to dance for me like she did at work. She happily went through her routine and it was very erotic. When she finished I sat her on the bed and asked if she would mind me kissing her. She said no, she didn't mind at all.

We proceeded through the various aspects of lovemaking slowly, freely, until dawn started to break. It was one of the most sensitive and magnificent sexual experiences I had ever had. Before I had a chance to bring her round she sat bolt upright in the bed and asked me what time it was. It was around seven. She got up, put on her clothes, thanked me, and left. I was so taken by surprise that I didn't have time to get her number, address, or anything.

I suddenly realized that she was probably still in a trance since I had never relinquished control of her. I rushed out after her, but she was gone. I went back to my room, ordered some tea and pondered the events of the night. I never caught sight or sound of the woman ever again. Was it a double bluff? Was she pretending to be hypnotized and just got a kick out of it? Did she fool me? Or, worse still, is there a hypnotized woman walking around out there?

If there is, all I can say is that I'm sorry about that and sorry that I can't remember your name. You're about five foot eight, black hair, attractive, around forty-five or so by now, Australian, possibly from Melbourne, and may have been in a trance for approximately twenty-seven years. Well anyway, better late than never. 'On the count of three, I relinquish all power over you. You will wake with absolutely no memory of what has happened to you, but you will feel happy, content and at peace. One . . . Two . . . Three . . .' Phew! I feel much better now.

Later during the same tour I hypnotized two girls in my room. This time I did close off the experiment properly, or so I thought at the time. Afterwards the girls followed me around everywhere in a semi-trance. They wore strained and perplexed looks on their faces and seemed genuinely distressed. I was really scared. Eventually, after a harrowing period when I worried that they might remain this way for ever, I managed to bring the girls out of their condition. Afterwards they seemed perfectly normal. But I became very frightened and have never messed with hypnosis again. Besides, there's enough brainwashing going on in the world without my adding to it.

Our final destinations in Australia were Melbourne and Perth.

My impression of Melbourne was that it was a pretty ordinary town. It reminded me of an old picture postcard of Brighton in the thirties. In Perth it was around 120 degrees during one of the shows. Like true stiff-upper-lipped Englishmen we still insisted on wearing those bloody red jackets. God, it was hot, so hot in fact that the insides of my amplifier melted towards the end of the show. But I did love the beaches, which were beautiful, and the Australian audiences were fantastic.

We moved on to New Zealand, then to Hong Kong and Singapore before heading for San Francisco and New York, where we did TV and press for our upcoming tour of the States later that year. *Hullabaloo* was one of the shows we taped.

We arrived back in England to promote 'Everybody's Gonna be Happy', which turned out to be a poor follow-up to 'Tired of Waiting'. It was based on a bass riff inspired by the Earl Van Dyke Band. Like many of our songs this one came about from messing with various ideas, jamming and improvising. First Pete popped out with this cool bass riff, then I started strumming out syncopated rhythmic jazz chords, incorporating the riff within the chord changes. Mick pounded away, pushing at important accents, and Ray wrote a song around it. A lot of songs grew out of strong riffs, and still do.

Our next single was 'Set Me Free', which sounded more like a Kinks record. I don't know why, but it's always been my least favourite. It seemed a little contrived to me, and Ray's voice uncomfortably high in places, although on reflection it now sounds quite charming. Our previous three big hits were in the key of G. But 'Set Me Free' is in A minor. It would have been too low in G. But I've always felt that the keys of G and E contain a special magic, a kind of rock 'n' roll voodoo.

'Set Me Free' was released quickly to try to counteract any negative effects caused by 'Everybody's' lukewarm reaction. I was very nervous about it being a single, but the night we performed it on *Thank Your Lucky Stars* in Birmingham I sensed that it would be a hit. Maybe our confidence had been shaken a little. Shaken but not stirred.

In March the Animals and the Pretty Things supported us on a few shows in England. I had a lot of admiration for the Animals, a really gritty band. Their song 'We Gotta Get Out of This Place' was great and would have been at home on a Kinks album. Alan

Price, the Animals' keyboardist, and I became friends later on. He was always hanging around the clubs and was good company. But Eric Burdon was usually too pissed to talk to, and after an evening of drinking, his Geordie accent would get so broad he might as well have been speaking in tongues. He was a great raver, though, and a bollocksy singer.

The clubs were the places to be late at night. The Flamingo was an earthy jazz club that became more R & B and blues-oriented. The Scotch of St James was a more upmarket club with a mainly music and show-business clientele. The Cromwellian was similar to the Scotch of St James but it also had a casino and dance room that was like a modern day disco without the flashing lights. These were the best places to pick up girls: models, actresses, wannabes. They went there to meet people like us.

I also struck up a friendship with Viv Prince, the drummer of the Pretty Things, who might have become our drummer if he had shown up for that audition a few years earlier. Viv understood the true art of self-abuse and had the stamina to be permanently stoned. Some days we hung out together and lost all track of time. We would take amphetamines in the morning and share two or three joints, followed by lunchtime drinking sessions in Soho pubs and drinking clubs, all of which knew him on a first name basis. In the evening more pills, some hash, perhaps a fleeting visit to the Marquee, but usually to the pub next door. It was great while it lasted, but our mutual quest to get higher than humanly possible was an empty dream. One day in De Hems, a pub near Chinatown in the West End where many rock journalists from the period congregated, Viv stumbled to a chair and lit up a Winston, cupping his hands and inhaling the cigarette as if it was the last joint on the planet.

'Viv,' I said, 'you do know that's only a cigarette you're smoking, don't you?' He blanked out for a few seconds before he replied. 'Yeah, so what? There's no difference in the end, is there?'

We couldn't have got any higher. I must confess that sometimes we would get so out of it that there didn't seem any point.

On 9 April 1965 the Kinks were to play our first ever Danish concert at the Tivoli Theatre in Copenhagen. We were very popular in Denmark and in Europe in general. During the afternoon we were invited to attend a press conference at a club called the Carousel, owned by Kai Postien, a wealthy local businessman. Kai had a daughter named Beden and a niece named Lisbet Thorkil-Petersen.

Beden and Lisbet both attended the reception. I was taken with Lisbet and Pete Quaife went with Beden. I think the first thing that attracted me towards Lisbet was her shyness. She had an air of sophistication but behind that exterior I sensed a kind of sexy innocence.

Although there was an instant magnetism and attraction between us, events during that day and night prevented us from sharing more intimate moments together. The band was checked in at a hotel called the Europa and I made arrangements with Lisbet for her to come to the show that night. The evening came and the band was ushered on to the stage to a loud and enthusiastic audience. The first few songs passed with the crowd jumping and screaming. Many of them had got up and made their way to the front of the stage. They were waving their arms and jumping in the air, a sight which by now we had become quite accustomed to. But it was obviously not one that the Danish police had come across before.

Suddenly a stream of Danish riot police armed with guns and riot sticks rushed in from the back of the hall. The crowd was going crazy to the music, which of course Ray, Pete and myself encouraged. The police started pushing some of the people around and though it was clear to us that the kids were just having fun and letting off steam, the police felt differently. The hall erupted into chaos, with angry police bludgeoning frightened kids, kids fighting back in retaliation. Girls screamed and ran terrified from the building. We stared at the scene in amazement, bewildered by the sight. The police were the most vicious and nasty I had ever seen.

As the riot worsened the promoter pulled us off the stage into the relative safety of the wings. By this time the angry and disillusioned crowd had started smashing seats, breaking windows, and ripping up everything they could lay their hands on. The scene now looked a wreck as arrests were made and others fled the building.

What had seemed like a scene of joy, excitement and music only minutes before had turned into one of grim devastation. After some time the riot subsided and we were led through the building and out towards a waiting car which took us back to the hotel. The foyer floor was littered with debris and shattered glass. There was not one piece of furniture left upright by the wave of anger that had swept like a small hurricane through the building, nor one window left intact. Ironically, only one picture remained hanging on the wall. It was a framed photograph of Jim Reeves.

Much to my relief, Lisbet had left the Tivoli Theatre before the scene had become really ugly and was waiting for me at the hotel. We sat in the bar and had a drink and reflected over the night's events. I remember feeling extremely angry and frustrated at the police. What right did they have to incite such violence, for which we would probably get the blame? Vicious ignorant bastards. They had ruined what should have been a wonderful and exciting evening by their own fear and lack of understanding.

As I drank I became more brooding and angry. I asked the waiter for yet another drink. As he began clearing up the tables I noticed a full bottle of my favourite brandy, Rémy-Martin, staring tantalizing at me from the bar shelf. I waited until the barman was looking the other way, then I reached over and took the bottle. Hurriedly I opened it, I poured the entire contents into a large pint glass. I swigged it down like a beer, as if to quench a long, hard thirst. I grabbed Lisbet's hand and asked her to come upstairs with me. The alcohol started to hit me, making my already inebriated condition about ten times worse. My head began to reel. Picking up the empty bottle of Rémy, I took one big swing and threw it with all my might and aggression at a large ornate mirror which illustriously adorned the back of the bar-room wall. I barely noticed the crash in the background in the mere seconds it took me to leave.

Once in my room I began to make clumsy and drunken advances to a bewildered Lisbet. After a short while, before I could remove any of her clothing, there was a loud knock at the door. I opened it to see three angry-looking security men frowning straight at me. One of them spoke to me in that very distinct Danish accent, where the words always seem to go up at the ends of lines and somehow hang in the air . . .

'Were you in the bar this evening, sir?' I could detect a condescending and patronizing tone in his voice.

'No, I wasn't. What's the matter?'

'One of your group has been in the bar and there's been an accident,' he replied.

Trying desperately not to slur my words, I said, 'Look, I don't know what you're talking about and besides, I can't imagine anyone in the band doing such a thing.'

One of the security guards edged his way into the room and noticed Lisbet sitting on the corner of the bed.

'Sir, I hope you realize that you are not allowed lady visitors in your room.'

God, I thought to myself, this is ridiculous. We're in Denmark, the land of sexual freedom and liberation.

He continued. 'Please, young lady, I must ask you to leave.'

I was starting to get really angry and stroppy. 'You fuckin' leave her alone, it's none of your business anyway.' I lunged at Lisbet's arm and dragged her out of the room. We got to a lift and descended into the lobby. As the doors opened I could see half a dozen or so armed police talking to hotel staff. I pressed the lift button eagerly, hoping to be whisked to the safety of another floor. But one of the policemen noticed me and rushed towards the lift just as the door closed and we ascended.

Lisbet had been silent all this time. This sophisticated young woman, who had probably led a fairly protected and organized life until now, was probably stunned into silence at what was transpiring. What a romantic encounter this was turning out to be.

We scrambled out of the lift on one of the higher floors and I drunkenly tried to find our tour manager, Jay Vickers. I started banging on doors at random, thinking in my stupefied haze that he must be in one of them. Strangers opened doors wiping their bleary eyes and wondering why a loud, drunken Englishman was noisily and obnoxiously pounding his way through the halls of this once quiet and sedate hotel. After I had knocked frantically on nearly every door on that floor, I made for the staircase and headed down to the next. To my surprise the Danish police were coming up the stairs towards me. I ran back up and went inside a small door that led to a maid's room. I turned off the light and waited. Outside I could hear the policeman's footsteps. The door suddenly burst open and the police violently dragged me out. I tried to reason with them, but it seemed that none of them spoke English.

Down in the lobby, to my relief, Grenville was waiting with Jay, who fortunately spoke some Danish. The police bundled me and Jay into the back of the police van. Grenville escorted Lisbet away. I shouted and cursed from the back of the van while Jay tried calmly to reason with them. By now the police were very angry and they started to beat Jay up. There I was, an angry drunk kid who had started this whole miserable affair, and it was Jay who was getting a beating. I went even more berserk, shouting and spitting abuse, then I was thrown into a cell. My arms swung pathetically in the air as I tried to punch one of the policemen. They put me in a 'choker' hold and the next thing I remember was waking to the clunking sound of the cell door opening. Grenville had bailed me out and managed to convince the hotel not to press charges.

When I arrived back at the hotel the main members of the staff stood on either side of the entrance hall, curious, no doubt, about my condition. As I walked down the hall I caught the hotel manager's eye and said, proudly, 'Fucking hotel. I didn't want to stay here anyway.' With this the small group clapped and smiled.

What a night. And what an introduction to this romantic and beautiful city. I wondered what had happened to Lisbet. I hadn't got her telephone number or her address. Wonderful, wonderful Copenhagen, friendly old port of the sea; was I ever glad to get on the plane and leave. Yet as I watched the city slowly become miniaturized below as the plane climbed its way through the sky, I couldn't help thinking about that pretty young Danish girl I had met the day before. I hoped I would see her again someday.

After the nightmare of Copenhagen we arrived back in England and performed at the *New Musical Express* Pollwinners' concert at the Empire Pool, Wembley. On the bill were the Animals, the Rolling Stones, Them, Tom Jones, and of course the Beatles. We played with the Beatles three or four times and they never liked playing on the same bill as us. We seemed at the time like a threat to everyone. Somehow we were always able to whip up a crowd to a frenzy. We had once played on the same bill together at the Liverpool Empire. The Beatles closed the show but the crowd was still shouting for the Kinks when they came on. That must have really put some grit in their teeth, especially in Liverpool.

As for Tom Jones, I never could understand his popularity. He was a really nice guy but he seemed so out of place among us rock 'n' rollers. He looked and acted like a much older singer from the fifties doing a Welsh Elvis or something. Like Frankie Vaughan doing Little Richard. That loud overbearing voice – excruciating. Odd, and not very cool.

At this concert, Epstein did a switch on us by insisting that we go on after the Beatles to close the show. At first it seemed like the ultimate compliment, but it was difficult to follow the Beatles. When we first appeared on stage the atmosphere seemed flat, but after a couple of songs the crowd started to get into it in the usual screaming way. I'll bet if Lennon were alive today he'd say that they wanted to go on before us to get home before the rush. But really I think they were wary of us.

I remember watching the Beatles' sound check in the afternoon before that show. I tried to make conversation with Lennon, guitar talk stuff, but he didn't seem very interested and kept insinuating that he didn't want anybody fucking around with his guitar. But I admired Lennon; I felt he gave them balls and earthiness. He was really the spiritual essence of the band in the beginning. The Beatles might have turned out to be just another pop group without his anger and cynicism, his special point of view.

I also felt Ringo was terribly underrated as a drummer. He had a certain feel that was so right for the time, especially since it was difficult then to find good 'feel' drummers. Even now, when we're recording in the studio, I might say to Bob, our drummer, 'Here Bob, do a Ringo,' meaning do that splashy side-to-side rock vibe.

Paul McCartney came across at the time as being a bit superficial. I felt that he held his cards close to his chest. George Harrison was a very quiet guy; I admired his playing but I never got to know him very well.

We didn't socialize much with the Stones or the Beatles except for casual meetings or chats in nightclubs. We were all quite competitive and while we were eager to know what everyone else was up to, nobody wanted to give anything away. Incredibly potent creative forces were at work – you could almost smell it and taste it.

After 'Set Me Free' we recorded one of my all-time favourite Kinks tracks, 'See My Friends'. I believe it's one of the most beautiful songs Ray ever wrote. And despite all its 'gay overtones', I always felt it was a song about tragic loss of a deep friendship that transcends words and defies explanation. Ray played me the song and we talked over several ideas for instrumentation. Because of its obvious Indian flavour we discussed the possibility of using sitars. There was very little Indian music around then, and I wasn't familiar with Indian instruments, so we messed around with different tunings to get the right kind of droning noises.

There was a great album out by an English blues/folk singer named Davey Graham, called, I believe, *Folk, Blues and*. He had a very individual way of playing that on the one hand was typically English folk but on the other demonstrated a wonderful variety of influences ranging from blues to Eastern styles. He used interesting tunings to create an ethnic feel using just a plain acoustic guitar.

I used to smile to myself when I listened to other records after 'See My Friends' was released, how everybody was buying sitars and trying to get into that 'Indian' thing. Especially since the instrumentation on 'Friends' was simply an old cheap Framus twelve-string that had been lying around for years, and my heavy electric guitar drone. I think that's why the record sounds so pure. It reminds me of my joyful experiences listening to Buddy Holly records when the drummer sounded as if he was just hitting a shoe-box. Minimal. Beautiful. Simple and totally expressive.

When we recorded 'Friends' we did a few takes then listened to the playback, expecting to be propelled into unknown dimensions of ecstasy. Instead it sounded flat and cold. We couldn't believe it.

'Shel, we're playing our hearts out down there, what's happening? Can't you do something?' we pleaded. It sounded good but there was something missing – not in the performance, but in the sound. The only effects the studios had at that time were reverb echo and tape delay. They had limiter/compressors but those were used only to try to level out the peaks and valleys of the music. In the end, the engineer came up with the idea of pushing the output of the multi-track (4trk) into the input of their two main compressors. He pushed the volume as high as it would go before audible distortion.

We went back into the studio and tried it again. It was amazing. Once Ray and I had laid in the vocals I knew we had made something special. Jagger said to me in a club one night that he thought it was one of the best records he had ever heard. One night at the Scotch of St James club, McCartney said, 'You bastards, how dare you? I should have made that record.' But he didn't.

'Friends' influenced the British music and record fraternity immensely at the time. Everyone went out and bought sitars. Brian Jones had forsaken his Vox guitar for one. And George Harrison bought an entire warehouse full, or so it seemed. I bet Ravi Shankar couldn't believe his luck. An Indian curry at the Shalimar in the Finchley Road on a Saturday night would never be quite the same again.

I was still living in my rented house at Connaught Gardens with Mick. The parties continued and I was taking a lot of pills. Uppers, mostly, and a great deal of alcohol. One evening I had arranged to meet a girlfriend of mine named Marianne at the Blue Post in Poland Street. We were drinking Scotch and Coke and I started popping pill after pill. Marianne was a sweet Irish girl I had known from my school days in Muswell Hill. After Sue and I broke up I started seeing Marianne and became quite fond of her. She was good company and even though I didn't think anyone could take Sue's place, I at least considered the possibility of making a go of it with Marianne. She was very pretty, petite and quite fragile, with straight black hair.

We had decided to go to the movies, but really I just wanted to get stoned. As we left the pub I hailed a cab, then got in and blacked out. I didn't remember a thing when I woke up the next morning with Marianne beside me. I was bewildered. I woke her up and noticed that she had a black eye and a fat lip.

'Marianne, what the hell happened to you?' I asked. She tried to smile but she seemed very hurt and upset.

'You really don't remember anything, do you?' she said. 'We were at the pictures. We saw *Beckett* with Richard Burton. In the middle of the film you stood up and started ranting and raving. I couldn't understand what you were saying, just weird stuff, gobbledygook.'

She told me how I started throwing ice-cream at the screen and how she managed to drag me out of the theatre. She was worried that I'd be arrested as I cursed and swore at every passer-by like a madman. We were in the middle of Leicester Square.

She continued. 'I pulled you into a nearby pub where you started to demand more drinks. You knocked over tables and other people's drinks and cursed at the publican for closing the pub. I thought for one awful minute you were going to take a swipe at him. He was about six foot six and almost as wide. I got you out of there and into a cab, where you passed out. The cab driver helped me into the house with you. You came round a bit after I gave you some coffee but you seemed like a total stranger to me, a monster. You started lashing out, hitting me. I was really scared.'

Marianne started to cry and I was overcome with self-disgust at hitting her and shock that I couldn't remember any of it. I had never hit a woman before and it appalled and disturbed me to realize that I had completely lost control of myself. I felt bad for Marianne, who left for good that day. I didn't see her again for many years, by which time she was married. I totally blew it with her. Marianne wanted a normal relationship and I frightened her off. This episode should have been a clue to me that maybe my drinking and drug-taking were getting out of hand, but instead I brooded.

I felt sorry for myself the rest of the day and thoughts about Sue flooded back. I suppose I was still emotionally pained by my experience with her. I hadn't got over it, even though I tried to push thoughts of her to the back of my mind. But Sue was always in my heart. Now, with Marianne gone as well, I thought about how I missed Sue and how maybe all I really wanted was a normal life with a normal job. I thought about the baby. Of sharing a little place with them somewhere, maybe going to see football at the Arsenal on a Saturday afternoon. Or going to Mum's with my kid on a Sunday for tea. I wondered about my stupid, unreal life and where the hell it was taking me. But it was too late, there was no turning back now.

I sat down and wrote two songs, 'I am Free', which appeared later on the *Kinks Kontroversy* album, and 'She's My Girl', which was recorded but never released:

Every single dress she wears, never really fits her well
A little girl with dark brown hair, she always laughs and never
seems to care

She's my girl . . . She's my girl and I love her all the way
She crawls around the floor each night, struggling but
keeping quiet
I've got to have her while I can, 'cos I'll die before my time
is through
She's my girl . . .

Tracey would have been around two years old. How I wished she and Sue had been with me then.

Our headlining UK tour took us all over the country. Other bands on the bill were the Yardbirds, Goldie and the Ginger-breads, and the Riot Squad. Pete and I were quite friendly with the Yardbirds, but Ray didn't trust them and thought they might steal our ideas. Goldie and the Gingerbreads became good mates. They were a lot of fun and mixed in really well with the 'rest of the guys'. Mick Avory even had something going with their drummer.

But it was a gruelling schedule with over nineteen dates in three weeks. We had been working constantly since our first number 1 hit and I think we were starting to feel the pressures and rigours of relentless touring. By the time we got to Cardiff we were becoming a bit edgy and bitchy with one another.

In Taunton the previous night, Ray and I had argued about the show. Something about me wanting to change the set and Ray not wanting to. I asked Mick his opinion and as usual he wouldn't say. By the time we got to our rooms the argument was becoming heated. I was upset that Mick was always so non-committal. He wanted everything to be easy, tapping away at his little drums and wanking. Looking back, I guess Mick didn't know how to behave, especially with Ray and me making most of the decisions.

All of a sudden our fight developed into a punch-up *par excellence*. By the time our road managers broke it up I had a sore lip and eye and Mick had cuts to the face and mouth.

By the following night, after we'd both had time to stew, our feelings were running very high as we took to the stage. A couple of songs into the show I looked at Mick and shouted at him, calling him a useless cunt. I said his drumming was shit and that they'd sound better if he played them with his cock. I sneered at him and kicked his drums all over the stage, then moved over to the mike and acted nonchalant. The next thing I knew I was lying flat on my back in the dressing-room with blood trickling down the back of my neck. Turns out Mick had lost it and hit me over the head with one of his cymbal stands.

Pete told me that Mick ran out of the theatre like a scared rabbit, thinking he had killed me. Thinking back on it, it must have looked quite funny: Mick on the run from the police in his hunting pink jacket and frilly shirt, trying to melt in with the crowd. I went to the hospital and had half a dozen stitches in my head and was driven back to London.

Mick and I made up and we were soon back on the road again. Later Mick admitted to me that he always regretted not coming forward and expressing his opinions more.

Another funny thing about that incident is that many of the audience thought that our fight was part of the stage show. It reminded me of an outrageous character named 'Beef' in the movie *Phantom of the Paradise* (a rock parody that came out in the early seventies based on *The Phantom of the Opera*). Beef was a very campy Gary Glitter type rock singer who performed in the theatre where the Phantom was hiding. During his silly act he was electrocuted by the Phantom. As they carried him offstage, frozen in a ridiculously camp posture with eyes bulging, the audience was cheering, 'Beef, Beef', thinking that it was all part of the act.

The Kinks were always ahead of their time. Once we started to get a reputation for fighting on stage, other bands copied us. I wonder if Pete Townshend was in the audience that night sussing it out. I can just picture Pete practising smashing his guitar in front of his bedroom mirror until he got it right.

The Who played with us a few times as the High Numbers. I remember thinking how deadly serious they all looked, with the exception of Keith Moon, who was not only a great drummer but a very funny character. Like a crazed younger version of Robert Newton, fresh from the set of *Treasure Island*. To give Townshend his due, he has been one of the few rock musicians who has openly acknowledged that the Kinks were a big influence on his career and that 'I Can't Explain' was directly inspired by 'You Really Got Me'. Later, the Doors did 'Hello, I Love You', which was obviously plagiarized from 'All Day and All of the Night'.

The chorus was melodically similar, with the same chord structure, and it was similar rhythmically as well. Our publishers wanted to sue, but we decided against it in the end. Ray and I thought it was so funny and so obvious that it didn't seem worth the trouble. There's no way that anyone could get away with it today. After all, I suppose it was the ultimate compliment. To be copied, not ripped off, I mean. Everything, in the end, is derivative of something else. But not always so blatantly.

After the Cardiff incident our managers were eager to get us back on the road. They were worried that the precious goose might start laying rotten eggs instead of golden ones. Or worse, commit suicide. The truth was, none of us knew how long it would last. Everyone agreed that the next important move was to go to the States. A tour was planned for June.

It was exciting finally to go to America and the first part of the tour went pretty well. But as it went on the dates kept getting shuffled around and at some gigs we had problems getting paid, like at the Cow Palace in San Francisco. We showed up but the promoters refused to pay us, so we refused to play. At other venues we were promised a certain amount of money, but the promoters would stiff us, saying we didn't draw the crowds they expected.

Our biggest problem, it seemed, was management. I never understood why Robert and Grenville stayed in England, when this was potentially one of our most crucial career moves. All the responsibility was left solely to Larry Page, who was too inexperienced to handle a tour like this, it seemed. He was also courting Sonny and Cher for Kassner, which really upset us. He underestimated the power of the unions and even abandoned us at one point to travel back to England on some flimsy pretext. We were left with Sam Curtis, our road manager, who did his best.

After this disastrous tour we were banned for three years from playing in the States. We never did find out exactly why, and some people attributed it to our wild behaviour, but I think it resulted from the consistent fuck-ups of our management, and black-balling by the promoters who had tried to rip us off. Larry Page was a music publisher, for heaven's sake, not a heavyweight like Allen Klein (an American manager who successfully negotitated deals for the Stones and later the Beatles), and definitely not an ambassador like Brian Epstein. Unfortunately, though he never admitted it, it was obvious to me that he was out of his depth. I liked Larry and I understood that anyone can fuck up, but during this trip my illusions faded and I began to think that maybe he was only with us to sign up other acts for Kassner.

I think Page must have manoeuvred Robert and Grenville out of the picture. Maybe Page thought that the Kinks were on a short fuse to self-destruct after Cardiff. We needed guidance, a strong influence, not weak-willed individuals motivated by self-interest who would run at the first signs of trouble.

Our first date in New York was at Manhattan's Academy of Music. Dave Clark was also on the show. We were billed as the KINGS. Mmmm. The crowd was great, just as enthusiastic as back home. We moved on to Philly, where we played a show with the Supremes and Clark again. By the time we got to Denver we received the full Beatle treatment: police escort from the airport, from the hotel to the gig, screaming girls tearing at our clothes, major security at the hotel to keep the crazed fans at bay. It was 'fab'.

Sonny and Cher joined the tour for a few dates and the shows went great. By the end of June we were checked into the Beverly Hills Hotel, Los Angeles. A dream come true. Hollywood at last, all the glitter, women, and fun of Tinseltown. We met and had drinks with Dean Martin at Reprise Records, shook hands with Warner executives and had dinner at the Brown Derby.

My stay in LA could have been ruined altogether. Before the American tour, somebody had loaned me a custom-built Guild guitar that had once been owned by George Harrison. In those days we carried our own instruments, and when we arrived at the airport in LA all the bags arrived except for that guitar. We were slated to do the TV show *Shindig*, and a runner from the show took me to a guitar store that he knew. I looked at all the new guitars and then noticed a bunch of dusty old cases stacked away at the back, including a triangular-shaped one.

'Let me have a look at that one,' I said to the proprietor.

'No,' he replied, 'you don't want that old thing.' That 'old thing' turned out to be a Gibson Futurist, also known as a Flying V. I asked how much it was.

'Two hundred dollars,' he said. I peeled off two hundred-dollar bills and bought it.

I used the Flying V for the first time on *Shindig*. It had been built in the fifties, but these guitars didn't become popular again until the early seventies. For *Shindig* we recorded back tracks to 'All Day' and 'Long Tall Shorty', which we sang live on the show. Also on the show were Bobby Vinton and Sonny and Cher. Because of union rules we had to use the house band. They were called the Shindogs and their guitarist was James Burton, one of my favourite guitar players, who played with Rick Nelson and many others. I couldn't believe I was recording a session with James Burton in the back-up band. I think my solo on 'Till the End of the Day' was inspired by that meeting.

One highlight of the tour was the night we played the Hollywood Bowl with the Beach Boys. At the time they were very much a kind of 'pop surf band', with Chuck Berry rip-off guitar breaks, but they went on to produce a body of work monumental in its scope and depth. The emotional intensity, the perception and musicality, the sheer warmth and joy expressed in their music, will be an inspiration for many generations to come.

Also on the bill were the Righteous Brothers, who were amazing, as well as Sam the Sham, who was silly but great, and the Byrds, who I thought were sensational. I feel that the Byrds were the first genuine American 'rock band' of the sixties. I liked their distinct, smooth harmonies and Roger McGuinn's unique vocal and playing style, not to mention the 'cool' rose-coloured shades. To me, Jim Morrison had a unique voice and obvious sex appeal, but the Doors never actually sounded like a band to me, more like session musicians playing together. American kids were desperate for some 'home grown' after the continuous bombardment of British groups to their shores, and the Doors fitted the bill just right, I guess.

I loved being in the States, even though most of the tour didn't go well. It was nonetheless a vibrant and stimulating experience. The people were so outgoing, and nothing was too much trouble. I had the feeling that anything was possible.

The one thing I noticed was that in certain towns the older generations seemed fearful of change. They didn't like us with our long hair and our rebellious, nonconformist attitude. The Beatles, you must remember, had a very smart clean-cut image and a very organized PR team. Even the Stones had their hair cut and wore ties. But we were pretty outrageous with our long hair and strange outfits. People said to me, 'Hey thar', are you a boy or a girl?' And I answered, 'Wow, neither. Are you a cowboy or a real live redneck?'

The States were fun, just like I had imagined. Cowboys and Indians in Reno. Big-titted glamour girls in Hollywood. Hamburgers to go, Coke and fries. The land of *I Love Lucy*, John Wayne, and Frank Sinatra. The place where most of my heroes, were born: Eddie Cochran, Buddy Holly, Big Bill Broonzy, Chuck Berry, Hank Williams. Twenty Flight Rock, Kentucky Fried Chicken, and pizza. Yeah, you couldn't get real pizza in England then. An incredible experience.

But I felt that after the novelty had worn off the Americans didn't really understand our music or our culture. Coming from a country where having central heating was considered posh and a refrigerator a luxury, Americans seemed to me to be strangely spoiled and 'old-fashioned'. They seemed lost in the forties and fifties. I expected to find Americans more forward and progressive but I was surprised to find many very set in their ways, just like their English counterparts. The sixties' cultural revolution was instigated by the English youth, and the Americans soon followed. We were resented by an older generation of Americans during the British Invasion because, after all, the Yanks invented rock 'n' roll, and here were some cheeky Limeys showing them how to do it. American audiences were still listening to Elvis and Bobby Vinton or the Kingston Trio, and it must have come as a surprise to see such bands as the Beatles, DC5, and ourselves take over the top spots on the charts. We, of course, were just offering our own interpretation of feelings, values, hopes and fears of a new generation. We were voicing its pain and frustration through rock music. During our three-year ban, the simmering cauldron of social and political upheaval would manifest itself in the Vietnam War. American consciousness was about to become drastically 're-fashioned'.

5

By the end of 1965, our time was taken up with extensive touring of Europe and recording sessions at Pye Studios. We recorded songs for an EP that was released in September, called *Kwyet Kinks*. It included a song that was a slight departure for us, a song that Ray put together while on holiday called 'A Well-Respected Man'. I believe the song was inspired by our manager Robert and his love of Noël Coward. This influence was to colour Ray's style of writing quite significantly. What was particularly interesting about this period was our growing musical diversity, which I've always thought has been one of the most important sustaining qualities of 'Kinks' music. We've always been difficult to pigeonhole, difficult to categorize. I feel that this has given our music a certain uniqueness, although it's created problems for us commercially.

As we continued to experiment musically, Pye became nervous about our departure in style and backed out of the challenge to release 'Well-Respected' as a single in spite of our enthusiasm. As was so often the case with us, decisions were made at an executive level that hindered our creative impulses.

We did include a song I had written during a moment of depression and reflection, 'Wait Till the Summer Comes Along', which was about loss and regret.

We also recorded and released 'Till the End of the Day' and the album *Kinks Kontroversy*. I had accumulated a fairly decent collection of blues and jazz records by this time, artists like Lightning Hopkins, Howlin' Wolf, Muddy Waters, Sonny Boy, John Lee Hooker, and Sleepy John Estes. I had a particular fondness for Sleepy John; his style was so laid back, his sound so rough and ready, the recordings so full of character and atmosphere.

One of his records had a track called 'Milk Cow Blues'. I

thought that it would be great to do a version of it for the album, so we altered the arrangement, made it our own, and recorded the song as one of the lead tracks on *Kontroversy*. If my memory serves, I believe we recorded it in only one take. We had very limited time in the studio in those days anyway, so we didn't have the opportunity to go over and over songs like you can today. But I think it worked for us. Exciting, spontaneous stuff with most of the rough edges left in.

The album took us only about a week to complete, mixing and all. I always considered *Kontroversy* a quirky kind of record, an odd mixture of styles and songs. I loved 'You Can't Win'. It used to give me chills when I listened to it and reminded me of the energy of the Everlys' song, 'Price of Love'. Another song I liked was 'I'm on an Island', which grew out of a riff I had introduced at one of our rehearsals – a strange riff, almost comedic.

I was surprised that 'Where Have All the Good Times Gone', which was the B-side of 'Till the End of the Day', wasn't released as a single. I thought it was an obvious stand-out track from the album. Its emotions were very close to the heart. Ma and Pa look back on all the things they used to do:

> *Didn't have much money but they always told the truth*
> *Daddy didn't have no toys*
> *Mommy didn't meet no boys . . .*

These lines always got me. Lines that contained a real and modest beauty.

It's such a weird paradox that Ray, who wrote that lovely song, would later become so abusive to me, so cruel and creatively draining. When I look back, many times I've become so exasperated by his contradictory nature, his unyielding and unreasonable behaviour. On the one hand he's sensitive enough to understand even the slightest emotion, to feel for the plight and frustration of the underdog, able to offer great insight and compassion. Yet at the same time he displays an almost resentful and sometimes condescending loathing for his past, his family. He is at times venomous, spiteful, and completely self-involved. A puzzling dichotomy.

In September we toured Sweden and Denmark again. Soon after we arrived in Copenhagen I decided to try and look up Lisbet, that lovely girl I had met on my previous visit. I didn't know where she lived, or her second name or phone number. All I knew was her connection to the Carousel club.

My heart full of hope and expectation, I took to the streets in search of it. As I turned the block I saw in the distance a young girl walking towards me carrying school books. I thought, could this be who I think it is or is it just wishful thinking? As we slowly approached one another we were both astonished and surprised at bumping into one another that way. She seemed extremely shy when I approached and said hello. I thought that maybe after our last meeting she might be a little embarrassed but I was sure she remembered me. After a brief exchange of words I realized that she had been thinking of me in the same way as I had of her. We were close to the hotel so I invited her back to my room for some 'tea'. Once inside we realized how strong our attraction was for one another. She was so soft, so sweet, so beautiful, so shy. The couple of hours that followed were glorious. Was I falling in love?

I called her my little Chinese doll. Her eyes had a slight oriental shape to them and when she smiled in her irresistible way her whole face would light up and make her look slightly Chinese. She was very beautiful.

After the show in Copenhagen I had two days off, so Lisbet and I spent them together, lost in each other's company. She showed me the Tivoli Gardens at night, where we ate in one of the prettiest and most romantic places I had ever been, and introduced me to Danish food, Tuborg beer, Aalborg schnapps, pastries, coffee, and Prince cigarettes. Her English wasn't great, but it didn't matter to me at all. We laughed and walked hand in hand through the gardens. The laughter of passing people, the noise of the happy crowd, the clatter of the roller-coaster, the clumsy way she smoked her cigarette, trying hard to impress me while being careful not to inhale, all these thoughts now serve to highlight wonderful and special memories of a time that I will never forget.

I left Denmark reluctantly and we promised to meet again. Now I was off to Germany and on that tour I made great friends with singer-guitarist Tony Sheridan, who had played with the Beatles in Hamburg and was full of bittersweet stories about them and the sleazy clubs and awful people he had had to put up with. He was an extremely angry and bitter guy – always popping pills, always ready for a laugh – who hated Germans with a particular flair. But I liked him and thought he was a talented man who had somehow missed the boat and had always been on the periphery of any real success.

He was very funny but crazy as well. During nights when there was a full moon he would lock himself away, claiming he suffered from moon madness. One evening after a show we were standing at the bar of a very crowded and plush hotel having drinks when all of a sudden he unzipped his fly, pulled out his cock, and started pissing over everybody, making Nazi salutes and swearing at the top of his voice in perfect German. I'm not sure if there was a full moon that night. Maybe a blue moon. Let's just say he was a very spontaneous character. And usually very stoned.

I think I was stoned the whole tour, since you could get great drugs in Germany at that time. On my first night I met a dark-haired girl in a club who spoke nothing but German. Despite the language barrier and with a little help from one of our German road crew I invited her back to my hotel. We smoked some hashish and since neither of us understood what the other was saying, there was only one thing to do.

We made love throughout the night. It was incredible, and the next day I decided to take her with me on the whole tour. We had sex constantly and explored each other's bodies to the fullest. And not once did we have a conversation. We didn't need to – our bodies were communicating just fine without the help of either German or English. Yes, I know that I had just left the woman I thought I was falling in love with in Denmark, but I was still only eighteen years old. Women were everywhere, and I had no thoughts about my future. I lived completely in the present and wanted to remember every last second of it. These were very promiscuous times, remember, before the dreadful scourge of AIDS.

Besides, I've always worshipped and adored women. I spent my childhood around beautiful women and I felt very comfortable with women of all types. Every woman has something special about her, no matter who she is, if you are prepared to look for it.

It was a pretty crazy time, not only for wild sex, but also for weird and silly haircuts. One of the bands on the tour was called the Lords. They were quite accomplished musicians but looked totally ridiculous with their long hair cut in true Beatles style. The joke was that on stage they looked like they were wearing German helmets. I don't think they appreciated us pointing out that fact. Hilarious.

Another band around at that time was called the Monks. While they were playing they looked like so many others with their perfectly trimmed Beatle cuts, but when they finished a song they would bow and reveal shaven bald patches in the middle of their crowns. Just like real monks. But very silly.

Girls' hairstyles were strange then, too, with their backcombed bouffants, hair matted and hardened by the constant spraying of large quantities of lacquer. Forget trying to run your fingers romantically through it. They'd just get sticky – or stuck. It was like matted cobwebs.

When we got back from our European tour I decided to sublet my house and move back temporarily to Denmark Terrace. Mick Avory had long since moved back to Molesey. Mitch Mitchell, the drummer with the Riot Squad, was looking for a place in London so I rented my house to him. But not for long. One day I went around to see how Mitch was getting on and the place was starting to look like a pigsty. As if it wasn't enough for the house to be filthy and unkempt, with dirty laundry all over the place, he kept pigeons, of all things, under his bed. There was pigeon shit everywhere. What a stink. I quickly kicked him out, pigeons and all, dirty sod. The next time I saw him he was playing with Jimi Hendrix. Mitch took flight with his birds and landed very surely on his musical feet. He was a nice guy, but his drumming style irritated me. In my opinion his style seemed fiddly and unnecessary. I suppose he must have been intimidated by Hendrix's energy, causing him to overplay. Hendrix probably didn't care anyway or even hear him half the time.

I met Hendrix only once, when we sat together on a plane from London to New York, but I considered him a fabulous rock 'n' roll character and a great and unique guitarist. He told me that he felt that 'You Really Got Me' was a major step forward for rock music, particularly the guitar sound. He was really interested in how we got that sound, which I related to him. It was clear that even though we didn't speak much – he was surprisingly very quiet and modest – we shared a mutual respect.

After the success of 'A Well-Respected Man', Ray came up with another gem in a similar vein, 'Dedicated Follower of Fashion'. This also gave us further opportunity to camp it up in public, especially at photo shoots, or on TV. My mate Quinn was eager to help furnish me with whatever outrageous clothes he could get hold of. The sillier the better.

One day I was looking in a ladies' hat shop on the corner of Carnaby Street and saw a purple and pink striped floppy hat, the kind that you can mould into whatever shape you want. It was by far the silliest item in the store so I bought it. Stretching it and pulling it into a point at the top and folding the base of it into a large brim, I placed it proudly and contemptuously on my head. I wasn't happy until somebody made some comment or the other about it, whether complimentary or not. It didn't matter as long as it was 'noticed'. I even wore the thing to bed.

One particular jacket I liked and wore frequently was a coat from Quinn's shop. It was kind of Edwardian in design, single-breasted, with yellowish raised flower shapes in velvet all over it. It hung long below the arse, with large lapels, and looked wonderfully silly. It was obviously made out of some old curtain fabric that had been lying around neglected in a Sandersons warehouse. There was probably wallpaper to match. If I could have found some I certainly would have repapered my bedroom to complement my dress. In fact I still have that jacket. My kids sometimes take turns wearing it for fancy-dress parties or retro-disco club outings.

I loved the theatrics and flamboyance of that period, the style and fun. I grew really long sideburns and enjoyed walking down the King's Road, Piccadilly, Soho and Carnaby Street with my friends, dressed to shock. Always looking for attention.

After a couple of unsuccessful attempts to record 'Dedicated Follower' we finally arrived at a version that we liked. It had a grating, brash, 'tinny' sound with a more open and 'changy' electric guitar intro, which sounded great on the radio. The earlier version sounded more ordinary, more folky.

This time Pye plucked up the courage to release 'Dedicated' as a single and it became a hit. On the B-side was a song that was virtually written and thrown together in the studio, 'Sitting on My Sofa'. I came up with a line, a riff or two, and a series of chord changes, and Ray embellished them and wrote a song based on them. Ray took all the writing credit. It didn't bother me at the time – after all, it was family – and we were enjoying phenomenal success. The adulation we received seemed more than enough for me. I never thought about the fact that the publishing rights would be so valuable or even cared about it. In fact, I never thought about money much at all, unlike Ray, who has to be one of the most thrifty people I've ever known.

My mum told me once that when he first went to the Croydon School of Art he was given a grant of £200 by the local education authority and she swore that he kept it and never spent a penny. She often remarked that our old man was mean, but I never noticed. He never shirked from buying a round of drinks in the pub, whereas Ray would somehow get called away at the crucial point in the evening when it fell to him to buy the drinks. Rosie always defended Ray's tightness with money, offering that he was only being 'careful'. But the truth is he's miserly with his money, and in later years he would be equally miserly with his emotions and affections.

Another time, according to Larry Page, he, Ray and Rasa were on their way somewhere and Rasa pleaded with Ray for the money to get herself a coat. 'Please, I need it, it's cold,' she said. But Ray refused to give her the money. Larry assumed that Rasa wanted to buy an expensive new coat, possibly a fur, and later found out that she merely wanted to retrieve her coat from the dry-cleaners. In contrast, I have probably always been too generous, always willing to help family and friends. Many years later, Ray's then wife Yvonne said to me, 'If Ray was a bit more like you and you were a little more like him, then both of you would have been better off.'

My wild, single life carried on as usual. At a party in Hampstead I met a petite, pretty, black-haired singer called Lesley. I was very drunk but not too drunk to fancy her. We talked about God, Life, Music, the World. The party drew to its end and Lesley invited me back to her flat. Many drinks later I was actually quite impressed by Lesley's ideas about the 'World' and 'Life'. I probably would have thought anything I heard was profound, just to get her in bed. Her flatmate arrived soon after, a very pretty and voluptuous blonde.

This lovely blonde started to roll some amazing joints. As we smoked the room moved and swayed. My speech became more incoherent and Lesley, seeing my condition, helped me into a bedroom where she undressed me and put me to bed. What an angel.

As my head hit the pillow I went into a serene and beautiful sleep. A sleep full of lush green fields, panoramic views of incredibly rich and luscious landscapes. Not one strawberry-coloured one in sight, though. After a while I was awakened by the blonde girl as she snuggled up beside me. She was naked.

We kissed and fondled, touched and stroked each other. She was a delight. This blonde Vampira licked my stomach and placed my penis fully into her mouth and began to suck on it like the Goddess of Whores. It was ecstasy. Then she sat on top of me and placed my cock inside her. She wiggled and swayed and pushed and pressed against me like a crazed and rampant slut, begging and pleading with me, 'C'mon David, do it, do it now.' In my somewhat helpless condition, what else could I do but comply with her wishes? Afterwards she left, and I fell asleep like a baby back into my dreams.

What seemed like only half an hour later I was awakened yet again by this ravenous woman. We made love, but this time I was on top and she talked me through it. It was strange but delightful. Again she left, only to return a little while later. This must have happened six times during the night. Although I'm sure I would have had trouble getting out of bed and standing up, I didn't seem to have any problems lying down.

As the dawn broke I arose from my slumbers surprisingly recuperated. I got dressed and wandered into the kitchen, where Lesley was making coffee. The blonde was nowhere to be seen. When I inquired about her, Lesley said that she normally slept late and wouldn't be up for some time. I'm not sure if she knew about our escapades or not.

I left, and as I walked through the streets of Hampstead I reflected with great pleasure about such an unexpected but thoroughly enjoyable experience. Later I ran into the blonde at parties and in clubs. When I tried to speak to her about that night she always avoided mention of it. It was difficult to approach her anyway because she was usually accompanied by a well-known rock singer who was a casual acquaintance of mine. I thought it best to let sleeping dogs lie. Although this particular dog didn't get much sleep that night.

By now, especially after our horrendous US tour, our management was unravelling. Early on in the formation of the Kinks, we had signed separate agreements with Boscobel, the company formed by Robert and Grenville, and Denmark Productions, the company formed by Page, with both sides taking management fees. Boscobel was now suing Denmark Productions for control of the Kinks. The pending court case plus our heavy touring and recording schedule was taking its toll on Ray. He became quite ill and our doctor insisted he take a rest.

Grenville had booked some dates in Belgium that he claimed we couldn't get out of, so he got Mick Grace from a local band called the Cockneys to fill in for Ray. We had never toured there before, so we thought we'd get away with it since Belgians had only seen pictures of the Kinks on album covers. I think Robert and Grenville were worried about Ray's long-term health.

We rehearsed with Grace and it seemed all right, so I agreed to the tour. But it turned out to be a disaster. Grace looked a bit like Ray, and as it turned out he was a manic depressive, so they had a lot more in common than I first thought. It was a miserable time and a bad move by our management. During the taping of a TV special which we were miming – luckily – Grenville was so panicked he made the cameraman avoid close-ups of Grace. At times like these when he was in a bit of a tizzy, he often reminded me of John Cleese from that *Monty Python* sketch, the 'Upper Class Twits Race'. When I watched the playback of the show later, I noticed that every time the camera would settle on Grace he would bow his head, trying at every turn to foil the approaching camera angle. It looked so ridiculous.

But there were some lighter moments, like one show near the French border. As I knelt down in front of the audience to do a solo, I saw a guy with an extremely perplexed expression on his face. He was staring ferociously at Mick Grace. After some thought he turned to me and said in broken English, 'Hey, Dave, he not Ray.' He wandered out of the building shaking his head in disbelief. I was laughing so hard I could barely sing after that.

When I arrived back in London I went to see Ray. He seemed a bit crazy and manic, but I was starting to get used to his erratic behaviour. Ray insisted I get my guitar and listen to an idea he had. A noticeably forlorn-looking Rasa stood by his side as he sat by the piano and started to play in octaves the descending line of what was soon to become the main riff of 'Sunny Afternoon'. He played the riff again, I doubled the line with my guitar, and he sang the first rough verse of it.

I got that now familiar chill up my spine and knew that this was something special. It was the same way I felt when I first heard 'You Really Got Me'. A mysterious magic had visited the three of us in that little house in Fortis Green.

In June 'Sunny Afternoon' became number 1 in the charts and it was turning into a truly wonderful summer. With some wild and crazy times, such as our experience with David Watts.

I am a dull and simple lad
Cannot tell water from champagne
And I have never met the Queen
And I wish I could be like David Watts.
Wish I could be like David Watts . . .

Ray wrote those words, based on an actual incident that happened to the band in the summer of 1966 in Rutland, England. David Watts, who was then in his forties, was a concert promoter, a Rutland dignitary who was obviously well in with the locals. On first meeting him, it occurred to me that although he had a serious manner, he was quite charming. He was very upright, lean, and fairly fit, with a disciplined air about him.

That summer, Watts produced a 'raving' outdoor show for us in Rutland. Everything went extremely well – in other words, we had the main ingredients for a good show: screaming girls and a cheering crowd so loud that it drowned out our puny public address system. We could barely hear ourselves play.

After the show and the usual backstage small talk, Major Watts invited us to his home for drinks. He lived in a beautiful Georgian manor house set in delightful rolling countryside. After our arrival he soon made us feel at home. Everybody was chatting and in good spirits as the drinks started to flow. David brought out bottle after bottle of pink champagne, to our delight. It was the first time I had ever had it. Pink champagne, that is.

Cannot tell water from Champagne . . .

After a while, there was a loud knock at the door. Much to our surprise some rather serious and rugged-looking men walked in. They were dressed in plain suits and raincoats. After brief introductions were made I came to the conclusion that these men may have been part of the local police constabulary. They were clearly close friends of David's.

Alcohol continued to be consumed in large quantities. Mick Avory, Pete and I were getting quite drunk. Never being ones to miss an opportunity to camp it up, we began dancing with each other in a very animated and suggestive way. Our frolicking became infectious. As the evening wore on and inhibitions relaxed, many of the men's personalities began to change. The previously macho policemen began dancing and kissing and frolicking around like camp schoolboys.

The transformation in our host, David Watts, was truly the most extraordinary. This smart, tough-looking disciplinarian type had, by the continued use of alcohol and hashish, gone through a staggering metamorphosis. Before our eyes this pillar of the community had become a delightfully funny, witty, flagrantly eccentric and flamboyant homosexual. With arms flailing theatrically in the air as he danced and pranced, Watts stole kisses from his police friends at every opportunity. His facial muscles flexed into absurd and contorted expressions that would not have been out of place in a Fellini film.

As for the women that night: we were all so drunk and busy taking the piss that it was quite late in the evening when we realized there were none in the assembled company. And by that time, the situation was much too far gone. Our night at David Watts's was turning into a wonderfully amusing party. The gay police strutted their stuff with total abandon in scenes that could have been right out of *Monty Python*.

Without the least provocation Mick started to strip his clothes off. As Mick displayed his wares to the delight of the assembled company like some screaming gay truck driver on acid, David took me aside to a quiet corner for a chat. He was extremely drunk. He leered lustfully at me through his big doggy watery eyes. He invited me upstairs to a small gym that he had built alongside his bedroom and asked me to work out on his exercise bicycle. I seized the opportunity like a true prick-teaser.

As I cycled and sweated and sweated, I could sense that David was reaching the perspiring limits of self-control. Now I understood how women felt when being leched at by some perverse and dirty old man. It was quite an interesting feeling of power, I must admit. After some strategic manoeuvring by David, we ended up in a full and deep embrace, his arms wrapped around me like a seething octopus.

> He is the head boy at the school
> He is the captain of the team
> He is so gay and fancy free
> And I wish I could have all that he's got . . .

Downstairs I could hear raucous laughter echoing wildly throughout the house. I suggested that we go downstairs and have another drink, thinking at the time that there would be safety in numbers. And at least Ray and the rest of the band would be down there, although who could guess in what state? Much to my relief, David agreed and we rejoined the happy and very drunken party – which had grown hotter by several degrees. I quickly shook off my ardent pursuer and began dancing around, sure that the issue was finished. Who knew what signals he heard in our music? I may have been responsible for the hard-driving instrumentation, but Ray tended to write lyrics that suggested at the very minimum some interest in the exploration of male–male couplings.

Nevertheless, I noted through my alcohol-induced fog that as I danced around David Watts's house, our host had fallen into a deep conversation with my brother. Was it possible Ray was defending my honour?

After a while, David – his ardour still not quite dampened – came over, put his arm around me and took me for a walk in the garden. We sat romantically on a double swing that rested beneath some beautiful willow trees. Our view was of a lake and the starlit sky. It was there that David Watts told me how much he cared about me. But that was not all.

'I'd like you to come and live with me,' he said with a blush.

I stammered out through my shock and surprise, 'I don't know what to say – it's all a bit sudden!' He seemed dashed and a bit confused. Whatever made him think of this, I asked.

'Ray says he's concerned about your future,' Watts continued. 'He made me a proposition.'

'A *what*?'

'You, for my house,' he said. 'This house.' His arms spread wide. Me, in exchange for a Georgian manor house. Wasn't that just like Ray, I thought, always the first to be concerned about my welfare. What an arsehole.

Watts stared at me with those puppy-dog eyes. He was utterly serious. The evening – which by now was turning to morning – had obviously got way out of hand.

'Let me think this over,' I said, trying to let him down gently. 'I'm going to need a few days to think this over.' This little bit of encouragement seemed to calm him. Quickly I rounded up Ray, Mick and Pete and we discreetly made our excuses among the Rutland crowd and left as the sun was coming up.

We didn't see David for some time after that, not until we'd finished recording a new album called *Something Else*. One of the songs on it was entitled 'David Watts'. Surprisingly, it came out more like many Kinks songs decrying the bourgeoisie than any direct comment on sexuality.

Wish I could be like David Watts
Wish I could be like
Wish I could beeeeee like . . .

It was our little code to Watts, an inside joke.

When we met Watts again he immediately understood the joke. We chatted and laughed and reminisced about the whole affair. He said he thought us perfect bastards, but I think he was really flattered nonetheless.

What stuck in my mind the most was the fact that my older brother, whose guidance and defence I had counted on, was ready to trade me for a bit of architecture. This time he had been thwarted. It was not the first time Ray had demonstrated his lack of regard for my feelings.

6

Much to my delight and surprise, Lisbet arrived in London and enrolled in a college near Goodge Street to learn English. Her mother had rented her a room in a house just up the road. Pete was still dating Lisbet's cousin Beden, but towards the end of that summer I noticed that he seemed to be unhappy with the band. Creative problems began to emerge – petty jealousies, differences of opinion.

During one afternoon rehearsal I started to play around with an idea. Pete jammed along with me. Ray came in and sat at the piano and Pete turned to him and said, 'Ray, listen to this song idea of Dave's.'

I started to play and sing, with Pete accompanying me. After the first verse Ray abruptly turned his head and said, 'I don't like it, it's silly.'

Before I could get a word out, Pete interjected: 'What the fuck do you mean? I think it sounds great.'

'Well, you would, wouldn't you, Quaife?' Ray replied. 'Listen, I've got a much better idea for a song.'

Pete threw his guitar down and said, 'You don't think anyone can do anything but yourself.' With that he got up and left.

I was very upset. Ray had always been difficult but this was the first time he had been so hurtful from a creative standpoint. Of course we had always argued over this and that since we were kids, stupid stuff like over points in a tennis match. My sister Peggy liked to watch us play because she thought our competitive aggression was amusing. And there was the David Watts incident, of course, and others like it.

But this was different. I had always supported Ray's musical ideas and now he was discounting mine as worthless in such a flippant and nasty way. I sat for a while in disbelief. Since Ray's illness just before the Belgian tour he had definitely been acting strangely. Maybe the pressure was getting to him, I thought. I told myself he didn't really mean it and that we would discuss the song another time, but that never happened.

But Pete didn't dismiss Ray's behaviour as easily. It must have been difficult for him to be in the middle of two brothers who did all the writing and got most of the attention when he was extremely talented himself. People often talked about sibling rivalry between Ray and me, but there was often a silent tension between Ray and Pete. They had been in the same class at school and Ray always managed to do everything a little better than Pete. They were both talented artists: Pete with his unique cartoons and graphics, Ray with his more traditional natural styles. They were also competitive at athletics, which were a big thing at William Grimshaw School. If you were a total shit at academics, it didn't matter as long as you were good at sport. I remember a photo from a 220-yard track race at school, which showed Ray as his chest was just about to break the tape. You could see Pete behind Ray, with a look of anguish and frustration on his face.

A little while after the hurtful incident with Ray, we did a show in Morecambe. Pete decided to travel back to Manchester in the van with our roadie, Jonah. At three in the morning the phone rang and Grenville spluttered out that Pete and Jonah had crashed into a lorry and had been taken to Warrington Hospital. Pete suffered multiple fractures to his right foot but apart from that he was left with only a few bruises and scratches. But Jonah had borne the full brunt of the impact and was in a bad way, with fractures to the ribs and pelvis, acute stomach lesions and, worst of all, severe injuries to his face and jaw.

We went to see them the following morning. The doctor would only let us see Pete, since Jonah was in intensive care. Quaife was really shaken up and even his usually cheeky sense of humour couldn't mask his fear. I was particularly upset about Jonah because I had grown up with him and we were good mates. His family ran the newspaper shop a few doors down from us.

Pete took time off to recuperate and we temporarily hired John Dalton to fill in. Jonah, however, was in hospital for a long time. I remember seeing him in those dreadful bandages, his eyes watery, trying his best to force a smile through his discomfort.

Pete was never really the same after the accident. He rejoined the band for a while before giving notice to leave in September.

The album *Face to Face* was released towards the end of October. It mostly contained recordings from various sessions. 'Party Line' was a song I wrote in Pete's hotel bedroom one night after a show. We were trying to call our Danish girlfriends and got snagged up with wrong numbers and operators' errors. Ray helped me with a few lyrics in the studio and there we had it. Complete with Grenville's posh voice at the beginning.

The song 'Rosie, Won't You Please Come Home' was about our sister Rose's move to Australia in November 1963. It was a horrible time, since she didn't want to go and neither did her son Terry. Terry had been touring with us for a while and we hoped he would end up becoming our road manager. But Rosie's husband, Arthur, insisted on going to Australia, so Terry and Rosie had no choice. I remember my mother read me a letter from Rose shortly after she arrived in Melbourne. They were staying at a relocation centre while waiting to be housed by the Australian authorities.

'Do you know, Mum, as we left Southampton, me and Terry stood at the back of the ship and watched the coastline slowly disappear into the horizon. When we couldn't see the land no more, me and Terry started to cry. I swear I cried all the bloody way there.'

Arthur was a very strict, serious man whom I sadly never really got to know very well. He had made up his mind to start a new life and that was that. And a brilliant idea it turned out to be . . . . Terry officially became an Australian citizen and he was called for duty in the army just as the Vietnam war was starting. He had to serve in Indonesia. Luckily he missed any action.

Some years later, after Arthur had died from cancer, Terry began to develop heart trouble and has been in and out of hospital ever since. I'm sure his troubles relate back to the time when he was dragged away from his friends, family, and homeland. I always felt that it literally broke his heart.

After the release of *Face to Face*, our fourth album, Ray, Grenville, and Robert flew to New York to meet with Allen Klein to discuss the possibility of renegotiating the Warner–Reprise contract. Pete went to Denmark to marry Beden and then returned to

London and was living in Muswell Hill at his mother's. Beden was pregnant.

I persuaded Pete to come to a recording session at Pye in November by telling him the band wasn't the same without him, and that we needed him. Indeed it wasn't, and we did. Pete's confidence was somewhat shaken, so I suggested that it might be a fun idea for both of us to play bass on one of the tracks, playing slightly different parts. One bass would sound twangy, kind of Duane Eddyish, and the other would sound more like a regular bass. The track was 'Dead End Street'.

'Dead End Street' was the epitome, to me, of what the Kinks were all about. A song full of character, pathos, yet containing an underlying sense of hope. Reflecting a fondness for the past but at the same time expressing a determination and yearning for change. Anguished voices calling to a heartless world. A world where the plight of the ordinary person mattered little. It was interesting to note that more than ten years later, the Clash did a song called 'London Calling' that seemed to be inspired by 'Dead End Street'.

'Big Black Smoke' was on the B-side, a perfect complement in atmosphere, sound and feeling. It tells the story of a young girl who leaves her country home in search of something more exciting in the city. She realizes just in time that maybe she was better off in the first place. I always liked that coupling – it reminded me of the Buddy Holly and the Crickets singles I used to buy, when B-sides were as good as the A-sides and there was a kind of continuity.

We shot a promo film for 'Dead End' in a mews near Kentish Town, north London. The BBC wouldn't show it because they thought it 'in bad taste'. Because it made fun of death and showed a corpse who suddenly awakes, jumps out of his coffin and runs aimlessly around the street and is chased by disbe-lieving undertakers. Very Keystone Kops. Really, how shocking.

By 1967 this party animal was starting to get tired. After one long evening of carousing, I took a good hard look around the room. People were lying on the floor, out of it. I was feeling disillusioned: the false talk, the false smiles, the superficiality. The hangers-on. I felt that I had no real friends, just people out for what they could get.

The following day I drove around London with Lisbet and she told me she was pregnant. She insisted it would be all right if we didn't marry, that she would be happy to have the baby anyway. I took a long hard look at her and inside at my own feelings. Maybe it would be nice to get married, have kids, and buy a house. After some thought I said that I would marry her.

The wedding took place in April 1967 in a small town hall in Fredericksberg, Denmark. When we arrived back in England I bought a little three-bedroom detached house in Cockfosters, near Barnet, north London. It was really nice, only ten minutes or so drive from Ray's and Mum's.

Ray was working on a new song and he played part of it to me. It was incomplete and needed a bridge, but immediately we started ad-libbing vocal parts around the chorus. I had a feeling that it was going to be a hit. The song became 'Waterloo Sunset'. Like 'Sunny Afternoon' it had a wonderfully hypnotic descending bass line contrasting magically with rising vocal harmonies, gentle but stirring textures. In fact, if it had been recorded then and there with just a piano and acoustic guitar it would have been perfect.

When we eventually got into the studio, we realized that after all the vocals had been laid in it still needed something. We messed around with various guitar ideas and sounds before we finally tried working the guitar part through a tape delay. It was almost like a fifties-type 'triplet' delay. It worked like a dream and the recording was complete. 'Waterloo Sunset' was released in May and became a massive hit for us in England.

One quiet morning I sat at an old upright piano at my mother's house in Fortis Green. That piano had outlasted many a familiar party and gathering over the years. It was never really in tune. I think it preferred to be perfectly off-key, it felt happier that way.

I messed around with various tunes, pondering my marriage, my days as a raver. I felt my life was like a circus performer's. I was always expected to be the life and soul of the party, whether at clubs, pubs or whatever. I was overcome with depression. Disenchanted. I felt foolish that people were constantly taking advantage of me, of my generosity, my nature, expecting me to act and 'be' a certain way. Not taking into account my real feelings.

I was feeling sorry for myself. I wanted more out of life than I had been getting. Suddenly the whole roller-coaster ride of the past three years seemed wearisome. Disconsolate, I felt like a cheerless clown, all painted up for fun on the outside, but hurting on the inside.

My fingers pointed out that simple, silly little tune. The words came into my head:

My make-up is dry and it cracks round my chin
I'm drowning my sorrows in whisky and gin.

A few days later we were in the studio recording it. Rasa helped with some sweet haunting la, la, la's, Ray helped arrange the middle, I wrote a couple more verses and there we had it. 'Death of a Clown'.

But we felt that we needed something more interesting at the beginning of the song, something different. After some thought, Ray came up with an idea. He leaned over the studio's large grand piano, a beautiful Steinway, lifted the lid and started plucking the piano strings with a guitar pick, playing that oh so simple melody. I loved it. We overdubbed it and, complemented by some delay echo; we now had a plaintive and haunting intro that set up the song perfectly.

The song was a metaphor for my real feelings. The pretence and illusion that surrounded me at the time. Finding myself squashed in between the unreal world of show-business and its parasites; its unquenchable demands on me, both socially and creatively, and of my inner shyness and personal insecurities. Robert loved it and, bless him, he pushed for its release as a single. The song's success was a numbing and exciting experience for me. I was overwhelmed by the attention it received. It became a massive hit all over Europe, at one point reaching number 3 in the charts. It was suggested that maybe I should leave the band and go solo, but although I thought about it, I decided that all I wanted was simply to be part of a band. The sense of unity and camaraderie was important to me. The Kinks had now become a crucial part of my life and I wanted to see it through to the end.

I think everybody was surprised by its success, especially me. Robert arranged for me to perform it on *Top of the Pops*. I had recently been in Berman's, a costume house, and came across a fabulous gold-braided, long, collarless, bell-shaped coat. King

Charles II style. Perfect. I hired the costume and was ready for my first ever solo performance.

For some reason I was extremely nervous the night before. Ray, Rasa, Lisbet and I were up at the pub with my Dad. I expressed some misgivings about performing solo on TV, and Ray said that if I didn't want to do it then he would call Robert and have him cancel it. Fortunately, Lisbet came to the rescue in her usual smiling and optimistic way and convinced me to do it. 'It will be fun,' she said. And she was right. It was a great success, coat and all. Lisbet always thought that Ray may have felt a little threatened by me doing it and by its possible success.

After 'Death of a Clown', Pye wanted more recordings. They also pressed for another Kinks album.

Robert booked a really small studio for me to make a solo album at Polydor for these sessions. It was more like someone's front room than a professional recording studio. They had these dreadful speakers that had coarse wire mesh wound around the front. I think they were called 'Electrostatic'.

I felt that I was being taken advantage of once again, being forced to make an album on the cheap. I got so upset I cancelled the rest of the recordings.

Ever since my near-electrocution a number of years earlier, Ray and I had always been experimenting with new sounds. We often tried playing tapes backwards. We played 'Death of a Clown' backwards and wrote a song based on its reverse melody. Shit, if Mozart could get away with it, why couldn't we? He may not have had the luxury of recording equipment but he did it nonetheless.

This concept opened up a whole new creative vortex of ideas. We attached some words to this hybrid piece of music, changed a few chords here and there, and we had a song called 'Shoemaker's Daughter'. It wasn't released because of the Polydor sessions I had blocked.

Another track from those sessions was called 'Creeping Jean', a song about a slut-girlfriend-drug addict. Sleazy but great fun. I liked the way Mick played on that record. Really free.

I have a great fondness for the *Something Else* album. There was so much love, humour and joy on that album. 'David Watts' grew out of that crazy evening in Rutland. My sister Peg was a

103

bit hard of hearing and sometimes she would come out with weird stuff that sounded either really stupid or really profound or both. When she first heard 'David Watts', she thought Ray was saying, 'I wish I could be like David was!' Yeah, sure, Peg.

'Funny Face' was a song about my feelings about Sue. Many times during my life thoughts and feelings about her would rise to the surface to plague or torment me. Unresolved emotions about a love that was never meant to be.

> *You're walking round in my memory,*
> *my love is getting stronger and stronger,*
> *smudged mascara and pill-shaped eyes.*
> *All the love you have was bought with lies.*
> *I see you peering through frosted windows,*
> *eyes don't smile, all they do is cry.*

I was still so angry inside because I thought she never really loved me. I could never understand how she could so suddenly not love me. 'Love Me Till the Sun Shines' was also about these feelings.

> *You don't have to look at me,*
> *rest your head upon my knee,*
> *as long as you just love me 'till the sun shines.*
> *Baby you can wear my clothes, play my records,*
> *stay in my home,*
> *as long as you just love me 'till the sun shines.*
> *Take my money, I don't mind,*
> *you can't leave such a helpless kind*
> *as long as you just love me 'till the sun shines.*

'Lazy Old Sun' was one of my favourite tracks – full of a strange and dark optimism. Now I was married and expecting a baby and I hoped and prayed that the ghosts would be finally laid to rest. Maybe having a family of my own would dispel my entangled feelings about Sue and the baby.

Ray had a song hanging around from the *Something Else* sessions called 'My Street'. It was a nice song but we were looking for something really special as a single. So we messed around with it a bit then played it backwards, and out came the inspiration for 'Autumn Almanac'. The middle section of 'Almanac' is the original version of 'My Street' in reverse. I think it worked beautifully.

The single was released in October and became a top three hit in England.

Later in November I played around with some blues licks *à la* Leadbelly, and came up with a chromatic riff that formed the basis of 'Suzanah's Still Alive', yet another song about Sue. It was recorded and released as my second single.

Oh, Suzanah's bedraggled
but she still wears a locket round her neck,
she's got a picture on the table of a man who was young and able.
She's got a doll with one eye,
that always cries when you try to get some sleep,
she's waiting for her soldier to come home,
but she'll cry and never die.
Oh, Suzanah's gonna cry.
Oh, Suzanah's still alive.
Whiskey or gin, that's all right,
there's nothing in her bed at night.
She sleeps with the covers down hoping somebody gets in,
it doesn't matter what she does, she knows that she can't win.

I never seemed to be satisfied, despite all the women that I had been with. I always wanted more. In a way I think Lisbet saved me from myself, although I really didn't take marriage very seriously at the time. Maybe I was irresponsible but marriage seemed more like an experiment than a commitment, even though I loved Lisbet very much. My first son, Martin, was born in September of that year. It was a truly wonderful experience, and my dad was particularly thrilled because Martin represented the first Davies male of a new generation to carry on the name. Ray and Rasa had two delightful daughters, Louisa and Victoria.

I started to realize to some degree the responsibility of having a family. Soon after Martin's birth I became fascinated with astrology. I read books, attended lectures, and took courses on the subject. I realized that within this ancient science there were keys that could open doors to the character and personality of a person beyond what I had previously imagined. In fact it was this fascination with astrology that led to my later interest in occultism, mysticism and metaphysics in general.

I threw myself into studying and after a while I could cast a horoscope successfully, together with the progressed chart. It seemed funny to me that I was so useless at academic work at school, especially maths and English, when the practice and study of astrology required good and reasonable knowledge of both.

I was able to lay down fairly concise information regarding a person's pattern of potential once I had the accurate date, time and place of birth. It's always struck me as strange that I was never able to obtain Ray's exact birth time, which is crucial in constructing a correct chart. My mother couldn't remember it, nor could my father.

At the end of 1967 we applied for visas to work in the States, but were denied. It was becoming increasingly frustrating not being able to tour over there, especially when there was a great deal of good music now starting to emerge. Apart from the Beach Boys, Dylan, and the Byrds, there hadn't been a lot of inspiration coming across the Atlantic. But this was changing with groups like the Lovin' Spoonful, Jefferson Airplane, the Steve Miller Band, and others.

'Wonderboy' was released in early 1968, a beautifully haunting and lyrical piece, but it was a failure in the marketplace – the start of a strange year for the Kinks. While our counterparts, the Stones and the Beatles, were making vast inroads in the US, we were left out in the cold because of the ban.

I found out that 'Wonderboy' was one of John Lennon's favourite Kinks songs. He liked to have lunch at a restaurant on King's Road called Aretusa, and I heard that he would make them play the song over and over.

Ray was writing prolifically. While other songwriters were metaphorically tearing up the 'old' in favour of the 'new', the Kinks were trying to point a way to a future where the good from the past could be interwoven with the new and radical. The revolution, we felt, if indeed there was to be one, could not happen purely by freeing ourselves completely from the ties of our past, our culture. It was obviously a question of integrating that of the old that still worked with that of the new.

In a sense the *Village Green* album encapsulated all these feelings. It was an album out of step with the time but in keeping with a broader realization that yearned for social, environmental and political balance. The feelings expressed in the song 'Village

Green Preservation Society' were like voices calling out of the darkness.

When you look around now at the terrible architecture in England from the mid to late sixties, it serves as a constant reminder of how thoughtless and naive post-war Britain was. They tore down lovely Victorian terraced houses all over London and replaced them with cold, ugly office blocks; they carved up beautiful countryside to build more roads. The architects and designers must have had their heads up their arses.

We are the Village Green Preservation Society,
God save little shops, china cups, and virginity.

Don't know about the virginity bit – Ray's purist streak taking things a little too far. Nonetheless *Village Green* is a very beautiful record.

It's sad that the English were always trying to compete with America. There wasn't that much wrong with us in the first place. We just needed to broaden our horizons, that's all. Eventually, by the 1980s, we became a society built on avarice and selfishness. Poverty breeds violence. If people growing up are told that self-worth is based entirely on one's ability to accumulate money, how can we seriously expect people who have nothing to be satisfied?

We'd come a long way from Denmark Terrace, where Mum used to leave the key in the door in case anyone wanted to pop in for a cup of tea. The local grocer would give Mum food if she didn't have enough money, with the promise that she would pay him when she could. My mother owned very little in her life, just a few ornaments and treasured photos that sat on her mantleshelf. But she was a very rich woman in her heart.

Preserving the old ways from being abused,
protecting the new ways for me and for you.
What more can we do?

It was around this time that I felt Pete was becoming dis-illusioned again, that he was drifting away from us. During the sessions, as a joke, he crossed out the word 'Days' on the tape box and replaced it with 'Daze'. It was as much a way of venting his jealous, resentful feelings for Ray as it was a demonstration of his frustration with the direction our music was taking. Pete left the band for good after the release of the *Village Green* album. I think in his mind its lack of success signalled the end for him and the Kinks. He couldn't have been more wrong. In a way, 'Days' waved a fond yet sad farewell to Pete.

The more diversified our music became, the more trouble we had with our management and agents. Because we were always taking chances with our music, and not churning out the same old stuff every time, I don't think they knew what to do with us. The lawsuit between Boscobel and Denmark Productions dragged on for some time, but the courts finally deemed in our favour that the contract between the two management companies was void. Apart from everything else, I was under-age when the contract was actually signed, thus giving adequate grounds for termination. Exit not only Quaife, but Page. Robert and Grenville continued to be our managers as we still had a contract with Boscobel.

In June, Barry Dickens, our new but sadly over-enthusiastic agent, booked us to play a tour of Sweden. Thinking we were playing 'Rock Festivals', we arrived to discover, much to our disappointment, that it was a tour of 'Amusement Parks'. We were far from amused. Maybe Barry had problems booking us, I don't know, but it did show a pitiful lack of imagination on the part of our management. One thing was certain – somehow the Kinks had to get back to America.

Those Swedish 'folk parks' were so depressing: parents strolling around with kids licking ice-lollies alongside genuine fans and party revellers. I had scary visions of us ending our careers on the cabaret circuit. It was a horrible, soulless experience.

Another odd thing happened that year. The winner of the Eurovision song contest was a Spanish singer called Masielle. The song was 'La La La'. It was a direct rip-off of the chorus of 'Death of a Clown'. I was surprised that nobody noticed what a blatant copy it was.

In October my worst fears were starting to become a reality. We were booked to play 'cabaret' dates in the north of England, the Club Fiesta in Stockton-on-Tees and the Top Hat in Spennymore. I drank more and more. Some nights I'd finish a whole bottle of Scotch before going on stage. The shows were only twenty minutes, and I thought I could easily manage that while drunk.

One positive thing that occurred during that period was the release of my third single, 'Lincoln County'. The song was inspired by Eddie Cochran and Leadbelly, and I also discovered that Lincoln County was where Jesse James lived and was imprisoned. But the main idea was based on an experience I had with Sue and my mum early on in our relationship. It was Sue's birthday and I walked to the shops in Muswell Hill to look for a present for her. In a little shop I saw this dark purplish scarf and I bought it for her. The lady wrapped the scarf in brown wrapping paper and I set back on my journey home. As I walked, I started to have misgivings: would she like it? Would she not? Outwardly I was very cheeky and arrogant but inside I was terribly shy and insecure. I became worried that she wouldn't like it at all, and hid the little package in between some bricks in a gap in a wall. Later that day Mum returned home from the shops, placed her shopping on the kitchen table and pulled out the very same bag with that dark purple scarf inside.

'I was walking through Princes Avenue,' she said, 'round the Broadway, and in between the crack in the wall I saw this. Lovely, innit, someone must have dropped it or something. Sod it, if nobody wants it then I'll have it.' She pulled the scarf out for all to see and put it on her head with much delight. I was so embarrassed that I just couldn't say anything. I never bought another birthday present for Sue that year and, in fact, I always had difficulty buying presents for her after that.

After 'Lincoln County' I recorded some solo demos in December, but I wasn't very happy with them. One song was 'Hold My Hand', which we recorded for a single. It was released in January '69 and though it did little or nothing saleswise or in the charts in England, I had some success with it in Germany, and I was booked to appear live on *Beat Club*, a popular German TV show.

I didn't really want to go, as I was thoroughly depressed by the record's lack of success. However, I left for Germany with guitar in hand, accompanied by a friend of mine who was a singer himself. He mixed with a lot of showbiz people and on the train he told me stories about Diana Dors, whom he had known very well, describing in detail her mirrored bedroom ceiling, her lust for men and general sexual antics. We drank and talked and laughed and by the time we arrived at the TV studios I was so pissed I could hardly walk. I sat stupefied by alcohol in the doorway while my friend made some local calls. He invited two 'girls' of dubious calling over to the studios. Meanwhile, the floor manager escorted me virtually semi-conscious into the main studio for a rehearsal.

He described to me exactly what they wanted me to do. It was a large set and at the top was a small round rotating platform with a long flight of stairs stretching down from it to a lower stage, where there was a girl I was supposed to sing to. I was then to take her by the hand and walk with her, lip-synching, the length of a long narrow catwalk-type of platform.

Because of the state I was in I told them that I was a little ill and that I would skip the rehearsal. I assured them I'd be fine for the show. I stumbled back to the dressing-room, where my friend was sitting with two large blonde German women. They greeted me eagerly and we opened wine and started to roll joints full of strongly perfumed hashish. At least that's what I thought it was.

I have never smoked such strong hash in my life. I felt absolutely wonderful, dreamy and floating. One of the girls undressed me and laid me on a couch. This voluptuous woman began to give me a massage. Her fingers delicately then firmly pressed into my shoulders and back. She was obviously very experienced in the art. As she moulded, squeezed and caressed my muscles I felt as if I was leaving my body. It was so relaxing.

I turned over on my back and she started to work on my front, again with exacting skill. My mouth was so dry I could barely speak and my head was reeling, but I felt wonderful. She moved her hand down to my stomach and stroked and kissed my abdomen with the gentle and sensual ease of a consummate artist. I felt her mouth on my penis and it felt as if her tongue was inside my head, touching and stimulating every nerve ending and sensory centre in my brain. Afterwards I fell into a deep, almost trance-like sleep.

I was awakened by a loud banging on the door. I tried to gather myself, but I was in a hopeless state. I looked around the room and it was empty save for half-filled wine-glasses and ashtrays full of cigarette butts. I opened the door with some difficulty. It was the floor manager telling me that I had to be on stage in five minutes.

Somehow I managed to throw on some clothes and used all the

power of my will to drag my body, which felt like a dead weight, to the studio. My head was reeling and I felt sick. Thoughts raced through my head: 'Why did I drink so much? Who were those women? What the hell was in those cigarettes?'

I looked across the studio at the small audience. It suddenly dawned on me, as I caught sight of the revolving platform and large flight of stairs, what was expected of me. There was no way I could go through with that bullshit. I could hardly walk, let alone prance around like some tarted-up crooner with gnashing pearly white teeth breaking into a broad and insincere smile, as I grinned down the camera, hoping to seduce the viewer with my charismatic and hypnotic performance of 'Hold My Hand'. If I ever needed someone to hold my hand, it was then.

Somehow I manage to persuade the producer that it would look much more natural and realistic if I just sat on a stool. And please to get rid of the girl, she would only make me laugh and I wouldn't be able to sing at all. Not that I could anyway.

I sat on the stool and performed my little song with the technicians and floor manager sneering at me from behind the cameras. As I sang I felt an overwhelming desire to go to sleep. I struggled to stay awake, praying inwardly, 'Please God, let it be over. Please.' I finally got through it and was led back to my dressing-room, where I fell into a deep alcohol- and drug-induced sleep.

All this time my friend was in the bar with the two hookers. I don't remember going back to England, but I must have. Of course I did, didn't I?

It had been a while since the Kinks had had a successful record and I quickly learned how fickle the public could be. While I was out Christmas shopping on Carnaby Street I went into one of my favourite shops, Lord Jim. Everyone knew me and the proprietor came up to me with the usual polite hellos. It was quite normal in those days for me to select some garments to take home, simply telling the shop owner to forward the bill. Sometimes they wouldn't even send a bill. But on this occasion, after I had tried on various jackets and decided which ones I wanted, the manager said that I would have to pay cash for them or I couldn't take them. I argued with him, but he said, 'Sorry, Dave. Come back when you have a hit record.' I threw his clothes at him and told him what I thought of him, then kicked over some clothes-racks before I stormed out of the store. The bastard, I thought to myself. Before, he had had his tongue so far up my arse that he could barely breathe, and now he was treating me like this. I never went in that store again, and in fact it closed about a year or so later.

Some years later I swear I saw that very same guy working a stall in Berwick Street market in Soho. I didn't say anything to him, but I did smile to myself.

Ray and I played quite often with a celebrity soccer team known as the Showbiz Eleven. The team had some great old pros, like Billy Wright, who had captained England in the fifties, and one of our childhood heroes, Jon Charles. I'd never seen a guy head a ball with so much power.

Bobby Smith and Bobby Moore would also play sometimes. Bobby Smith was really funny: before a game he would open a half bottle of Scotch, drink half of it and rub the rest on his legs to warm up. If I started to get a bit cocky he would joke that he could have me and a bottle of Scotch for breakfast if he wanted.

One of the greatest footballers I played with during that time was Danny Blanchflower. Although he was getting on in years, he had such craft, such skill, the sort of abilities that you rarely see from the terraces but that have a profound effect on certain players and on the way a team functions. I remember him telling me one day during a fairly competitive match at Leeds United football ground (we were playing an ex-Wolves eleven): 'Stop looking around for the ball when you're running forward. Just run towards the goal and don't worry about the ball.' I listened, and as I ran forward ever closer to the six-yard box, this perfectly flighted ball would pop over my right shoulder and land exquisitely in front of me. What a great player, always making other players look good. Others on that team were Tommy Steele, a great winger, and Jess Conrad, our goalie. Mike Cox was our strike, Ray played right mid-field, and I played inside-left, left mid-field.

Once, when we played a charity match in Jersey, Jess, Mike, Ray and I were asked to judge an annual beauty contest. Of course we eagerly agreed. As we assessed the preliminary rounds, we agreed for the fun of it to vote for the plainest girl in the contest. When we got to the final there were three really attractive girls and one fairly plain little dumpy one, who of course got our unanimous votes. She was about sixteen, and totally surprised. You should have seen the faces of the other contestants, the looks of strained disbelief and bewilderment. But we all tried our best to make it up to them in 'other' ways later on that evening.

Jess made up pet names for everybody. Harry Fowler, the actor, was called 'Harry the Horse' because he was hung like one. I was called Dave 'We Can't Make It Without You' Davies and Ray was Ray 'I Spent a Pound' Davies, referring, of course, to Ray's meanness with money.

Our next single was 'Plastic Man', which we loved, but again it failed badly. It was about this time that I noticed the trend of DJs waffling about this and that instead of just playing the music. Many of them had these inflated egos, when all they were doing was playing other people's music. I always found those types offensive. There were some DJs I liked, such as John Peel, funny, droll and intelligent, or Bob Harris, a hippie but a great DJ. Pete Murray had great respect for the music he played, as did David Jacobs. Really old school but respectful.

When we finally got back to touring in the States, one of my pet hates was to visit radio stations, which were mostly populated by what seemed to me as obnoxious, self-aggrandizing children. During one visit to a radio station in Boston, the DJ was obviously not interested in who I was or why I was there and made really stupid comments about our music. In the end I couldn't stand it. 'You useless fucking cunt,' I said to him on the air, and took a swing at his head. I was promptly ushered out of the building by our tour manager. Some days later I heard that the station had been temporarily shut down because of the incident. Arseholes.

But there were a few DJs and stations who had respect for musicians, like Scott Mooney at WNEW in New York and Pierre Robert at WMMR in Philadelphia. And today, things have generally improved all over.

I had a friend from Muswell Hill, Ewin Stephens, whom I spent a lot of time with during this period. Ewin was tall and had long black hair, and he had a kind of squashed face that looked as if it had been caught in the door. His mother left him a little money when she died and he spent it with alacrity. We got on great together. He was really a good laugh, ready for anything. He had a lovely young wife, a quiet girl who didn't seem to care about his behaviour. In fact, she was very broadminded. Ewin had a good heart. He shared everything with me, including his wife.

Ewin was also a frustrated rock singer. He didn't have a very good voice, but got away with a Dylanesque type of vocal. He desperately wanted to make it in the music business and spent his money on instruments for his band, studio time and, of course, hoards of drugs. Everything from Mandrax to heroin.

During one very stoned evening I said I would write him some songs and produce them. Ewin booked some time at Marque Studio, then hired Elton John's rhythm section and the guitarist Albert Lee. A great player.

The first day in the studio I routined three of the songs with the guys. It went well, so we had a break and Ewin and I went to the pub next door. We popped a couple of amphetamines, and knocked back some beer and whisky chasers. After a while we went back to the studio and began to lay down the back tracks. Ewin rolled joints as the engineer and I got the sound together.

After the back tracks were laid down I thought it wise to get all the guitar and keyboard parts on before attempting to lay in Ewin's vocals. I sang some rough guide parts so the guys had a better idea of the songs, and Albert Lee started laying in guitar parts.

I was starting to feel really out of it. Ewin kept feeding me beer, pills and joints and by the time Albert started to play his solo over the last song, I was really quite 'gone'. I kept asking Lee to play solo after solo – in my state I kept thinking the next would be better than the last. He had some great licks. It's funny, I can't remember the song but I can remember the final solo we chose, note for note. He had already played a 'blinding' solo some ten takes back, but we just wanted to listen to him play. We were getting off on it. But he was getting pissed off, so I finally let him go for the day.

It was time for Ewin to start singing. He was so out of it he could hardly stand. I was so out of it I didn't care. We did a few passes and I realized that Ewin was well past it and was starting to sound like a pissed duck trying to do a Bob Dylan impersonation. Frightening. I was also starting to lose it, so I

114

mustered up my last ounce of energy and tried to call it a wrap for the day. I sat at the desk with my shades perched on my nose in true Rock Star fashion, a real 'cool' producer. 'OK, guys,' I slurred, 'that's it for today. Catch yer later.'

With a pleasant stoned smile Ewin looked up from his horizontal position on the floor and waved at me like a camp marionette before falling into a drug-induced coma.

I willed myself to the door, still trying my best to look as cool as possible. I reached the door and walked through it with great relief. I noticed that all of a sudden it had become really dark. I couldn't see anything as the door closed behind me. I thought that I had gone blind.

'Help!' I shouted, totally blowing my cool. As I waved my arms around looking for the door I hit something with my arm which crashed to the floor. The door suddenly opened and the engineer switched on the light. He stared at me. I looked around and noticed I was standing in a broom cupboard.

'Oh, hi, man,' I said to the engineer, looking like a fool. The guy politely led me out into the street. As I walked, feeling like an idiot, I thought to myself, 'OK, now all I've got to do is find my car. Shit, where did I park it?' I spent the next half hour searching before I finally found it.

Lisbet hated Ewin. When I arrived home from our binges I was always so out of it. One night I came home late. Lisbet was so upset she wouldn't even let Ewin in the house. She put on the table the dinner that she had lovingly prepared some hours prior to my return. I could hardly speak, but I thought I had better make the effort to at least pretend to eat something. As she placed the food in front of me I collapsed on the table, smashing the plate and knocking the table to the floor. There was blood all over the place. I had broken the plates and cut my arms quite badly.

Lisbet reluctantly looked after me and laid me on the couch. The wounds weren't as bad as first thought. I dozed off into a drug-induced sleep. I awoke to find that Lisbet had gone through my pockets and was in the process of pouring the entire contents of my drug bottle down the sink. I struggled with her as I frantically tried to pick the dissolving drugs out of the sink with my fingers. I went into the garage, brought a tool-box into the kitchen and set about dismantling the U-bend and the pipes below the sink. I had never been particularly adept at plumbing, but this night, even in my stupefied condition, I would have put an expert to shame.

I managed to retrieve some of the pills. It was pathetic. Lisbet was quite distressed watching this desperate figure on his knees, almost in tears as he tried to recover what was left of his drug hoard. God, what a sad picture it must have been. Poor Lisbet, she didn't realize what she had let herself in for, but God only knows what I'd have been like if I hadn't married her and settled down, if you could call it that.

Some time after the recording sessions at Marque Studios, Ewin organized a photo shoot for himself. He begged to borrow a pair of boots I had recently purchased. They had been hand-made at Anello & Davide, thigh-length in tan leather, with a large Cuban heel and a narrow Spanish-style toe. They were skin-tight and came right up to my crotch, with a loop-strap at the top of each boot where I could thread a belt. They were really expensive, definitely a one-off, and I loved them. I was about to go on tour in Europe, so I reluctantly lent them to him. After all, he let me borrow his wife, so how could I refuse him this one small favour?

After I returned to England some time later, I got a call to say that Ewin had died of a heroin overdose. I just couldn't believe it. I was devastated. I felt really bad for his wife, as she had a little boy from a previous relationship. It was so tragic. Poor Ewin, he was so young. God, how I loved those boots, but I just never had the heart to ask for them back. I wonder where they are now?

7

The summer of 1969 was significant for two reasons: one, we got word that our ban was lifted and we could tour again in the States; and two, we recorded the *Arthur* album. *Arthur* has always been a special record for me. After the setbacks of our last few records I really sensed that we were back on course, that our music was more purposeful, more motivated than ever before.

The album was inspired by my sister Rosie's husband, Arthur, who had become disillusioned with his life in England and dragged his family to Australia where, it turned out, life wasn't any better than it had been before, even though he was convinced it was. Arthur felt that the world had somehow passed him by. Even though he had a good management job in a plastics factory in England, it wasn't enough. I think he had a difficult childhood. His brother, an RAF pilot, was killed in the Second World War. Arthur also wanted to be a pilot and follow in his brother's footsteps, but he failed the medical test because of his weak eyesight and was forced to spend his war years in the RAF in ground staff, personnel. To Arthur that was tantamount to failure. He was a handsome man; he always reminded me of Alan Ladd. But he was frustrated and I always felt uncomfortable around him. Ray, of course, had spent much of his adolescent years with Rosie, Arthur and their son Terry and was extremely close to them. Arthur was flattered that we had based an album on him, and just before he died prematurely of lung cancer he told Ray how much he always loved *Arthur*.

Ray had got together with the writer Julian Mitchell to do a script for a television play based on the *Arthur* concept. Granada TV was going to produce it. Half-way through production the whole deal fell apart and Granada backed out. There was talk

117

that the Who were doing a concept album and maybe that scared them off.

Ray had a friend at the time called Barry Fantoni, a writer/ musician. He was also a friend of Pete Townshend's, and while I thought Barry was a funny guy, I was sometimes suspicious of him. He was always hanging around Ray, and I felt that he might be undermining us by conveying our ideas to Townshend. Who knows?

John Dalton, whom we called Nobby, was fitting in really well as Pete Quaife's replacement. He had a much more stable personality than Pete, more down to earth, and he was rhythmically a more rooted musician, which also helped Mick's playing. John and I did have our ups and downs, and it wasn't until much later that I realized and appreciated the importance of his collaboration and involvement in the band.

I really enjoyed recording *Arthur*. I remember that the day we did the vocal parts on 'Young and Innocent Days' I had chills running up and down my spine and was brimming with emotion. It is such a gorgeous song.

'Some Mother's Son' is also a beautifully poignant song, telling of the futility and dreadful suffering of war, of loved ones lost in meaningless slaughter. We worked really hard on the arrangements and I think it showed in the performances on the record. I have always believed that it is so important to have solid arrangements before attempting to record. Sometimes a song's meaning, vitality, and enthusiasm can get lost during a long recording process. I've always preferred to spend more time on the arrangement and as little time as possible on the actual recording to gain the maximum effect from a piece of music.

'Australia' was a sardonic and wry track, full of humour and cynicism, with an underlying anger. It expressed our rage about a country that had enticed our sister and dear friend and nephew away from us. Losing Rosie and Terry to Australia broke a family bond that would never be repaired. I remember singing the choruses to the title track, 'Arthur', with tears in my eyes. Even Ray, who had always been much better at concealing his true emotions, couldn't hold back his pain.

'Shangrila' was released as a single, and much to our surprise it was greeted with derision and negative criticism. For some reason the media, critics, people in general, had got hold of the wrong end of the stick. They thought it was purely a put-down of certain social attitudes and behaviour of the time, when in fact there was an underlying sympathy for the role played by middle-class Britain.

'Driving' was a reflective song about our childhood. My dad saved up and bought this old car, a black Vauxhall 12. It was always going wrong, but we loved it anyway. Dad called it 'Betsy'. At first Arthur was the only family member with a driving licence, so every Sunday the family would get together, bundle into old 'Betsy' and have a day out. I would have been around eleven or so. On a typical outing there would be Rosie, Arthur, Terry, Ray, Bobby, Jackie, Mum, Dad and me all excitedly squashed in the car. We'd go to Southend, Ramsgate, visiting aunts, or just take a drive through the countryside.

Some weeks Dad and Arthur would take me and Ray on overnight fishing trips to the river Ouse, near a small village called Offord in Cambridgeshire. Sometimes we would camp there and just stay up all night catching eels. The following morning we would drive back to London and Mum would cut them up to make eel pie or jellied eels. I used to think it so weird to watch her cut up live eels. Even when they were in pieces they would still wiggle around. Eventually Ray stopped coming, and when Dad got his full driving licence only he and I would go, which I loved. We sometimes stayed at this funny little cottage beside the river that belonged to a woman. I'll always remember that smell of freshly made tea at six o'clock in the morning. Smells of the river, the morning dew and dampness. Mum always hated Dad going to that house; she used to joke around, saying that Dad was knocking off the woman who owned it. Everybody would laugh, but knowing my dad, I wasn't so sure. I wouldn't have put it past him.

I had a great relationship with my dad but he and Ray never seemed close, especially when Ray was a child. Dad was a man's man, and since I was a cheeky little rough and ready kid, I was ideal company for him. A real chip off the old block. The only shame was that he was so much older than I, he could have been my grandfather. That's one of the reasons I wanted to have children young, so that I could enjoy them when I was still comparatively young myself.

There is one distinct memory about my dad that I have from

my childhood. It came about when Mum refused to buy me some sweets from the shop next door, probably because she didn't have the money. I rummaged around my parents' bedroom and in a wardrobe I came across a small oblong wooden box with a screw at the bottom of it. I found a screwdriver and undid the screw. Inside I discovered a wad of pound notes. Neither of my parents kept bank accounts in those days. They didn't trust them. There must have been about £100 or so. It was evidently my dad's savings. Excitedly I tore one of the pound notes from the small bundle, put the rest of the money back in the box, replaced the screw and placed the box back where I found it. I crept out of the house, went to the sweetshop and bought the sweets I had earlier been denied. I sat at the back of the garden eating them, but was so overcome with guilt and shame I didn't know what to do. I never told Dad that I had taken the money, but many years later I told Mum about it and she laughed. But the experience had such a profound effect on me that I never stole anything from my parents again. Even now I get a sinking feeling inside when I think of it. My father, although he was a bastard to my mother, had worked hard all of his life to provide for us and *I* stole from him. I couldn't forgive myself. I know it seems really trivial but I carried the burden of shame for many years. The two things my father detested more than anything were stealing and people he called 'con' men.

After finishing the *Arthur* album we started our tour of the States. Our ban ended as mysteriously as it began. Fortunately, it hadn't completely ruined our careers. I've always wondered, though, how different our fortunes would have been if we hadn't been prevented from touring America for those three crucial years.

The first stop on our US tour was New York, at the Fillmore East. Everything had changed so much in three years. Instead of screaming teenage girls in the audience, there were thoughtful 'potheads', some curiosity seekers, and of course our faithful fans, who had waited patiently for three years for our return.

Not really knowing what to expect, we were under-rehearsed and nervous. It was apparent that this tour was going to be hard work. It was like starting all over again. A long, hard slog back.

Warner Brothers had packaged the *Village Green* album with 'God Save the Kinks' buttons and plastic bags full of English

Me aged two, with my sister Rose in
the back garden at Denmark Terrace,
Fortis Green.

Eleven years old.

Me as a boy with some of the women of the family. Clockwise, from upper
left: Joyce, Amy Kelly (my father's mother), Gwen, Mum, Jackie, Irene.

Mum and Dad playing up to the camera. They knew how to
have a good time.

On the beach at Ramsgate, around June 1957. Left: Jackie, Rene's son Bobby,
Terry, Ray and me. Right: Gwen (left) and Rene.

A double-exposure shot of Ray and me, taken in 1993 at Saratoga Springs, NY.
Photo: Martin Benjamin.

Tracey as I never knew her,
aged eight.

With Tracey, when we first met.

UFO-spotting in north Devon in the late eighties.
Note my classic Citroën H-van camper!

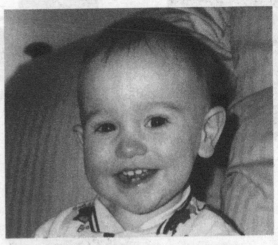

...y and me with Daniel and Lana, 1991.

Eddie at Christmas time, 1994.

With Lana in 1989. I'm wearing
my costume for the
'How Do I Get Close?' video.

Clockwise from lower left: Christian, Simon, Martin, Russell, in the early eighties.

Teaching Russell the guitar in the late eighties at my cottage in Devon.

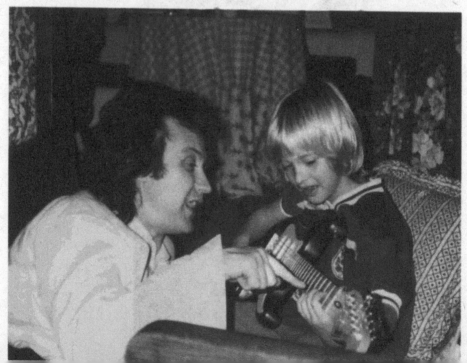

Lisbet in the late eighties. On the left is her cousin, Beden, who was
Pete Quaife's first wife.

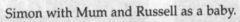

Simon with Mum and Russell as a baby.

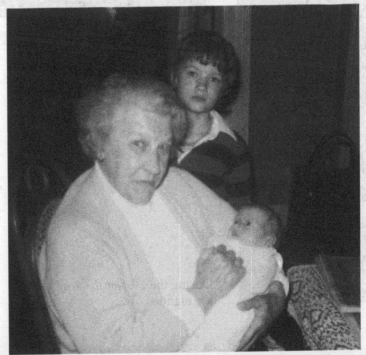

With my beloved Citroën Light 15, London 1988. It was built in 1947, the year I was born.

During the *One for the Road* tour in the eighties.

A portrait of me with Ray, taken in 1989. *Photo: Paul Cox.*

On the *Schoolboys in Disgrace* tour in the US, 1976.
Above: me. Below: Ray.

The Kinks as the Muswell Hillbillies. Outside the Flask, Highgate Village.

Me solo, in the early eighties.

Lisbet's and my first son, Martin, as a baby. Christmas Eve, 1967.

Fortis Green, 1968, just after the success of 'Death of a Clown'.

In 1966, just after our return from Australia. Pete Quaife is in the background.
Photo: Marc Sharratt.

The Kinks in late 1969. From left: Ray, me, Mick Avory, John Dalton. Note my lace shirt. *Photo: SKR Photos International.*

Dedicated follower of fashion: in the dressing room on tour in Denmark, with Mick Avory adjusting himself. *Top of the Pops* photographer Harry Goodwin also took a portrait of me then in my trademark gingham shirt.

With my first guitar, bought from Selmer's on hire purchase.
We were just starting to go places.

An early cigarette, camping in Cornwall when I was about 13.

The football team at St James Primary School, 1957. I'm in the middle row on the far right. I still love football, and I hate missing Arsenal matches when I'm in LA.

grass. The kind of grass you actually find on lawns or on a village green. Of course everybody thought it was the other kind of 'grass' and some fans tried to smoke it. It probably did very little to alter their perception of the world.

Our first shows were a little awkward and we were a bit sloppy. It was hard to imagine what the audiences really thought of us when we played songs like 'Village Green', 'Well Respected Man', 'Victoria', 'Mr Churchill Says', in the midst of 'heavy' American bands playing stoned, with tedious over-indulgent solos that seemed to stretch long into the night. But most of our audiences were out of it. Stoned. So maybe they got more out of it than they expected.

Our bill at the Fillmore East was odd, to say the least. Opening the show were the Bonzo Dog Band, followed by a band called Spirit, a deathly serious dirge-like rock band. The audience must have been at least as confused and as baffled as we were. At that time there were a lot of American bands around like them who smoked pot, tuned up for hours – they were really into their music, man.

The Bonzos, a British band who combined rock with comedy, were hysterically funny, but the audience didn't seem to know how to react to them. During their first set the audience sat open-mouthed and gaped in disbelief. You have to remember that *Monty Python* was just gaining popularity in England, and American kids hadn't seen anything quite like this before. They didn't get it at first. They seemed so bloody serious, reading into everything and anything. They watched in stunned silence as Roger Spear played his solo on a plastic woman's leg. Hmm, there must have been some real deep meaning behind it, man. Others were so stoned they probably thought that Roger was performing an incredible 'feat', or should I say 'foot'.

Drugs were easily obtained in all the cities we toured in the States; you only had to look as far as the local groupies, who were always well supplied. I never really liked 'grass', but preferred a good stiff drink and some uppers.

I met a beautiful young black girl in New York called Diana. We met at a bar on 8th Avenue called the Haymarket, a place that attracted a mixed clientele: everyone from dancers from the local theatre district to gays, drunks, and simple lonely Englishmen in search of Bass ale. Diana was a sexy woman with a shapely body and perfect arse. She was sweet, and we chatted and drank wine before going back to my hotel.

She introduced me to a drug called Angel Dust, which I hadn't had before. It seemed fine when I was lying down, but trying to walk was really difficult and trying to cross a street – well, forget it, that was another matter. I think it was intended to be used when you were so stoned and drunk with everything else that it would be the only thing that would effect any noticeable difference. God, it was wretched stuff.

During these first tours back to the States we were re-establishing ourselves. We didn't make a lot of money, so our tour budget was limited and to cut back on expenses we all had to double up in rooms. On that tour Grenville and I were sharing a room at a wonderful hotel on 42nd Street. That's wonderful spelt D-E-P-R-E-S-S-I-N-G. We had become quite good friends. Grenville spoke with a perfectly cultivated and punctuated upper-class English accent and he synchronized his facial expressions in accordance with his range of vocal tones and skills. Very animated sort of geezer, you know. On this particular night, Grenville had sloped off somewhere. He was quite a loner, a secretive sod who often went off into the night on his own. A bit of a mystery man. He acted very snobbish and aloof in public, but deep down he was really all right. A bit of a cynic with a dry and sarcastic sense of humour and a sense of the ridiculous. I remember that when he first heard of Pete and Jonah's crash, he said, 'Good, good, anyone dead?' I suppose it was his way of dealing with things.

Diana and I had made love and were lying in bed drinking wine when we heard the sound of keys outside the door. The bedroom door burst open and in trotted Grenville, showing signs of wear and tear that indicated he was more than just a little drunk. He was wearing his usual pin-striped suit, white shirt and black tie. Now that I think of it, I don't remember him ever wearing anything else. He was a stockbroker before he and Robert became our managers, and I think he really enjoyed his smart, well-dressed wealthy Englishman image. But on this occasion his shirt was unbuttoned and his tie askew.

'Hi, Grenville,' I said from my lying position, sipping wine casually, unperturbed by his entrance. 'How are you doing? This is my friend Diana.'

'Oh, good, good, how are you?' he replied as he started to take off his jacket. He shook Diana's hand as a good gentleman should, of course. I offered him some wine and he cheerfully poured a glass and sat at the end of the other bed.

'Grenville,' I said, 'why don't you get in bed with us? Diana, you don't mind, do you?'

The poor girl looked at me in shocked silence. She was too embarrassed to say anything.

'Yeah, OK, why not?' Grenville answered, as he ripped off his shirt and tie to reveal a clean and well-laundered white vest. As he took off his trousers his previously gentlemanly poise now turned into an expression of leering lust, and he played the part to perfection. He threw his trousers to the floor to reveal a large pair of spotless white baggy underwear. Very unmacho, very unsexy. The sort of underwear that could have been specifically designed by overprotective mothers in order to quell instantly, on sight, the sexual desires of any advancing female who may have improper designs on the male in question.

Grenville pulled aside the bedcovers and slid into the bedsheets alongside Diana. Diana, who was completely naked, huddled closer to me.

'Right, come on, you bitch, what you need is a jolly good pumping,' said Grenville, as his hand reached towards her. I was trying so hard not to burst out with laughter that I forgot about the poor girl's embarrassing predicament.

Diana turned to me and said, 'Look, I can't do this. What do you think I am? Get away from me!'

Grenville continued his advance toward her. 'C'mon, you'll love it, you bitch.'

Diana jumped out of bed and grabbed nervously for her clothes. 'Dave, what are you doing, I don't do this kind of thing!' I could contain myself no longer and erupted into uncontrollable laughter. Almost on cue, so did Grenville and we both lay there laughing.

Diana angrily huffed as she got dressed. I got out of bed and apologized. In the back of my mind I had just wanted to test the potential of the situation, but on reflection it was a cruel thing to do. I escorted her out of the room and the hotel and got her a taxi home.

I had lunch with her the next day and we joked about it. She

was fine, but I still mused to myself how interesting it might have
been if things had gone the other way.

By the time we got to Chicago we were still very much feeling
our way with our new-found audience. At the Kinetic Playground we played with the Who. They, of course, had had the
good fortune to have been touring the States during our ban and
had obviously built up a strong following. Woodstock was a key
move for them, resurrecting their somewhat ailing careers and
restoring them to their rightful place in the rock 'n' roll arena.
They headlined the Chicago show and it was good seeing them –
fellow Brits far away from home and all that – but there was
definitely some tension mixed in with the camaraderie.

I was a little depressed after the show. I felt homesick and I
wasn't happy with the way the tour had been going. I started
drinking heavily and ended up back at the hotel, after an
extensive outing at the Rush Street clubs and bars, with a woman
I didn't even fancy. Once inside my room, realizing I was too far
gone to enter into a rite of passion, especially with a girl I didn't
like, I went into a tirade. God, those horrible hotel rooms. I
promptly started trashing it. As usual the lampshades were the
first to go. Then I smashed the mirrors, and promptly followed
that by upending the tables and beds. After a while I was ranting
and running like a madman up and down the hotel corridor. At
the end of the hallway near the elevator there was a glass exit
sign. With one almighty blow I smashed my right hand against it
and shattered the glass. Blood started streaming from my hand.
It was a terrible mess.

I went to the hospital for an examination but was relieved to
find that I hadn't damaged any tendons or ligaments. I had
simply torn the skin from the tops of my knuckles. I received
several stitches in my hand and the doctor recommended I take
at least a week off in order for it to heal. We weren't making
enough money in those days to afford to take our wives or
families on the road with us, so the next day I flew to Copenhagen to join Lisbet and Martin, who were visiting Lisbet's
mother. A couple of shows were cancelled, then I flew back and
picked up with the tour again in November in Detroit at the
Grand Ballroom. We were on the bill with Joe Cocker and the
Grease Band plus the James Gang.

My hand hadn't completely healed, but the stitches were out and I could move my fingers quite easily. I don't know what happened with the hotel in Chicago, but I assume they sent a bill for damages. The tour continued through Cincinnati and by the time we arrived in Los Angeles we had started to build up a following again.

Hollywood seemed such a different place from before. The drug culture had really taken hold and all kinds of drugs were available, from the weakest weed to acid, black bombers, and various assortments of uppers and downers to please even the most discerning junkie. Cocaine was becoming a more popular drug and you were considered uncool if you attended a party and didn't get high. It was a real 'trippy' time, man, and I did my best to make up for the time spent away in England during the ban. But I think that I was probably becoming a serious alcoholic and a drug addict.

The Kinks were booked to play at the Whiskey on Sunset, but we had four or five days to settle in. Or, rather, to get out of it. Well, at least me. Nobby and Mick were more into drink than drugs. I preferred to mix the two. Ray was more serious, more into the business and giving interviews. I suppose I was becoming a slave to my excesses. It was odd, because I really did enjoy my family life and I hated being away from home. I think that if my wife and son could have travelled with me, I might have stayed out of trouble a bit more. At least I wouldn't have acted in such a self-destructive way.

We stayed at a hotel north of Hollywood Boulevard near Vine called the Hollywood Hawaiian. It was a fairly cheap place so we each had a small apartment. I met a girl called Norma in a local club and we were very well matched. We drank ourselves into oblivion the first night, and had lustful hungover sex in the early hours of the following morning. Norma was a lot of fun; she was very into drugs and had access to everything.

The hotel manager was a big fat black guy named David. He was a fun-loving type and a good laugh. I would sometimes loan him records and sit in his apartment smoking dope. We always had plenty of albums, as it was the done thing in those days for record companies to give away large quantities of freebies. We had everything from the Band to Frank Sinatra. Actually it was quite a kick being on the same label as Frank. I loved the Band,

125

and Norma and I would stay up listening to them until the early hours.

It didn't take me long to realize that David, in addition to managing this somewhat sleazy establishment, was also pimping for some of the ladies who inhabited the upstairs apartments. One night I popped into his room to drop off some records and found him naked in a drug-induced sleep, with a quite attractive semi-naked middle-aged woman sitting calmly and happily beside him smoking pot. He had the biggest cock I had ever seen. It was like a tail of a python resting between his legs. She seemed happy enough.

Late one night Norma and I arrived back at the apartment drunk and stoned. We opened a bottle of Mateus Rosé wine, which was my favourite at the time. She opened her purse and showed me some small white pills. They were acid. Although I had probably taken every other drug known to man, I had never taken acid before. She told me that she had tripped many times and that this stuff was really good and untainted.

'Don't worry, Dave, it'll be fine. I'll babysit you if there are any problems,' she assured me.

I was drunk anyway and didn't need much prompting. So we swigged down two tablets each with a glass of rosé and waited. We lay silently on the bed and I pulled long and hard on a Marlboro. After about fifteen minutes nothing had happened so I poured two more large drinks and sat at the end of the bed and we talked. I took another cigarette and lit it. As I started to inhale I felt as if there were two of me inhaling two separate cigarettes, each of 'me' experiencing two different and quite distinct effects. And then it hit me: the classic acid awakening.

I was suddenly transported into another dimension or, I should say, dimensions. Before me I could see the universe and all it contained and I was rushing at the speed of light into what seemed the very heart of it. At first it was a phenomenal sensation of travelling very fast when, in fact, I was virtually motionless.

Norma spoke to try to calm me down and her voice took on a strange multi-layered quality as if there were many voices inside her. I was so high that none of this strangeness freaked me at all, at least not yet. I was lying there able to see through my eyelids into the vastness of space. I examined a chair and could sense the

126

pulsating radiations from its atoms, hidden from normal sight. A world of 'energy' opened up to me, everything throbbing with relentless life-force, breathing, vibrating in every molecule. This was the most incredible experience that had ever happened to me. Explosive, completely revealing, enlightening, illuminating and exciting, but strangely sad. During this 'trip' I would lapse into profound moments of excruciating and unbearable sadness. Then I would be suddenly lifted into mystical realms of ecstasy, where answers to the riddles of life would be answered in an almost alien, ineffable language of mind energy. Truly 'cosmic', man.

During the whole experience I sensed a being above my head who talked me through it all. He told me he was my Captain. He explained so much to me, and helped me out of my tangled moments of confusion. He showed me, in a scintillating, almost cinematic way, that all I had ever learned would now have to be unlearned. I looked over at Norma, who was lying on the bed transfixed on an invisible point in her own world. She looked like a reptile. Normally, it would have scared the shit out of me to see this, but for some reason her appearance made some surreal and subconscious sense. The acid had triggered primeval messages in my brain, memories conveying genetic information from an ancient past into the present.

The furniture breathed, doors swayed almost painfully from the constriction of being modelled unnaturally by man into a strange form. Wood became rubber. As were the walls . . . My body now, bodies. Being pushed in and out of each other. There is no sleep, sleep and waking are the same, dreaming and reality are interwoven. Ideas become real. Talking to me from somewhere is the Captain. He tells me what to do, what is right, what is wrong, what does what to me. A cinematic box opens in my forehead. I see everything, everything is new, strange. The movie continues . . . I am helpless to its purpose. To its cause . . .

I walked out of the room and into the pool area. It was early morning and the world was asleep. People looked like they were made of Plasticine. The man at the front reception looked dead; everyone seemed as if they were dead. I felt terribly alone. Everything seemed funny, but I still felt unbearably sad. Oh God, now I started to wish for it all to end. I didn't want to see any more. I went back to my room. Norma was trying to get herself together, explaining to me that she had never experienced a 'trip' quite like it before.

'It must have been powerful stuff,' she said. She tried to calm and relax me, but I was extremely restless and irritable. I pleaded with her to give me something to make it stop.

'Is this ever going to end?' I kept saying over and over. I drank a bottle of wine, but it had little effect. The alcohol just increased my paranoia. I started ranting, asking questions that had no answers.

Norma gave me some strong sleeping pills and after a while I slept. The days that followed were terrible. I felt like an alien who has suddenly been dumped on a hostile and frightening planet. I drank more and took more sleeping pills.

All of a sudden it was the day of our first date at the Whiskey. The thought of performing filled me with fear and trepidation. Backstage before the first show, Nobby told me that I looked really strange. 'You look like your body's there, but your soul is somewhere else,' he said. I laughed it off, but he was probably right.

We got on stage and started to play. I thought it so odd that everybody seemed to be playing a split second later than I. I just couldn't understand why everything was so disjointed. Half-way through the show I couldn't stand it any more, so I left the stage, put my guitar in its case, and left the building. I walked all the way down Sunset to my hotel, telling myself that I couldn't live in this crazy unreal world any more. Hopelessness pulled at the core of my being.

By the time I reached the hotel I decided I was going back to England on the next available flight. I would start a new life. A life away from the falsehoods and pretences so eloquently crystallized in form by 'Them'. I felt I was seeing through the 'ultimate deception' that toyed with us as mere unconscious puppets, stupefied by ignorance. I felt we were just going through the motions, pleasing some hidden dark force. There was a strange rationale to this new paranoia of mine, or was it a new 'truth'?

As I entered the hotel, Norma was anxiously awaiting my return. We talked for a while and I told her about my plans. Grenville came to my room and tried to persuade me otherwise, but I had made up my mind, or so I thought. I took two sleeping pills and slept for nearly two days. The remaining shows at the Whiskey were postponed.

I was alone when I awoke in my room. The afternoon sun shone brightly and hopefully through the window. I felt like shit. Mentally, physically, and spiritually. I was in a terrible state and knew I needed help. I felt lost and confused. I went to Ray's room to talk, to find some comfort in my misery. He seemed like a total stranger to me, unemotional, uncaring. Maybe it was just me, maybe I was lost in my own world. I explained to him that I had had it and that all I wanted to do was go home, that I was tired and mentally and emotionally disoriented.

He turned to me and said, coldly, 'Look, Dave, you should see it through to the end. There's only one week of gigs left at the Fillmore West in San Francisco, and then we can all go home and rest and contemplate our next move, or whatever.'

I really needed Ray to come through for me on that occasion. I was empty inside, my world had been thrown upside down and my mind was in disarray. He was acting detached and was being his usual 'practical' self, as was normal for him when confronted with an emotionally abrasive situation. I suppose Ray has always had a problem with his emotional life. But I needed him. I smiled to myself, shaking my head in disbelief. As I turned to walk out the door, he stopped me.

'Dave,' he said, 'before you go I want to tell you about a dream I had last night. I was walking down the street in the early hours of the morning. I looked across the street and saw an old man with his head bowed. He took a brief look at me, opened the door to his house, walked in, and slammed the door behind him. It was as if he had closed the door on the world.'

I looked at Ray wryly, then left and went back to my apartment. It was so typical of Ray to use words as an emotional device to get me to do what he wanted or what he in his mind thought would be best for me in the long run. I suppose I should feel grateful that he tried, even in his sophisticated yet really exasperating way. But I would have been happier with a hug or a more open demonstration of love and support. A day later we went to San Francisco, completed the remaining dates and headed back to England. Mentally and emotionally I was in a bad way. But I was very happy to get home to my family.

My interest in metaphysics, particularly yoga and spiritualism, became much more intense. One day I went to a psychic and she told me that the experience I had had with the Captain was my higher self watching over me. I threw myself into a search for my inner self. I had to try to find the reasons for my private 'madness', the voices I was hearing, the weird impressions I was getting. I was experiencing a kind of mental-psychic breakdown.

I was much too scared to tell anyone about my private hell. I even shielded Lisbet from the more disturbing aspects of my condition. Lisbet was always so wonderfully cheerful and optimistic and supportive. I don't know what I would have done without her during this period. I truly started to believe I was going crazy.

Unbeknown to me at the time, this psychic metamorphosis was to last some two years and would get much worse before it got better. Like a snake that slowly and painfully sheds its old skin to make way for the new, I had to rebuild my inner life step by step. The abuses of the previous years, the drugs and drink, were now truly taking their toll.

Around this time I composed some poems which I gathered together in an unpublished book of writings. Here's an excerpt from one called 'Chair':

> The subtleties of this world are awe inspiring,
> the foreverness of this moment is wonderful beyond
> belief. Beyond what is seen to the naked eye.
> Truth takes shape of my chair . . .
> Mind assumes the forms around . . . I am the tree . . .
> I am the ground. A sound. A note . . .
>
> Secrets humbly await recognition.
> My mind takes a leap . . . Words stumble on my tongue.
> Thoughts are too fast to hold. Too many holes. I am sitting.
> The chair is breathing. Who is asleep . . .
> All is dead.
> I look around. This stillness is full of both noise I
> understand and noise that I can only absorb.
> The mind's a box of tricks.
> A tree . . . A chair . . . A box . . . A screen . . .
> Now the harlequinade materializes adequately detailed.
> A mental landscape full of colourful meaning.

KINK

Illusion dances hopelessly in the sun with Plasticine
soldiers. Naked. Smiling. Oblivious to the battle.
Their waxy features melt into mush. The war rages
unseen in the mind, memory takes a back seat.
I am still here . . . where . . . Here . . . sitting . . .
just sitting . . . On this chair . . .

8

K I N K

Illusion dance- hopelessly in the sun under Plastimac
soldiers. Nickel. Smiling. Oblivious to the battle.
Then waxy features melt into mush. The marionette
frozen in the mind, memory takes a back seat.
I am still here . . . where . . . How . . . sitting . . .
just sitting . . . On this chair . . .

Early in 1970, Grenville suggested that it might be a good idea to
try out a keyboard player on stage. Ray played keyboards in the
studio, so it seemed a logical step to hire someone to play them
on stage. One afternoon we auditioned John Gosling, who was
then a student at the Royal Academy, and it seemed to go well. I
immediately got on well with John. He seemed a bit shy and
nervous but was a decent sort. We soon became friends.

During a rehearsal at Ray's house I introduced a chord pro-
gression which a week or so later became the basis of 'Lola'. Ray
never gave me any credit for partly inspiring the piece. It may
have been Ray's lyrics, his story, but they were my musical ideas
that formed the foundation of this song. Working in a band, the
creative process is usually a collaborative one. Sometimes you
come up with ideas that contribute significantly to the overall
structure of a piece of music to a greater or lesser degree. When
my son Simon later formed a band of his own and they started to
write songs, I suggested that everyone who contributed to a song
should have equal credit. In the end it would save a lot of
arguments.

In May we started recording 'Lola'. Again, as with previous
successes, I sensed something special in the air. We changed
studios and recorded various tracks that were later to form part
of our last album for Pye records, *Lola Versus Powerman and the
Moneygoround*. Although the album was greeted with mixed
reviews, it was nonetheless a great opportunity to express many
pent-up views and emotions stored in our hearts and minds. Ray
used it as a forum to punch, jab and shout at the mistreatment we
had received from certain more unscrupulous quarters of the
business. I wrote a song for the album called 'Strangers', about
friendship, reconciliation, and unconditional love. About the

realization that we all, at various times in our lives, have to give up a part of ourselves for the benefit of something greater to become part of a greater whole.

STRANGERS

Where're you going to, I don't mind
I've killed my world, and I've killed my time,
So where do I go, what do I see
I see many people coming after me.
So where are you going to, I don't mind
If I live too long, I'm afraid I'll die,
So I will follow you wherever you go
If your offered hand is still open to me.

Strangers, on this road we are on,
We are not two, we are one.

So you've been where I've just come
From the land that brings losers on,
So we will share this road we walk
And mind our mouths and beware our talk,
Till peace we find, tell you what I'll do,
All the things I own I will share with you
If I feel tomorrow like I feel today
We'll take what we want and give the rest away

Strangers . . . (chorus).

Holy man and holy priest,
This love of life makes me weak at my knees
So when we get there, make your play
Cause soon I feel you're gonna carry us away.
In a promised lie you made us believe
For many men there is so much grief
And my mind is proud but it aches with rage
And if I live too long I'm afraid I'll die.

Strangers . . . (chorus).

Gosling was integrating well as a band member and was also showing much promise at the pub as a serious drinker. John was actually a very funny guy, and in spite of his classical training he was a talented musician who possessed a genuine enthusiasm for our music and had a unique creative flair. He was also an exceptionally awkward sod. A klutz par excellence. I shall always remember how Nobby would continually tease and wind him up. Nobby renamed him John the Baptist. After all, he did look like John the Baptist, or what we imagined John the Baptist would or should have looked like. One evening we were in the pub having a pint or two after a session and Nobby asked Baptist for the time. Baptist is left-handed and was holding a near full pint of beer in his hand. He promptly turned his wrist to view his watch and without thinking poured beer all over himself. I guess stupid is as stupid does.

Nobby was always pulling pranks like that. He was generally very down to earth and practical but he had a cheeky and mischievous sense of humour, which was a godsend. The band seemed to be coming together with a feeling of real unity and camaraderie that we hadn't had since Pete Quaife's departure. The Kinks seemed like a 'band' again. Things were starting to feel right and we regained the joy of playing and performing together. I believe that humour really saved us from possible self-destruction and frequently delivered us from the depths of despair and even insanity. I know it saved me. If there is a god of humour then I will become its number one devotee, disciple, and worshipper.

The *Lola* album includes one of my favourite Kinks tracks, 'Get Back in Line', and it contains some of Ray's best lyrics. To me the emotions and sentiment echo deep into our background and our upbringing, a tribute to the difficulties of the working classes. I really believe that if it hadn't been for the good fortune of being in a successful band, I most probably would have ended up working in a factory.

Music became a great device for us to express so much that would otherwise have remained dormant or suppressed or, worse, forgotten. We were able, through our music, to communicate the struggle of the ordinary working man trying to survive in a greedy and purely materialistic society. As the song goes, 'All I want to do is make a little money and take you home some wine.' Obvious, melancholic simplicity. A great song that's full of yearning, full of feeling. I have always believed that the world, or rather people, can never really change until the word 'feeling' is truly understood. Feeling connects us to the spiritual part of our being. And Kinks music, with its characters that may seem quirky at times, or even sad or fragile, or sometimes weak and clumsy, is always hopeful. We must never lose hope.

The song 'Top of the Pops' was a piss-take of the British TV pop show which is still being aired today. I never really liked that song – it showed a bitter side of Ray's writing that has always disturbed me a little – but it was fun to perform. We performed another cut from that album, 'Apeman', for the real *Top of the Pops*, and since it was Baptist's first TV show with us we jokingly demanded that he dress up for the occasion.

We convinced him that for this inaugural TV appearance he had to wear a full gorilla outfit. Apart from the fact that he looked so wonderfully stupid with all six foot three of him tucked neatly inside this ridiculous outfit, it was so hot under the studio lights I was surprised that he didn't suffocate.

After a number of rehearsals during the day the big moment came when the show was to go out live to millions of viewers. As the cameras panned, music blared out from the monitors and the audience danced with their usual enforced enthusiasm. Baptist looked sillier than ever. He had just spent a few hours propping up the BBC bar and was more than a bit tipsy, but he was ready for his close-up, Mr De Mille. Just as the camera moved forward to take full view of the gorilla playing the piano, Baptist tripped over a cable and fell off the podium. Baptist's first television close-up ended up being a shot of a wall. But a very nice wall it was, with coloured lights shining on it. It was hilarious watching a drunken gorilla holding his back in agony while kids danced and cavorted in excitement, staring adoringly at their much-admired pop stars who by now were trying desperately to hide their hysterical tears of laughter behind the swagger and veiled sincerity of their performance.

Needless to say, Baptist passed his initiation with flying colours – or at least with flying gorillas. To his great relief and humiliation the show was finally over and much laughter shared by one and all. However, Baptist didn't know that due to his great success as a gorilla he would be asked to repeat his impressive performance at a promotional film shoot a few days later, which to this day is perhaps one of the silliest things we have ever done. Baptist bravely swigged back a large brandy, and with a true blue English stiff upper lip he put on his gorilla head once again and gave a devastating and tear-jerking performance.

John had still not performed a live show with the Kinks, and he was starting to get worried that this gorilla thing might get out of hand and become more than just a prank or a wind-up. A US tour was looming up and he must have wondered if it would taint his image or credibility as a serious musician. Was the big break he had so desperately been looking for tragically backfiring before his very eyes? Was he to become a mere pawn – or I should say, gorilla – in the hands of the terrible, cheap-laugh Davies brothers? The Kinks would again make an almost triumphant, if not humourless, return to the USA that year.

All of a sudden, or so it seemed, the sixties were over. I was married to a beautiful woman, I had a young son and another on the way (my second son, Simon, was born on 10 June, 1970). As if by magic, or maybe through the power of a sorcerer's dream, I had arrived in my early twenties. I felt reflective and a little sad, even though I had already fulfilled so many of my dreams and much more at such a young age. But I felt that there was something missing in my life. The last year had taken an emotional and spiritual toll on me and I felt lost. What had become of my old friends, I wondered? I thought about my mate George Harris. What was he doing now? In my depression I felt that although I was probably the envy of many, I had spent my teenage years in a weird, alien cocoon. I had been isolated from the life that perhaps I was meant to live.

I decided to try and look up some old friends. I knew it was dangerous to try to recapture the past, but I felt as if a part of my growing up, my youth, had been taken away from me. I walked out of my front door and looked at my posh sports car, a Citroën Maserati. It was odd, but I felt kind of ashamed to own it. It meant nothing all of a sudden. What was I trying to prove? It was nothing more than an elaborately designed lump of metal that stared somewhat arrogantly and smugly back at me as I stood in my drive. I felt uncomfortable, I think, having money. Sometimes you wish all your life for material things and when you get them you wonder what all the fuss was about. I also owned a small red

Austin Mini, which I had bought a few years earlier when I passed my driving test. I got into that instead and drove to Muswell Hill to visit my mum.

'Hello boy,' Mum greeted me as I walked into her front room. 'You must have smelled the tea brewing. Sit down, I'll make you some.' I sat and looked at some old photos of me and Ray, other family members, and friends, that were huddled together affectionately on the mantlepiece. From the kitchen Mum shouted, 'I've just come from Wylie's the baker's, I got a lovely farmhouse loaf; shall I make you a cheese and pickle sandwich?' Since I was a small boy, cheese and pickle sandwiches had been my favourite. Trust Mum to put a smile on my face.

'Yeah, I'd love one, Mum,' I shouted back. In she came moments later with her giant yet familiar brown china teapot, cups, saucers, and of course the cheese and pickle sandwiches. Crusty fresh doorsteps they were, oozing with generous portions of pickle. Mum always said that tea tasted better out of either a china or porcelain cup, but that china was best. We sat and chatted, and she gave me the local gossip. She said she had seen George's mum round the shops several months ago and she had told her George had been taken into hospital to have a kidney removed, but that he was recovering fine. I knew it was his drug abuse that had landed him there. The last time I had seen him some years before he had still been very heavily into drugs, much, much more than I. Drugs were fun to me, but to George they had become more a way of life.

I recollected for Mum how I enjoyed going to George's room at the top of his house to listen to blues records and jam with him till the early hours of the morning. In those years I had always dreamed of George and me making a record together. During our school days, George's dad would pay me a few bob to teach George guitar. George later became a fine guitarist, and my dream was partially realized when I rented time in a small studio in Soho after I had started to make some money in the early days of the Kinks. We recorded a few songs – covers of blues standards and a couple of Spider John Koerners songs – but nothing more ever came of it.

I told Mum that after I finished my sandwich I was going to look up George.

'Dave,' she said, 'I also saw Sue.' My heart started to thump. I think part of the reason I had made this visit was to get some news about Sue and our daughter, Tracey. Mum went on to tell me that Tracey, who was then about seven, was getting on fine. She reluctantly showed me a picture of her, the first I'd ever seen. She was beautiful, with lovely chubby little cheeks. But she had that melancholy Davies look around her eyes. Sue had got married, and she and her husband and Tracey had moved to Hatfield, but Mum didn't know exactly where.

I found out many years later that Sue often visited Rasa when Ray and I were on tour in the early days. I didn't know it, but she also wanted to know how I was doing. It's a shame, really, that our parents caused us to think that we didn't care about one another when, at the very least, I could have had a father–daughter relationship with Tracey instead of just some fleeting glances at photos and an emptiness in my heart.

Mum had become quite tearful watching me gaze at Tracey's photo, but she pushed back her tears with a joke as she often did and placed the photo back neatly and securely in her handbag. As I looked around at the various family snapshots, she shook her head, smiled, and said, 'Oh David, you were such a lovely little boy, but what a sod you were. You had beautiful blond hair and when the sun shone on it you'd swear you'd see a halo on the top of your head. I always thought, yeah, one day that bloody halo'll slip round his neck and strangle him.'

'The tea was great, Mum,' I said. 'I think I'll take a walk round Muswell Hill. Maybe I'll pop back later.'

'Don't dig up the past, David,' she warned. 'You've got a lovely family of your own now. Let bygones be bygones.'

I left Mum's house and walked to Fortis Green Avenue, the street where George lived with his mum and brother (his father had died while we were still in school). As I approached the house I was full of excitement at the expectation of seeing George again. I knocked several times, but after a while it became obvious that there was no one in. I continued walking. I passed the corner near Princess Avenue where I had first met Sue all those years ago. Our favourite coffee bar, the El Toro, where we would meet our friends, and where Ray and I would play occasionally, was sadly now a Chinese restaurant.

I ventured further up the road to where that lovely old Victorian building, the Athenaeum Ballroom, had once stood.

We did one of our first shows there as the Ravens. I remember that we were really nervous, as it seemed such a big gig for us at the time, and afterwards the management told us that we were terrible and that they wouldn't have us there again. The building had been torn down some years before to make way for the ever-expanding Sainsbury supermarket chain. Inexplicably, I decided to go in. I picked up a Coke and headed for the check-out. Standing at the counter was none other than George's mother. I couldn't believe it. We started to talk as best we could in the crowded store. The Harrises had moved out of their house as it was too big, and had taken up residence in a smaller flat. Mrs Harris told me quite coldly and in a matter-of-fact way that George had died. After coming out of hospital he had seemed to be recovering well, but one day the phone rang and it was the police. George had been found dead, lying at the side of the road in the West End. His death had been caused by a drug overdose. I found out later that it was a lethal concoction of heroin and methedrine. Because of the crowded shop I left with Mrs Harris's phone number and promised I'd get in touch with her later on. I never did. Every time I'd think of it, it just seemed too painful.

I was stunned. George couldn't have been more than twenty-one years old. I walked back to my car, got in and drove. I drove up through Barnet on the A1 towards Potters Bar and Hatfield. I drove around the streets of Hatfield almost as if dazed. I kept driving up and down the same streets, thinking that maybe I'd come across Sue walking with Tracey down the street. Then all of a sudden it hit me. George was dead. Really dead. Gone forever. I had loved and admired him, he was so talented, so unhappy, and I wasn't there for him. He was such a purist, he always made fun of our commercial successes, and although his comments were sometimes tinged with jealousy we were really good friends. I had lost a good friend, the second one to be taken away by drug abuse. I should have kept more in touch.

I drove solemnly back to my house in Barnet. I parked my car and went into the house, where I was greeted by Lisbet and my lovely young son Martin. I picked him up and gave him a tremendous hug. Tears welled up in my eyes. Maybe I wasn't so badly off; maybe my life had changed for the better. Maybe destiny had something special in store for me. I felt so bad about George. Maybe Mum was right. Don't look back. Let bygones be bygones. I couldn't help but think that I might have been able to help George, and now it was too late. I wanted so much to see Tracey, but I couldn't impose on her family now. She had a father. And I had my own family. I later wrote a song about George called 'Georgie Was'. It was never released, although it was recorded. It was an odd song about the tragic dangers of drug addiction, a song that would never see the light of day. A 'love song' for a friend, written and recorded for George, that no one was to hear. I remember thinking that he probably would have preferred it that way.

We toured the States again in the summer of 1970. Baptist tasted life on the road with the Kinks for the first time, discovering for himself the tortuous rigours of rock 'n' roll: sleazy hotels, groupies, purple vodka, rum, Scotch.

'Lola' became a massive worldwide hit for us. There was one little glitch with its release, however. While we were touring the States we got word that the BBC took exception to Ray's use of the word 'Coca Cola' in the song, so he had to fly back to England mid-tour to re-record it as 'cherry cola'. It seemed awfully silly and unnecessary, but after all our problems with bans and the like, we didn't want to stir up any more trouble.

Our US tour would take us to the Whiskey in LA and back again to 'Frisco, where we played the Family Dog and the Fillmore West, with Elton John as our opening act. It's funny how through the seventies and early eighties it was considered lucky to open for the Kinks. It seemed so strange that a number of bands, such as Steely Dan, Blondie, the Hooters, INXS, and others became big after touring with us.

It's probably no surprise that we had quite a reputation in those days as heavy drinkers, especially in the States. Some fans in New York nicknamed us the 'Juicers'. And with Baptist in the band we had an added dimension, if you could call it that. On one flight back from Iceland, after a gruelling stint of shows, Baptist, Mick, Nobby and I had been drinking excessively and were acting like hooligans on the plane. I had bought a large furry sheepskin coat at Reykjavik airport and I insisted on crawling up and down the aisle of the aeroplane with it on my back pretending to be a wild animal, biting people's legs. The crew were getting really pissed off, so they sectioned off a corner of the aircraft for us and continued to feed us large quantities of alcohol, to pacify us, I guess. But their efforts were futile. Grenville was getting very angry and I think he was finally becoming disenchanted, especially after spending most of the year in America with us and putting up with our gross, self-destructive and, to him, childish behaviour.

During the flight the captain threatened to land the plane at Glasgow and throw us off if we didn't behave. So for about an hour we managed to restrict ourselves to the odd shout of abuse across the aisle at the occasional passing passenger, especially ones that looked to us like Frank Sinatra, Lionel Jeffries, or the English newsreader Reginald Bosanquet. Isn't it funny how ordinary people start to look like famous personalities when you're really out of it?

Things had finally started to return to normal when all of a sudden Nobby got up and staggered into the cockpit with a stern and mean leer on his face. During the whole trip he had complained about the fact that our late departure had caused him to miss playing in a local football match. Nobby jokingly requested the captain to put the plane down in Cheshunt, near where the match was going to be played, but the crew wasn't amused. Two stewards dragged him back to his seat and we were severely cautioned by the captain that our behaviour could have drastic and serious consequences. The bar was immediately closed and we were put under close watch by the stewards until we finally landed at Heathrow. On our arrival we were escorted off the plane and out of the airport by armed police. The officer in charge warned us that if there was any further trouble we would all be arrested. By this time Grenville was out of his mind with frustration and embarrassment. At one point I started to question the authority of the superintendent, saying to him, 'Who do you think you are, God?' Grenville stepped in grace-fully and defused a potentially difficult situation. But it was the beginning of the end of our relationship with Grenville and by the time we reached LA for yet another tour in November, things were really coming to a head.

It was our third tour of the States that year and we stayed once again at the Hollywood Hawaiian. We had a day off, so we all decided to go to the shops on Hollywood Boulevard, except for Ray, who stayed behind to do interviews. We found a wonderful clothes shop that was also a costumiers and joke shop. I bought a replica .45 gun, hat and gangster suit. Baptist bought a Viking helmet, a cape and a horn. With his long hair and beard he looked like a fugitive from Wagner's *Die Götterdammerung*. Mick bought a clown outfit with make-up kit, and Nobby got some '50s clothes and dressed up as the Buddy Love character from Jerry Lewis's movie *The Nutty Professor*.

That evening we decided to take Hollywood by storm by visiting the various clubs dressed up as our respective characters. By the time we ended up at a club called Filthy McNasties, we were well into the swing of it. I met this pretty young dancer and together we moved with our entourage into the Whiskey. Mick was hilarious dressed as a clown doing somersaults in the air, dancing with all these really cool groovy kids from Hollywood.

Nobby swaggered around chatting up all the chicks, cocky and ultraconfident. 'Hey, baby, put it there,' he'd say, offering his lips to a woman at the bar. 'Do it, you deserve it, you'll feel better,' he'd say in true Buddy Love style.

I saw some record company executives sitting at a booth showing off for some girls, and I decided to threaten them by waving a very lifelike gun in their faces. They were not at all happy until I assured them that the gun was really fake. The look on their faces was a treat. The look on mine must have been equally amusing when I found out later that the record company people were our own. Shit, what the heck.

Baptist was just content to dance the night away like all good drunk Vikings do, horns and all. I decided to leave them to it. I took the girl back to my hotel, where she stripped and danced for me on the table. She had a lovely body. We made love and then went to sleep.

Mick and I were sharing the apartment and when I awoke in the morning I discovered him in the next room lying on his bed with clown make-up running down his cheeks. He was groaning.

'Mick, what happened to you?' I asked. He told me that he had tried to do a back flip on the dance floor and ended up crashing into a table, nearly breaking his back. Poor sod, he was in agony. A truly sad clown if I ever saw one.

By the afternoon, Grenville had got word of the previous night's antics and called a meeting. Ray and I sat with Nobby and

Mick in Grenville's room. Ray was obviously concerned but had not yet been informed of all the facts. Grenville was furious.

'Look,' he said, 'you simply cannot go on like this. This outrageous behaviour has to stop, I won't put up with it. I just will not stand for it any more. You're destroying your careers.'

We sheepishly agreed that maybe things were getting a little out of hand and that we should really think about the consequences of what we were doing – knowing full well, like the true overgrown schoolboys we were, that we intended to do the very same thing again.

Just as Grenville seemed reasonably content that his point had been made and we had convinced him that things would change for the better, the door suddenly burst open. It was Baptist, drunk, still wearing his full Viking's costume, but this time with an even larger horn. Full of proud excitement, he lifted the horn to his lips and with all his might blew into it. It let out a loud, rasping, ear-shattering blast of noise.

'Look what I found,' he exclaimed proudly, 'isn't it fabulous?' Baptist slowly scanned the room, wondering why everyone was so silent, so unimpressed by his great discovery. His look of joy turned to confusion as he observed the distinct lack of enthusiasm shown by the assembled company. After a few quiet and uncomfortable moments, everyone, unable to control themselves any longer, burst into hysterical laughter. All except Grenville, who was flabbergasted, shocked, and totally disgruntled.

'That's it, I've had it,' he said. He got up and hurriedly left the room, muttering inaudible words of disbelief. I think that was the last straw for Grenville. It wasn't too long before the differences that had gradually built up between Ray and Robert, coupled with Grenville's disillusionment, found us without management. This wouldn't be the first time – or the last.

Nineteen-seventy was also the year that we were commissioned to do the music for an English movie called *Percy*, an appallingly silly film about a man's penis transplant. Ray wrote some truly beautiful songs, including 'The Way Things Used to Be' and 'God's Children', with touching, thoughtful words and haunting melodies, but they were completely wasted on that awful project. It's a miracle we survived it at all.

9

By 1971, I had lost my confidence to play live and was mentally in very bad shape. Tours to Germany and Australia were postponed or cancelled due to my illness. I felt fine in the comfort and security of the studio and enjoyed recording, but touring and travelling constantly was really starting to get to me. I was extremely paranoid and depressed on the road. All I wanted was to be in the studio or with my family.

Looking back now, I think I really should have sought treatment for my worsening mental and emotional state, but I was so terrified that there might be something seriously wrong with me, in my mind – or worse, my brain – that I stubbornly refused to get help.

On the road I felt scattered and confused. I was drinking very heavily. In an effort to get to the root of my problem, I started to read up on the occult, books on mental health, schizophrenia, black magic. I really thought I was going insane.

At home I felt fine, but I hated being in strange places with people I didn't know. Although I was unhappy and distressed, the Kinks continued to tour up and down the UK and we went to the States in March and April.

The shows in and around New York went fine even though morale was low. By the time we got to LA I was again in despair and was continuing to experiment with hallucinogens. We had three or four days off in LA and I spent the entire time in my room drinking wine and taking mescaline. I had with me a strange little dark woman whose name I can't remember. She continually ran errands for me. Maybe she was a homunculus conjured up from my mind, for she seemed half-reptile, half-human. Maybe she popped in from another dimension. Wherever she came from, she was a strange person indeed.

After those few days I never saw her again. Weird.

Ray had flown back to London for the break and by the time we reassembled and were to play our first California show in San Diego, I was far too ill and we had to yet again cancel shows. On 10 April we returned to England, and the remainder of our dates were cancelled.

There was one particularly humorous show, however, that I recall from that tour. We were in New York to play the Philharmonic Hall. It was a beautiful place and had a very plush backstage area. We even had a full-sized grand piano in our dressing-room. There was great excitement and anticipation before the show. I had a few stiff drinks before I arrived, in the hope of shutting out the voices in my head and the merciless cacophony of noise that was just New York's crazy way of welcoming a fragile, if not oversensitive, visitor. New York talks to you like no other town in the world; it constantly screams for attention from every street corner, never allowing one to rest.

Spirits were high backstage as we rehearsed a few songs sitting around the piano. It was soon time to go on stage. After about two or three songs I noticed Ray struggling a little, kind of swaying from side to side. We continued the set to an excited and enthusiastic crowd. About half-way through the show Ray started to look extremely rough, as if the tequila had suddenly taken its full effect. He took a step back and lost his balance as if the floor had vanished from under his feet. He started to totter backwards towards me. I thought I had better step out of the way. As I moved to one side Ray fell and crashed into my speaker stack, bringing the whole back line thundering to the floor. He picked himself up and staggered around while the band continued to play quite nonchalantly. A roadie appeared on stage and tried to help him, but by this time he was totally out of it. Some kids from the audience got up on stage as well, and one of them pulled Ray's mike away from its lead and ran out of the building with it. Ray desperately held on to a roadie's arm and continued to sing down an empty mike cable.

I moved over to my mike and invited members of the audience to come up on stage. All of a sudden the stage was full of people singing, laughing, and shouting. I looked around and saw Mick struggling with a couple of guys who were trying to make off with his drums. The place was in chaos. There were kids trying to sing into microphones, budding keyboard players banging away on the piano. Nobby was threatening anyone who came near his gear, and I stood in total disbelief, watching it all as if it were a movie. To any other band but the Kinks this night would have been considered a disaster. But to us and our fans it became a night to remember long into the future. The management, of course, were not quite as amused and we have never been asked to play the Philharmonic Hall again.

Another memorable event from that year was when Arsenal won the double. Ray and I knew someone who worked at the club, so we easily got tickets for the matches. We travelled all over the country to watch games, from Goodison Park to Loftus Road.

Charlie George was such a great player; the spontaneity and skill he demonstrated were awesome. A true character, an entertainer and a naturally gifted player. We cheered the team on from the stands: George Graham, Bob Wilson, Ray Kennedy, John Radford, Peter Storey (elbows), Pat Rice, Peter Simpson, Georgie Armstrong, Frank McLintock, Nelson and the rest of the boys. We became so involved in Arsenal's quest that we temporarily neglected our own careers. If a match happened to fall on the same day as a gig, we would think nothing of cancelling the show under some pretext or the other just so we could go to the matches.

The highlights of the season were watching Arsenal beat Liverpool in the FA Cup Final, 2–1, when Charlie scored a tremendous goal and when Ray Kennedy scored the clincher at White Hart Lane against old rivals Spurs that settled the league title. What wonderful moments they were.

To me it was like watching England winning the World Cup against West Germany in 1966. That day we had been booked to play a show in Exeter. These were the days before the M5 motorway, so the drive usually took about five to six hours. We watched the match on the telly at home and planned to leave directly after it was over. We thought we would just have enough time to get to Exeter for the gig. But of course the match went into extra time and there was no way that we were going to miss it.

It was an incredible afternoon. When you looked out into the streets it was as if the Blitz was on. There wasn't a soul in sight;

everybody was indoors glued to the telly, watching the game. Eventually, of course, England won what was to become not only a memorable match but also an historic one.

Ray, the band and I headed towards the West Country hoping to get there in time for our show. Unfortunately we didn't get there until around midnight, due to exceptionally heavy traffic. When we did arrive at the gig, everyone was packing up and the last of the crowd were wandering off home. God, was the promoter pissed off. I remember us standing on the stage looking out into the debris of where our audience had once stood, discarded Coke cans and pieces of paper littered all over the place. The promoter was speechless with anger. He came up to Ray and kicked him up the arse. Ray fell off the front of the stage – it was only a few feet high so he didn't hurt himself – but it was hard for us to contain our laughter.

Ray held his arms out in an apologetic way, trying to hide a smirk that was building up on his face, but the damage had already been done and there was nothing more to be said. On the way back in the car we joked and laughed about the incident. We felt bad about the audience; after all, it really wasn't very nice. But I mean, what were we supposed to do? England had won the World Cup, for Christ's sake!

By the summer of 1971 we had signed with a new label, RCA, and by August we began rehearsing material that was later to become part of the *Muswell Hillbillies* album, a very special record to me. It was an affectionate recollection of characters from our past, and its theme was inspired by the working-class families who were forced out of the inner city and rehoused in the cheaply built suburban New Towns that were to become the slums of the future. But once again, the album didn't get the commercial success we hoped for and only reached number 100 in the charts.

Robert and Grenville were gone for good, and I was saddened by their departure. Ray was becoming increasingly more difficult to handle. While I was retreating into myself, becoming more withdrawn, Ray was becoming more outward, more flamboyant and narcissistic. He had become a much more astute business-man after our management problems in the past, and was tired of feeling that people were ripping him off. He wanted more control. I felt this only made him meaner and more selfish.

Robert confided to me some time later that Ray's changing behaviour and attitude at that time was due to the fact that he was always listening to the wrong people, people that sucked up to him and 'yessed' him. He didn't listen to the people who really cared. Ray had told Robert that he was angry at the way we had been treated and was determined to make everybody's lives as difficult as possible in order to get what he wanted. Some of Ray's bitterness was excusable, in a way, what with publishers ripping him off, and management taking more than their fair share. Those greedy fucks. But for all Robert's faults I regarded him as a good friend and loyal ally. Grenville and I had become good friends as well, but he had recently married an heiress of sorts, and I think he wanted an excuse to get out without looking like a 'cad' or a 'bounder'.

Ray was happy they had left and believed that we didn't need anyone else's help; that we could manage ourselves. I wasn't so sure, and was much more insecure about it. It's all very well when you're riding high, caught up in the euphoria of repeated successes, but when you stumble a bit and you're struggling, it can be a terribly lonely world out there, without the emotional and creative support of people around you that genuinely care. I began to lose heart, I think, but I nonetheless went along with Ray and followed his instincts.

But Ray was becoming more and more distant and, I felt, was over-extending himself. We continued to tour, the show now augmented with Mike Cotton's brass section. We recorded some of the US shows at Carnegie Hall in New York and these recordings became part of a double album which was released later in '72, called *Everybody's in Show Biz*. On that album there was a song that was to become a Kinks anthem, 'Celluloid Heroes'. The lyrics show the most beautiful and sensitive side of Ray's character. Sentimental, charming, fragile, a yearning for lost innocence. I've always felt that Ray at his best seems like a soul which is looking for the pieces of life that are constantly being cast aside by an arrogant, relentless and uncaring world. He collects and analyses those pieces, and tries to put the fragments back together in order to make some sense of it all. A typical example shows itself in the lyrics of 'Autumn Almanac'. He's sensitive to the small things that most people overlook.

'Celluloid Heroes' shows the flaws and fragility of stardom.

It's a truly inspired piece. It gets me in the gut every time. That bastard, Ray. He is so good at manipulating your feelings. When it's in a positive way, like in this instance, he can really put you in touch with the more sensitive side of your nature and I applaud him.

'Celluloid Heroes' was a typical Kinks single: when first released it was a flop. But I felt that it didn't matter at all. You can't judge the long-term importance of a piece of art by the level of its short-term commercial success. Yet it did eventually become one of our most popular and requested songs, and continues after all this time to put a large lump in my throat whenever we perform it live. Everyone can relate to it. We are all 'failures' in one way or another. Simply because the world is in such a mess and it is our world.

We recently performed the song in Japan, in May 1995. There was a young girl in the front row – she couldn't have been more than seventeen – with tears streaming down her cheeks as we played it. I was very moved, even though I embarrassed her by gently poking fun at her. But to see that kind of emotion was nice. To be able to transmit these feelings from one generation to another like that, to share such special moments, to touch a complete stranger that way, it was odd but it kind of made me feel invincible. It's moments like these that keep me going.

By 1972 we had acquired a strong if not unusual following as we continued to tour the States: straights, gays, groupies, transvestites, transsexuals. There was a group of outrageous tranvestite dancers and singers called the Cockettes (à la Priscilla, Queen of the Desert) who followed us everywhere. I remember one particular guy, a transvestite from San Francisco and part of the Cockettes entourage, who constantly went on about having a sex change operation. We became friends, and I was always trying to dissuade him from the idea by telling him that I was concerned about the post-op psychological trauma, etc. But eventually, against everyone's advice, he had the operation. The last time I saw him he seemed fine, but I was saddened by what he had done. Then again, if it made him happy, I suppose that's all one can ask. When I saw him walk out of the hotel lobby, I thought to myself, 'Oh God, what have you done?' I'd never noticed before, but he had a pair of the broadest shoulders I had ever seen on a woman.

RCA threw us an amazing party at the Hyatt House in Hollywood. It was wild and very funny. It seemed as if all the freaks in LA had come out of the woodwork for the event. We probably seemed the most normal people there. Once again, our reputation led people to imagine the worst.

Everyone who was anyone was there: actors, actresses, sexy buxom wannabes, record company executives mixed with transsexuals, junkies, misfits from all walks of society. Someone put acid in the butter in the restaurant downstairs and I heard later that people had to be carried out to the hospital. It was a resounding success, I guess. Unfortunately, I was too far out of it to remember very much. But people who were there still refer to it as the most outrageous party they've ever attended.

Around that time we discovered this eccentric, totally insane classical singer and violinist named David Sewell, who would accompany himself while performing Wagneresque operatic duets. He would start playing a dramatic classical piece (it was obvious that at one time, before he went 'barmy', he was quite a good violinist), then mimic the male singer in a loud and expressive fake German accent. You know, 'Ich lieber mein, shafter trousen cleavage haven.' That sort of thing. Then he would run across the room and take on the voice and persona of the female. The duet would continue for a while as he ran from one side of the room to the other, playing out some great operatic tragedy, which I suppose it was, really. Gradually the performance would become more frantic as the drama increased and eventually it built to a climax where the male would strangle the female in a fit of rage. Of course he would finish up screaming, with his hands around his own neck, throttling himself before falling to the floor, dead. This always had us in hysterics. I often remember Mick and myself writhing around in collapsed laughter on the floor.

We took David on the road as a support act. But sadly he didn't go down too well. I remember his first night at the University of California at Berkeley. I was much surprised when the audience started to boo and hiss half-way through his act. He never even got to finish.

We eventually recorded his act at our studio. Sound only, which made it even funnier. I suppose it was like having a ventriloquist on the radio. Actually in the fifties on the BBC a ventriloquist did have his own radio show. I always thought it bizarre as a kid, but nobody ever said anything about it. It was one of the most popular shows around, *The Peter Brough and Archie Andrews Show*. In case you didn't know, Archie was the dummy.

Of course we G-ed him up, saying things like, 'David, that was a really moving performance, it brought tears to my eyes,' and such. It was hysterically funny seeing him running across the hard wooden floor doing each movement on either side of the stereo image, while performing the duet with himself. It was even funnier listening to the playback afterwards. Very silly, great fun. It turned out that David wasn't quite as daft as he made out. He eventually ended up with his own TV show, even though it didn't last very long. Everybody's a star.

The final gig of that US tour was at a college and had been added at the last minute. None of us really wanted to do it, as everyone was eager to get home. We all drank a little too much before the show. I was so pissed that my guitar roadie sat me on a chair at the side of my amps. During a song called 'Alcohol', Ray started spraying beer all over the stage and the front row of the audience. While performing a balancing act with a beer bottle on his head, Ray slipped on the wet stage, fell, and cracked his head on the floor, rendering himself unconscious. Two stage hands ran on stage and carried him off. I got up from my chair and started playing a blues riff. Baptist and I kept alternating solos in the hope that Ray would eventually come back on stage. It was starting to develop into one of the longest twelve-bar blues jams in history. During one solo I bent down and a guy in the front row shouted to me, 'Is Ray dead?' At this I fell into uncontrollable laughter. I was so drunk I must have looked a real prat. Eventually Ray bravely came back on stage. By the looks of it he was suffering from concussion and was sporting a large bandage on his head. He looked ridiculous singing 'You Really Got Me' done up like the Invisible Man. God, it was awful.

After the show, Gosling was so upset and distressed that he ran from the building crying. I don't know where he thought he was running to, maybe he was trying in his drunkenness to run all the way home to England. Our tour manager chased him and slapped his face to calm him. He was like a hysterical child.

Afterwards I drank myself into oblivion. The next day I

boarded the plane back home with a hangover supreme. Baptist was so drunk they wouldn't let him board the plane and made him wait three hours for the next. It's sad, really. But ya gotta laugh, haven't you?

We spent much of the spring of 1972 recording and mixing the *Showbiz* album. It was the last time we recorded at Morgan Studios, as we had earlier in the year acquired a building in Hornsey, north London, where we had started work on building our own recording studios. God, it was a struggle getting it off the ground. The construction and the equipment weren't the problem. The biggest hurdle was getting Ray to countersign the cheques. Jesus. I remember waiting an hour and a half one morning downstairs at his house, trying to persuade him to countersign a cheque I was holding for the down payment on a Neve mixing console after we had already ordered the damn thing. It was like pulling teeth. I took care of the technical side of things and Mick helped me supervise the building work. It was very important for me to get the studio operational, as I saw the obvious potential of it, something for the future. We named the studio Konk.

It's around August 1972. I'm in New York a horrible hotel on 8th Avenue.

That awful hotel, like a soulless prison. That fucking orange carpet. What demented fuck thought of the décor? God, I wanna get out of here. I'm fearful of everything. People are so crazy in this city, the city won't let me sleep. The more weak you get the more paranoid you become, the more the voices come to torment you, to GET you.

During this trip to New York my inner problems really came to a head. I was confused, dysfunctional, hypersensitive, and drinking. I just could not get out of this weird state of mind. Feeling isolated and alone, I walked the streets; the vibe of the city made my head reel. It felt like a radio set where all the stations are switched on at once. I would pick up people's thoughts and think them my own. All I wanted to do was to go home. What was I doing here on tour with the band, I thought, when I should be in a loony-bin, a hospital, anywhere else but here. I was too tormented and too fearful to discuss my problems with anyone, particularly anyone I knew.

I went back to that fucking hotel room. I felt I could trust no one. 'They', by their subtle influence, would manipulate anyone who would try to help me, making things worse. A dreadful feeling of foreboding came over me. 'They', the voices, lurked around every corner, awaiting any and every opportunity to attack. To goad me, confuse me, muddle my mind, my concentration. I thought, 'How can all this weird shit be just my imagination?' The thought of being ridiculed by friends only added to my feelings of insecurity and paranoia. Also, I thought, 'How could everyone around me act so normal? Couldn't they hear those awful mocking voices?' Obviously they couldn't.

As I entered my hotel room I began to feel as if I were being devoured by a dark psychic swamp that was dragging me into its secret world in all its subtle and insidious power. I looked around the room and was overcome by an acute loneliness as I gazed out of the window and into the rain-soaked street below. By now the glass was streaking and dribbling with rainwater, like furious tears. How could this be happening to me? How could I fight it? Who could I turn to for help?

I frantically tried to reason. I had to find some logic to it all. Was this just one prolonged hallucination? I wondered if I had maybe suffered permanent brain damage from the drugs and alcohol. Why wouldn't it go away? Why wouldn't 'they' go away? I thought I'd end up like one of those weird street people, the 'crazies' that wander the New York streets shouting obscenities into the air. Down and down I was dragged, further and further into a mental and emotional mire. The cityscape glared soullessly back at me through the window. Black, wet, dripping shadows of a world I no longer understood or wanted to be a part of. Soggy characters toiling against 'time' without making even the slightest impression on it.

An unopened bottle of Johnny Walker sat on the table, tantalizing me. God, is this what it's like to be an alcoholic, I wondered? I shuffled and paced the room, anxious and afraid. *That guy, what was his name . . . yeah, the guitar player with Sha Na Na . . . I met him in London. Johnny, yeah, that was it. 'Dave,' he said to me, 'always remember wherever you go, that's where you are.' Yeah, great help. Gotta keep moving . . .*

I continued to pace the room, too scared even to close my eyes. *Huh, fucking great help, Johnny. A week after he returned home he committed suicide. Very perceptive, Johnny, where did you get that from, from the back of a matchbox or out of a Chinese fortune cookie? Johnny . . .*

I became startled when I realized that I was talking aloud to myself. I laughed, thinking how fucked people were, the world and everyone in it. *Get out of my fucking head, you bastards. Leave me alone. Wow, that's really great, now I'm talking to myself, perfect, that's just what I am supposed to do now, isn't it? Of course it is . . .* I laughed out loud again. *Hello, is Dave there?* I tapped my knuckles on the sideboard. *Hello, it's me . . . is Dave there?* More nervous laughter. *Dave, how are you? Well, you know, Dave, I'm just fine and dandy. Dandy, dandy, where ya gonna go now, who ya gonna run to . . . Yeah, I'm just great apart from the fact that I'm losing my fucking mind and falling uncontrollably into a dark and bottomless abyss . . .*

In a state of panic, I desperately tried to reassure myself that everything would be OK. I was thinking that maybe I should talk to someone about what was going on. Then the voices started again. *Oh hi, Mick, John, guys, I was wondering if you could give me a hand with these voices that are running amok in my head.* I knew that if I wasn't taken seriously the demons would surely get what they wanted. I tried to pull myself together. At least I could try to pretend that I was normal. Shit, I wasn't normal even when I wasn't crazy. I put my head in my hands and cried. I looked over at the window again. The voices said: *Jump, go on. There is no other way. You can never go back to the way you were. It's too late. Jump.*

I closed my eyes and silently prayed for help. Surely someone, something, could help me. As I got up and walked over to the window there was a knock on the door. I opened it to find an old girlfriend of mine named Linda. I hadn't seen her for some time, but she had heard I was in town and decided at that moment to come over for a chat. We sat and talked for a while and she could tell that I was in a bad way. Her voice was calming, soothing. She told me that she had taken up nursing and had been on a special course, so she couldn't get to shows like she used to. Recently she had been training in the psychiatric wing of the hospital where she worked. If ever I needed a nurse it was then. Or an angel.

I told her about my confusion, or tried to. It wasn't easy. She told me she was on her way to see her young nephew and pulled a handful of black spiders from her pocket. I jumped up, startled, until I realized they were only plastic ones from a joke shop. She laughed. For a minute I had thought they were real. I burst out crying and laughing at the same time. God, the relief. I thought, maybe there is a God after all. How close had I come to actually jumping out of that window? I'll never know. The intervention of an angel saved me. I truly believe that. I know that I have been helped many times in my life, sometimes quite inexplicably, as in this case. I no longer believed in coincidence and from that day forward I started to believe in God.

What I experienced that day was the beginning of what I call my 'psychic death'. After that incident I had to clear my heart and mind of many 'demons', and believe me, they come in many varied forms and guises and there is no set way or orthodox method in which to deal with them. Whatever works, works.

I stopped doing acid and all other hallucinogens. I finally realized that the body can only take so much before things go wrong. When I was in my teens I felt that I was indestructible. I had always been sensitive, but pouring so much poison into my system was starting to have adverse effects. I also changed my eating habits and became a vegetarian. I developed an aversion to meat.

It was only through certain mental, spiritual and psychic practices that I was able to rebuild my inner life, and the key word that kept me going was hope. One must never lose hope and give in to despair. Hope is one of the most powerful weapons we have against the darker forces of the mind. I remember some words from an Indian spirit-guide, given to me through a psychic medium at that time: 'Hope creates a light in the spirit-world that our guides and helpers gravitate towards. Despair is like a dark cloud that covers the light of the soul and is a difficult vibration to penetrate.' My feeling is, never lose hope, eventually someone will see the light and come to your aid. Reject nothing – keep the realm of possibilities open. Sometimes help may come to you in the simplest way – the smallest thing can change a mind. Even the most childlike thought or action can produce an effect in the mind that would confound the devil himself.

Mental illness has since fascinated me. I feel that by the use of certain mental techniques, combined with the use of tonal (music-oriented) therapy, we can help alleviate some negative mental conditions.

I was only beginning to unravel the many mysteries of the world and the mind. I learned from this terrible situation that I had the strength of will to cut through the crap, but it didn't happen overnight and it was an extremely gruelling – yet enlightening – process. I was about to embark on an inner journey that would eventually completely change the way I felt and thought about myself and the world around me.

10

By early 1973 the studio was coming along nicely and we had begun rehearsing material for *Preservation, Act One*. I wasn't taken with the idea at first, and believed at the time that it was simply a piece of self-indulgence on Ray's part.

Briefly, *Preservation* is a story set in a semi-surreal world of both the future and present day. Mr Flash is the current leader in power. Mr Black is the political leader in opposition, a tyrant and a dictator who wants to create a purely totalitarian society. He is grooming his ranks and preparing his armies for a coup to completely overthrow Flash's corrupt style of government. He boasts of a new world order, a society where everyone works for and serves the system. No ideologies save that of the governing authority.

Flash is a bit of a wide-boy, a spiv who grew up on the wrong side of the tracks. He is a gangster, a cheat, a liar who gets away with all kinds of treachery and crime. But Flash is the 'lovable villain' type, living a life of crime, running prostitution and the rackets in the city. He is full of deceit yet is generous to his followers. He rules by the fist and the gun with one hand and with the other palms off false promises and lies on the public. He is a charmer, with a pleading and seductive rhetoric. Persuasive, a kind of mixture between Nixon, Luciano and Max Miller. In spite of Flash's flawed character, a part of him truly resents Black's vision of the new world order, feeling that this regime would turn people into zombies and destroy what's left of their culture and history. His beloved homeland would become a 1984/Big Brother-type society.

Mr Black goes on TV and talks to the media to promote his campaign, giving powerful speeches to expose the treachery and villainy behind Flash's regime. Eventually he succeeds, to great effect. Flash realizes that the world he has created is starting to crumble around him. He has terrible visions of what may happen to him (like Scrooge's visitations). In torment, Flash kneels and prays for forgiveness. He solemnly promises that he will change his ways if only he can get rid of Black. Black and his People's Army take over in the end and we see the demise of Flash, a forlorn and remorseful character arrested and imprisoned.

Mr Black's government ushers in a new era of discipline, restrictions of personal liberties, rigorous rules of conduct, austerity and complete compliance to the new order. Maybe the world that Flash had created wasn't so bad after all. Although his change of heart came just too late, maybe the world would have been better off under his rule. What we are left with is a society devoid of all emotional and creative expression. The new world order produces people who are like robots. The dilemma is that maybe power corrupts at every level. All systems have a worm at their core eating away at it, but which do we prefer? What system is more favourable? The question nags.

I thought it was an interesting concept with great potential, but I felt it should have been explored as a theatrical piece or as a movie. (Perhaps it may yet happen. The movie, I mean.) Regardless of my feelings, we started rehearsing some of the material. I was active on the engineering as well as the performing side, mainly because it seemed that I was the only one who understood how to use the studio equipment properly. I enjoyed being involved with the technical side of our music.

I was also feeling better emotionally, although my confidence was still shaky and my self-esteem was low. One day, during rehearsal at Konk, we were messing around with ideas. I had been writing some songs at home and I played Ray a musical idea I had come up with using a different guitar tuning, a twangy, open-stringed sound with a kind of Indian-blues feel. The following day Ray came up with an idea for a song called 'Daylight', which was to be the opening track of *Preservation*. It was based on my guitar part, the drone and de-tuned thing. But Ray gave me no credit for contributing to the song, for coming up with the musical ideas.

In fact, Ray and I were drifting further and further apart. He was becoming more self-involved, while I had become more reclusive and withdrawn. At one of the rehearsals I suggested to him that we should write some of the songs together, since I felt I could support his ideas, themes, concepts and lyrics with musical ideas of my own. I was totally flabbergasted by Ray's reply. He said, in an extremely dismissive way, 'No, I don't think so. Anyway, anyone can write songs.'

I was really hurt by that. Of course his dismissal of my ideas didn't stop him from using them, as in 'Daylight'. It seems petty now, but at the time I was already disillusioned. I was often overcome with feelings of hopelessness. Ray behaved as if he were living in a world of his own, becoming increasingly self-focused, appearing to have little or no regard for others' feelings or ideas, as if in his mind everything and everyone was there merely for his sole use.

During a light-hearted drink one night, Ray let something slip in a casual conversation that played on my mind at the time. We were talking in general about personnel, people we knew, etc. Ray mentioned 'so and so', saying that he really liked him because he didn't mind being 'used'. The instant Ray said that he looked at me in a way that suggested he had said something he shouldn't have, and yet it was too late to retract it. He fluffed it over and promptly changed the subject.

As time went on, Ray became at times an almost vampire-like drain and pull on my creative and emotional energy. I would receive little or nothing in return. I felt that Ray was becoming increasingly more ambivalent towards me. He had become ruthless, manipulative, and selfish, and everyone suckered up to him. All except for me. I couldn't do that. And I couldn't treat people the way he did, in that condescending way of his. I wanted to help people, not take from them. It wasn't just my paranoia, either. Others agreed that Ray, for reasons known only to himself, wanted to grind me into the ground.

I felt that I had always been supportive of his ideas and had encouraged him throughout the ups and downs, yet he was becoming more distant and much less receptive. The insults, the put-downs, the constant criticisms, were really getting to me. At some shows he started making insulting remarks in front of the audience. At first I pretended it was nothing and just laughed it off, but this eventually led to a lot of resentment on my part.

Later on there were various occasions on stage where I would take the bait, lash out at him and feel a prat afterwards. 'I would now like to introduce my brother, the silly little sod,' he would say. I'd lose it and run across the stage towards him with the intention of hitting him with my guitar. He would promptly turn to the mike and say with a sarcastic grin, 'Only joking, Dave.' Then he'd go on, 'You'll have to forgive him, he's a little uptight today. Let's hear it for Dave "Death of a Clown" Davies.'

I would seethe inside when he'd pull this kind of a stunt, the bitch. What the audience didn't know was that I had to put up with this type of mental and emotional abuse from the bastard on a day-to-day basis. I think he really used to get off on it. There were so many instances, particularly in the studio, where he would deliberately provoke an argument so that I would eventually release my anger in front of everybody. After the shouting and verbal abuse had died down he would often look very pleased with himself. He always has to have an audience, and always has to have attention.

Many years later, towards the end of Ray's relationship with Chrissie Hynde, he was in a really bad way and had to have a male psychiatric nurse with him around the clock. I lived just down the road in Maida Vale and got a call from Ray's nurse saying that I should come and see Ray right away. Chrissie was on tour in Australia and Ray, it seemed, was in a terrible state and asking for me. When I got there the three of us sat in the kitchen and had tea. After a while, Ray started in on me in his usual manner, shouting, insulting me, goading me for no apparent reason except that he was obviously distressed by what was happening between him and Chrissie. At one point he brought up a business issue and started screaming at me, accusing me of not having been available to make a decision. The male nurse turned around to Ray in shocked surprise and said to him, 'Hey, Ray, you can't talk to your brother like that!' I remember thinking, 'What's the matter with him?' I actually thought Ray's behaviour was normal.

At all costs I was not going to allow Ray's cruelty or his selfishness to cloud my inner view. I needed to replenish my ailing energies somehow. I did what was necessary during the recordings of both *Preservation One* and *Two*, although my heart was not really in it. I tried to rebuild myself mentally and spiritually. I felt inside that I didn't really want to be a part of this business any more after seeing what it appeared to be doing to

Ray and realizing what it was doing to me. It was destroying my insides, my soul. But what else could I do? I didn't know how to do anything else. Since the age of fifteen I had been on a merry-go-round that I knew one day might stop, but now I felt that maybe it was merely going to throw me off. I felt weak and isolated, strangely alienated. I was in a downward spiral that I felt would eventually erode my creative instincts.

Even my familiar surroundings and people I had known all my life seemed as if they were changing. I clung to my family, but nobody really knew the torment that was going on in my heart and mind. Lisbet would ask me what was wrong, but I wasn't able to confide in her, even though she was always tremendously supportive. The sanest I felt during this time was when I was with my children. To be in the presence of children, in the aura of their purity, their trust and innocence and, above all, their honesty, became a great inspiration to me.

I came across three books that were of great help: *Hatha Yoga* by Theos Bernard, which I still have; *The Middle Pillar* by Israel Regardie; and *Raja Yoga* by Swami Vivikeneda, a book I carry with me to this day, which is a virtual map of the workings of the 'mind' and offers practical methods that anyone lost on its vast ocean can use to navigate its sometimes hazardous waters.

Regardie was Aleister Crowley's secretary at one time and later became a renowned occultist, psychoanalyst and meta-physician. I didn't like Crowley's work, but I found Regardie's little black book *The Middle Pillar* particularly helpful, as it explained in quite straightforward language various ceremonial rituals based on the ancient teachings of the Kabbalah and the Golden Dawn that were specifically designed to create certain psychic and psychological effects on one's consciousness. I practised and studied the rituals and even spoke with Regardie on a few occasions. I was very impressed by his energy and his clear and haunting voice.

I wish I had had the chance to meet Vivikeneda; *Raja Yoga* is a concise and practical little masterpiece. It was he who brought it home to me that the only difference between Good and Evil is selfishness and the only real difference between white and black magic is 'Motive'. Where love is absent, beware. I feel that the true understanding and practice of Karma Yoga can equip anyone for the seemingly insurmountable problems that one may face. Regardie suggests that 'the occult student at the outset is besieged by hundreds of books, full of promise and ways of bringing him to the attainment defined. By the very wealth of material he is overwhelmed. In the end the tendency is to do "nothing" but "read". Reading does very little to bring a person to the realization of his or her divine nature.' Vivikeneda reminds us in his book *Karma Yoga* that 'the whole secret is practising – No one was ever really taught by another, each of us has to teach himself, the external teacher offers the suggestion which rouses the "internal" teacher to work to understand things.'

On 21 June 1973 I got a call from Ray. It was his birthday and he was in a terrible state. Rasa had left him and run off with the children. I knew that over the years he had treated her badly, taking her for granted. She had ceased to be her own person any more and had become merely 'Ray Davies's wife'. I couldn't blame her for being unhappy, but the way she left was particularly cruel.

I felt awful for Ray. I'll never forget how he looked that day, as I walked down the gravel path that led to his front door and peered at him sitting by himself in the front room. He was like a lost child, abandoned and alone. Many years later my mother was to stare sadly through that same window in the days close to her death, as she waited in vain for her son Raymond to return to her so that she could see him one last time. It was the same house that only a short time before had been full of so much creative energy, inspiration and joy and now was merely bricks and mortar. A cold lifeless shell, emptied of love.

After a few days my sister Joyce and I made plans to go up to Bradford in an effort to talk to Rasa and try to reason with her. As I sat and talked to Rasa it hit me all of a sudden that it was a wasted journey, that it was all over between them. Rasa was weird and strange; she was not herself any more. It was as if she had been brainwashed. Poor Rasa. Her family – in particular her older sister, who always seemed cold and manipulative and whom I had never liked or trusted – had got to her and had been instrumental in planning the whole thing over some time. The idea of walking out on him on his birthday definitely came from a sour and bitter mind. Although I firmly believed that it was not in Rasa's nature to act in that way, I have never really forgiven her for it. Her actions had a devastating effect on my brother and my family. Yes, Ray wasn't exactly the perfect husband, and life goes on, but it was the manner in which they split up that was particularly nasty.

We all tried to comfort Ray as best we could through the weeks that followed. But during an open-air concert on 15 July at the White City Stadium in London, Ray, to everyone's surprise including my own, sadly and emotionally announced his retirement. 'I'm fucking sick of the whole thing, I'm sick up to here with it,' he said. I thought he was joking at first. But I didn't know that before the show he had taken a whole bottle of amphetamines.

Ray left quickly after the show, without a word, and I went home a little bemused by the day's events. Late that night I got a call from the Whittington Hospital in Highgate. The staff nurse explained that Ray had been taken ill, suffering from a drug overdose, and that he was in a bad way. They had pumped his stomach and apparently he was over the worst of it.

When I arrived at the hospital he looked terrible – forlorn and pathetic – and it was all I could do to prevent myself from bursting into tears. I got his things together and Lisbet and I took him back to our house, where he spent the following weeks recuperating. Lisbet was fantastic; she nursed him back from the brink of despair. She cooked and chatted to him in her usual positive and optimistic manner. I shopped for books and records for him. For hours he would listen to Mahler's Second Symphony, 'The Resurrection'. After a while he began to seem a little better and we would play old Chuck Berry records and mess around on our guitars. It seemed as if time had taken a shift backwards and we were reliving the many hours we had spent some years before, practising and playing music in Mum's front room, before all the bullshit had taken its toll on both of us.

After about a month we decided to go back into the studio to finish off some recording. I felt a lot better and more optimistic about the future. In some strange way this experience helped bring Ray and me closer together for a while.

During these sessions Ray came up with a beautiful song called 'Sweet Lady Genevieve'. It was quite obviously a bitter-sweet tribute to his relationship with Rasa. The song always makes me cry, and I've never liked performing it. It's just too sad.

Unbearable. It was recorded very simply, and it reflected all the joy, sadness, and regret that Ray was experiencing at the time.

Rasa moved to south London with Louisa and Victoria. Ray wanted a place where it would be convenient for the girls to visit him and bought a second home in Surrey.

For some time we had been toying with the idea of setting up our own production company and record label (named Konk, like our studio) and eventually we signed a distribution deal with the US label ABC and started looking for acts to record. I was extremely excited about the idea. I thought it was an opportunity for me to get involved gradually in other aspects of the business that would enable me to spend more time with my family.

I also started producing some tracks with John Gosling and we formed a production company called Dazling. We co-produced albums by folk-rock singer Andy Desmond and a band called Café Society, of which Tom Robinson was a member. They were a good group but there were a lot of petty jealousies and squabbles that marred a lot of the recordings. Tom, who later became well known as a post-punk gay activist, was very talented in my opinion, but it was obvious to me that he drew much inspiration from Ray. Tom had an over-inflated sense of his own importance, but together as a band Café Society had some really good material. Tom eventually went his own way, which I suppose was inevitable, and found success with the song 'Glad to Be Gay'.

Before the relationship between Ray and Tom became bitter and catty, I remember one occasion when Tom and the band were rehearsing some songs while waiting for Ray. Ray, as usual, kept Tom waiting a very long time, and when he eventually arrived Tom promptly went into a sarcastic rendition of 'Tired of Waiting for You' which really spelled out the end. Ray derives great pleasure, it seems, from keeping people hanging on, waiting around, postponing decisions until the very last minute. It must be the Cancerian in him: never let them off the hook if you can keep them hanging on. Ooh! Ray can be totally exasperating. He is such a control freak.

Later he did have the final word when he wrote a song called 'Prince of the Punks' for a Kinks B-side. He never openly admitted it, but I always felt it was Ray's way of having a dig at Tom. What a couple of bitches.

By the end of 1973 the Kinks had finished mixing *Preservation Act One* and had started *Act Two*. Early in 1974 we made plans to tour the States. By this time we had acquired a large brass section and two girl singers. The albums weren't commercially successful but they received critical acclaim.

Privately, I was continuing my exploration into spiritualism and I studied under a trance medium in north London who channelled information from an ancient Egyptian child king. Everybody thought I was crazy, round the bend, but I didn't care. It was all part of my inner growth, a spiritual and psychic metamorphosis.

Ray was always very dismissive of my interest in metaphysics, even though I know he's very psychic himself. But he'd never admit it. I think deep down he was afraid of it all. Lisbet was also concerned about my behaviour and about the 'things' I was getting involved with. But something was churning inside me. I had an incredibly insatiable desire to know about the 'subtle worlds', about metaphysics in general. My interests ranged from astrology to Zen Buddhism. I was like a hungry child, desperate for knowledge, for spiritual food.

By the end of March 1974 we had completed work on *Preservation Act Two*. We toured the States in April and May and introduced some songs into the act from *Preservation*. In April we hired the services of a fellow Muswell Hillbilly, Tony Dimitriades, to act as business manager for our newly formed Konk Records.

I found touring more tolerable this time around. We toured with bands such as Lynyrd Skynyrd, the Tubes, Maggie Bell, Kansas, even King Crimson and Aerosmith. I was finally starting to feel more motivated, but by the time we arrived back in England around the end of May, I was beginning to get frustrated and bored with Ray's concept ideas. I really wanted to get back to playing straight ahead rock 'n' roll again. I thought that surely Ray had had enough of this self-indulgence by now. Our albums weren't selling that well, although we had a tremendously loyal following in the States. Frankly, I was concerned about our direction.

Then Ray thought of the most egotistical, but actually the funniest, concept of them all: a soap opera about himself, *Starmaker*, which was originally produced as a thirty-minute musical play for Granada Television. At first it seemed quite amusing: a story about an ageing rock star who is totally wrapped up in himself taking on the persona of Mr Average and exchanging lives with him. His name is Norman, as in normal.

I thought to myself that maybe, just maybe, Ray could exorcise his personal demons through this once and for all. I patiently went along believing this to be the case. But on the day we filmed *Starmaker* for Granada it suddenly hit me that maybe the Kinks were really finished as a band. Maybe I had taken a back seat for too long. Ray seemed so caught up in himself and I feared that the band would never be the same again.

The Kinks were shown into a small corner at Granada's Manchester studios and we set up. We were treated worse than a house band. The sound was atrocious, there was not one camera line-up for the band during the whole broadcast, and I had to sit and play stuck in the corner with the others while Ray pranced around the studio like a ponce, as if lost in a megalomaniacal trance. He was playing out what I felt at the time was the final act in a great tragedy, the death scene of a once great British rock band.

As I drove back to London that night with our tour manager I felt really hurt, yet also angry with myself. I thought that it was time for me and Ray to go our separate ways, that maybe Ray's ideas had become too large for the limitations of our small band and maybe he just didn't know how to let go. Whatever the problem was, I felt like a side man, humiliated and used. I just wanted to get out.

We finished off the year completing the remaining dates as scheduled, promoting the *Preservation* albums in the US. In New York I confronted Ray about the problems I was having, particularly regarding our live work. He was thoughtfully concerned, especially when I told him that I wanted to leave before any further tours were planned, as it was mainly the touring that was getting me down, as well as the fact that I felt like a hired hand. We agreed to talk again when we got back to England.

New York had a good club scene then. I especially liked a place called Nobody's, where bands, groupies, and music people in general would congregate. Janis Joplin and Johnny Winter would often be there. I liked Janis a lot. She was a really nice person with a good heart. There was an amazing amount of love in her. And could she drink! She could out-drink most of the guys in the place. In the end, of course, she became another sad casualty in a hard and unrelenting business.

One night I was really bored so I called up my friend Linda, the woman who had helped me so much that awful day in the hotel room. After a few drinks we decided to have a bit of fun. I dressed up in her clothes and she in mine. She did a great job with my make-up and when the final touches were in place, wig and all, we hailed a cab and descended on the bars and clubs in Greenwich Village. We finally ended up at Nobody's at about three in the morning. I'd dressed up in women's clothes before, but never quite so publicly. It was very interesting the way men would look at me. I must admit I got a bit of a thrill out of it.

Linda slicked her hair back and she really looked the part. It was quite a turn-on seeing her act in such a butch way. I really got a kick out of the fact that no one knew who I was. It was fantastic. I could observe the world from a totally different perspective. As a voyeur. It was like acting. Pretending to be someone else had great therapeutic value, particularly pretending to be a member of the opposite sex.

Linda and I sat at the bar and ordered drinks. As I looked around the smoke-filled room I saw Baptist, drunk and acting like a fool as usual. At a table opposite I saw Mick really pissed, sitting with some friends and chatting up a girl. I got up and sat next to the girl and started to eye up Mick. He looked over at me and I was surprised that he didn't recognize me. The dirty old man was leching and leering at me. God, now I realized what it must be like for a woman! I continued to flirt with Mick in the dimly lit bar. I slowly stood up, spread my legs, lifted up my dress, and sexily guided my hand down the front of my underpants and grabbed at my crotch. Suddenly it hit Mick who I was. He was stunned, with mouth agape. You should have seen the look on his face. It was a treat, a gem. He was really taken aback.

After I arrived back at the hotel in the early hours I reflected on the events of the night. I had really enjoyed being someone else. Shit, maybe I was becoming a little too self-absorbed, a little too serious.

11

Back home in London I continued to produce and record acts with Baptist for our Konk label. John and I worked well together and I really enjoyed it. He was a real romantic at heart, the soft old thing, and people sometimes took advantage of him.

We had a road manager at the time called Colin, whom we nicknamed Colin the Scrap (he had once been a scrap metal dealer). He was one of Mick's cronies from Molesey. Scrap was a mad sod who always persuaded Baptist to drink too much and do silly things. Baptist was far too gullible and often fell victim to Scrap's often derisive sense of humour. On one occasion Baptist had lost his suitcase and the airline gave him money as compensation. Scrap took Baptist to the shops and insisted that he buy the silliest clothes they had. Baptist went through the whole tour dressed in a variety of garments that wouldn't have been out of place in a circus. At least it kept us in laughs. Scrap helped keep our spirits up when morale started to hit rock bottom, but he was often a bit over the top.

Scrap and I were both terrified of flying, so he concocted a special drink called 'Château Scrap' especially for plane trips. It was a whisky bottle made up of all the free drinks from various airlines, the miniatures, and he would carry it with him at all times. It was really potent stuff and definitely not for the faint-hearted. I went through a phase of being so petrified by the thought of getting on a plane that Scrap and I would do almost anything to avoid it. We'd get up at the crack of dawn to drive 400 miles to the next gig, or spend fifteen to twenty hours on a train then drive straight to the sound check. However, it became so exhausting that often the only answer was to get out the bottle of Château Scrap, go to the airport, and face the music. But sometimes even Château Scrap couldn't cut through the fear. I liked Scrap and he was often good company, but he was a bit of a crafty sod and in the end I felt that his habit of constantly looking for a joke in everything became draining. He was starting to do the band more harm than good.

I was also still having problems with Mick, who would never say much about anything at all. Although he could be supportive at times, I found his lethargy quite boring and an irritation. Almost negative. He was always agreeable – in business or just matters in general. He was friendly enough but it was obvious he merely wanted an easy life with as few problems as possible.

Whenever Ray, Mick and I would have business discussions, Mick would always take Ray's side if there were any conflicts. This often created bad feelings between us and later led to more aggressive confrontations. Mick knew which side his bread was buttered on and he never wanted to fall out with Ray. I remember Scrap saying to me on one of those seemingly everlasting train journeys, 'Mick'll never make any waves. He's on to a good thing and he knows it.'

For his part, Ray is very manipulative and can be quite intimidating when he doesn't get his way. When I'm pushed too far I tend to react and possibly cause a scene. To be fair, it must have been difficult for Mick stuck in the middle of Ray and me, but he could have shown a little more spunk.

It was time to rehearse *Soap Opera*, which was the album based on *Starmaker*, and I decided to try to enter into the spirit of it. Some of the ideas were very funny, yet it was a searching and questioning time for us. I wasn't sure where the concept albums were taking us as a band, if indeed they were taking us anywhere at all. It was obviously a very creative time for Ray. But at the time these ideas meant little to me, aside from the humorous side of them. I was content to just go along with it, but in private I was pursuing my own personal spiritual interests.

I suppose on reflection that *Soap* was a novel idea. The early seventies were a creatively barren time in general. With the exception of Roxy Music and David Bowie, and perhaps a few others like Marc Bolan or Little Feat, there was very little innovation, I felt.

The Kinks had always been considered outsiders, and we were becoming even more isolated than ever from a business we had never really felt a part of to begin with. The vast heaps of bullshit that were forming in and around the music industry at the time needed more than mere bulldozers to remove them.

There were and still are so many people in the industry, including performers, who live their life as if in a dream world, or a bubble. A bubble that is often fiercely protected by their egos. When the thin veil that separates them from 'the real world' is penetrated, it often reveals quite weak and sometimes sad individuals.

It's a business that can be extremely exploitative, cruel, back-handed, two-faced, snide, and nasty. A world where reality often takes a back seat. There is too much money in the music business. Money is such a great deceiver; it can act as a buffer that shields and protects you from the outside world. There's too much wealth and too much deception in the world as it is. I believe that public figures – artists – have a responsibility to express honestly their views about the world, be they political, philosophical, spiritual, or whatever, to constantly question social conditions and what is going on around them. The wealthy should use their resources to create better conditions in the world. Thankfully, there are some who do. Really, how many cars do we need? You can only drive one at a time. How many houses can you live in at once? How much land do we need – and is it really ours to own in the first place?

I had a friend who was a millionaire many times over, a very practical and astute businessman. One day we were driving in his brand new Rolls Royce to some expensive restaurant in the West End, when we looked out of the window and saw a poor filthy old homeless guy lying at the side of the street. I said, 'Shit, look at that poor old bugger, he looks dead to me.' My friend just drove on and said to me, 'I really do not feel any pity or feel that I have anything in common with people like that. There is equal opportunity in the world; I was born into a poor family and I made a success of my life, with pure determination and hard work. People are lazy.'

I was shocked by what he said. I couldn't understand how this man, with the brains and mentality to make his way to the top of his profession, couldn't fathom the simple concept of com-passion, that we are all part of one 'human family'. When I confronted him with this he just smiled in an arrogant way as if

170

I was a fool. I felt deeply saddened. Money makes people crazy, makes them lose touch with reality.

I think all genuinely talented artists have great concern about humanity. Yet once they obtain wealth and success it sometimes prohibits them from doing anything about it, apart from appearing in the occasional 'high-profile' charity show. Most live in outrageous comfort when they could be trying to change the world.

In an age of communication everything has become 'show-biz', especially politics. In my view, politics has become an outmoded concept for solving our problems. It rarely takes into account the emotional and spiritual needs of an individual, always browbeating, bullying, cajoling, and only deals with a part of the problem. It always deals with the 'money' side of things: 'materiality'. Its focus is on the 'outside' and rarely on the 'inside'. It is inside people where all the real problems and solutions lie, I feel. We cannot 'buy away' the misery in the world. We need to expand our views of the world to encompass and include the spiritual needs of people.

Money also creates 'power'. Power is the greatest deceiver of all. Money and power help create delusion. Delusion about ourselves, about the world and our place in it. I have a lot of sympathy for stars like Michael Jackson, who have at times suffered at the hands of the media and press, but then again I wonder. He is a role model for thousands and thousands of kids, and they don't mind that he is considered 'odd'. Probably because they simply love the music or believe the hype, or both. He is obviously talented and has become successful and im-mensely wealthy. People think him quirky and funny, eccentric. If he were poor, people would likely consider him 'insane'. I use the word 'insane' in the context of what is generally considered acceptable social behaviour. What's normal, anyway?

One of my favourite send-ups of the deceptions of fame was done by Larry 'Legs' Smith from the Bonzo Dog Band, one of the funniest guys I ever met. The band appeared in a late sixties TV comedy show in England, called, I think, *Do Not Adjust Your Set*. In his act he would pose as a super-show-biz star, appearing on stage dressed in a white silk suit. He would walk down a flight of stairs crooning in a smug, slimy, self-adoring way to a song entitled 'Mr Wonderful': 'Look at me, I'm wonderful, dooby doo

waa, I'm not like "you" or "you", I'm a super-show-biz star . . .'
When he reached the bottom step of the staircase, still singing, he
would fall through the floor with an almighty crash and vanish
from sight with arms flailing desperately in the air.

Another artist I really liked who made fun of the whole
business of celebrity, vanity, greed and hypocrisy in show-biz
was Frank Zappa. *We're Only in It for the Money* is a great album
and still one of my favourites. It shows a streak of jealousy in
Zappa's personality, a personality which was also thankfully full
of anger, rage, and cutting wit, but it really stands the test of time.
It's a truly wonderful piece of work that shows another side of
pop culture and in particular exposes the falseness of the hippie
movement in America in a very funny way. God bless you,
Frank. Gone, but definitely not forgotten. Compulsory listening.

Soap Opera was an obvious opportunity to make a commentary
on how ridiculous life can be in 'show-biz', particularly the
people in it – the so-called 'stars'. When we began routining for
the stage show, it was fun to dress up in high-heeled boots and
glittery shirts, silver and pink Afro wigs and gold satin suits,
Glam-Rock style. It was really daft and actually hilarious at
times. Luckily recording the album didn't take too long, which
was a blessing in a way, but there was not enough attention
given to the arrangements and the sound. It remains my least
favourite Kinks album, but I do urge the reader to check out
'Holiday Romance' and 'Ducks on the Wall'.

I recently met a black musician in LA who had worked with
Ray Charles. He told me that he had persuaded Charles to
rehearse 'Ducks' with the intention of using it in his set. Evidently Charles is a tremendous fan of the Kinks. The guy went on
to say that he was ashamed of the way the music industry in
general had treated us, in his words, 'like Cockney niggers'. I
laughed, but I knew exactly what he meant. I would give almost
anything to see Ray Charles perform 'Ducks' or hear a recording
of it. Please, Ray, do it – the other Ray, I mean. 'Holiday
Romance' is nostalgic, extremely silly, irritatingly cute, funny,
and somehow, despite itself, quite beautiful.

After touring with *Soap Opera* I felt much more confident about
myself and my playing. We hired a new engineer at Konk who
seemed to fit in perfectly, named Roger Wake. He was sensitive
and knew how to record the band. He was a very sweet and

amiable guy, who enjoyed a drink. He would arrive at Konk around ten, a couple of hours before the band would get in, and ask Sarah, our office girl at the time, to go up to the local general store and buy a large bottle of Woodpecker cider, a six-pack of Guinness and two ham sandwiches. He did this every day and devoured the lot before noon. Roger never refused a drink. Somehow it didn't seem to impair his judgement. I suppose practice makes perfect.

Roger's first project with us was the album *Schoolboys in Disgrace*. In my view it was a fabulous little album, although underrated at the time. The concept was drawn mainly from Ray's and my experiences at school. Ray's observations and feelings about education, and Sue's and my explusion from school, were all blended together with Ray's preoccupation with the character Mr Flash from the *Preservation* albums. I love the track 'Headmaster'. The chorus after the guitar solo is pure magic. So full of emotion, regret, and anger. Poignant. All the bittersweet memories of that time came flooding back.

We rehearsed the songs at Ray's house as in the old days and I was very excited about the project. There was a good spirit again. But inside I began to believe that I would never be free of my feelings for Sue and for that time in my life. I wondered if it was going to haunt me and torment me forever. For all the new knowledge I was acquiring about the inner workings of the world, about the occult, about my own inner life, it seemed that I would never be able to shake loose those old feelings.

Roger Wake did a great job in the studio. He really knew how to record guitars and vocals and had a good overall sense of sonic placement. The band also played really well. The song 'The First Time We Fall in Love' is a beautiful track if you ignore the Elvis and Doo Wop parodies and showy arrangement. It actually has a sweet verse *à la* Mike Love/Beach Boys which is really moving, despite the fact that it's clothed in humour. 'Hard Way' is pure classic Kinks. 'No More Looking Back' finishes the album on an ironic note, as another phase of the Kinks' career came to a close. *Schoolboys* was our last album with RCA and it also signified the end of the Concept period.

Ray soon struck up a fortuitous relationship with Clive Davis at Arista. He was a big Kinks fan who understood our situation and knew, as I did, that we had to make a more straight-ahead rock album in order to re-establish ourselves commercially. Clive was instrumental in persuading Ray that this was the right course to take. As he said, 'Sometimes you have to take two steps back to make one step forward.' But I was of the opinion that it would be a step forward anyway. It was the first time since Robert and Grenville's departure that I had felt so positive about the future.

After completing tours in the States with *Schoolboys* I really started to enjoy my playing again. We were still using our brass section but the show was becoming more of an out and out rock show. By May '76 a new recording contract was on the table with Arista and final negotiations were being made. By June we had officially signed with Arista. Clive flew to London and we held a sedate press party at the Dorchester Hotel.

We started recording *Sleepwalker* and John Dalton decided to leave the band. He had been getting fed up with touring and I don't think he liked America very much. In fact when we toured the States he always kept his watch on English time, and always tried to judge when his mates would be going up the pub, or when and where his local football team would be playing. It was quite sad to see him leave, particularly in view of the fact that he had been with us through some difficult times and now things seemed to be getting better. I think his wife had been giving him a lot of stick about being away from his family so much. By that time I had three children of my own – Martin, Simon, and Christian, who had been born in April 1972 – so I could sympathize with his feelings. It's always hard being away from loved ones for long periods of time. Especially when your kids are young.

We auditioned several bass players before we found Andy Pyle. Pyle had been around for a while and had played with Savoy Brown, among others; he seemed an amiable sort, so we gave him a try. He played bass on the track 'Mr Big' from the *Sleepwalker* album, which has always been a great favourite of mine.

I also recorded some solo tracks with him using a drummer friend, Nick Trevisick, whom I had got to know through the sessions Baptist and I produced for the Konk label. Nick was a good 'feel' drummer, and being a songwriter himself he had a good hook on what was needed. Those initial backtracks sounded great. There's something really interesting about a three-piece band; it can often sound much heavier than a four- or five-piece. I loved Johnny Kid and the Pirates in the late fifties/ early sixties. They were basically a three piece with a front man (singer). They sounded great. The Big Three were a great little band from the sixties and of course the Police were a three-piece unit that sounded cool.

There was one track from that session, called 'Islands', that I particularly liked, but for one reason or another it never got finished. It was a song about lost friendships – how people go their separate ways in order to find something new and sometimes become isolated. Islands. During this period in the seventies I recorded quite a few tracks that never saw the light of day. For some reason I would spend a lot of time on them at my new home in Southgate, north London, where I had my own drum-kit and eight-track set up. I'd make well-arranged demos playing all the instruments myself, but when I got into the studio with other musicians I'd have problems communicating with them and the songs never really turned out how I wanted them.

I think one of the reasons why Ray and I have worked so well together, in spite of our personal difficulties, is that over the years we have developed a certain telepathy. Many times Ray and I would just get together and things seemed to happen. But when I worked with other musicians whom I didn't know as well, somehow it just wouldn't come together. I felt that I had to explain so much to them about what I wanted that the naturalness seemed to ooze away. I was quite nervous and I couldn't seem to convey my ideas properly. I expected people automatically to know what I wanted. A frustrated musician might say to me, 'Dave, what the hell do you want me to do, read your mind?' 'Well, yes, it would make things a lot easier, wouldn't it?' I'd want to reply.

When you spend a great deal of time in close proximity to the same people there can be an empathetic vibe that can really help galvanize a performance, give it a certain 'feel'. I couldn't seem to replicate the 'feel' of the demos when I used other players. Something was missing. I love the feeling you get with demos, the freshness, the vitality and newness of creating and building a song up for the first time. It is really special. There can be 'magic' in a demo sometimes, with all its faults and rough edges. Many times that intangible quality can get lost when translated into a full-blown studio situation.

At the same time, the Kinks completed *Sleepwalker*. It contained some great songs, like 'Brother', 'Life Goes On', 'Stormy Sky', 'Sleepless Nights', among others. On the one hand, the song 'Sleepwalker' is about Ray's problems with insomnia, but it also gives some insight into how sensitive Ray is. I love the Draculaesque vibe to it: 'When the sun puts out the light I join the creatures of the night.' I remember that some years ago an astrologer friend of mine was writing a book about rock stars' astrological charts. She said that midway through doing Ray's chart she decided to stop as she felt as if he could sense her doing it and it freaked her. It amused me, but I knew exactly what she meant. He is so sensitive at times it is uncanny.

After the *Sleepwalker* album had been released we had these weird followers in Massachusetts, of all places, who firmly believed that Ray and I were vampires. One of them was a witch and she was always casting spells and stuff. You have to be careful with that – you can evoke a demon to carry out some dark and sinister retribution on an enemy, but watch out that it doesn't turn around and bite you back. And usually when you least expect it.

'Brother' is an exceptional song about unity and brotherhood; it is very beautiful. I sing a song on the album called 'Sleepless Nights', written by Ray. It is a fun kind of thing about a lovely lady who lives next door to a guy who is mad about her, but she never notices him. She keeps him up all night making love to her boyfriend and it drives him crazy. But I am sure if it had been Ray, he would have been up all night whether she lived next door or not. 'Stormy Sky' is a favourite Kinks track of mine. It is atmospheric, delicate and comforting. Kinda kosy. A lovely little song.

In the song 'Juke Box Music' there is a passage that I sing in the middle. It starts, 'It's all because of that music, that we slowly drifted apart, but it's only there to dance to, so you shouldn't take it to heart . . .' It is so emotional, so sad. Maybe Ray and I would have been better brothers to each other if we hadn't been brothers.

During that time we also acquired a new manager, Elliot

Abbott. He was from Chicago and seemed positive, businesslike, with a pleasant laid-back manner. He worked with a guy called Chip Rachlin, a New Yorker whom we had known on and off over the years. Elliot had been managing Ry Cooder and Randy Newman. Ray and I both liked him so we took the plunge. It was a crucial time for us and we all felt that it was essential to have management, particularly in the States. Record companies seem to feel more secure when strong management are involved. With new management, a new album, a new record company, *Sleepwalker* was greeted with good initial airplay and pre-sales were promising. It charted at 21 in *Billboard*.

During the first *Sleepwalker* tour I struck up a friendship with one of our girl singers, Shirlie Roden. Baptist never really liked having girl singers in the band and I would often catch him grimacing at me from across the other side of the stage during shows. Baptist and I named their singing style 'Posh Rock' because both girls had posh accents. We would often make comments and jokes about them, taking the piss. They were good sports and just laughed it off. During rehearsals or sound checks, Baptist and I would mimic their singing, stuff like (sung in an upper-class accent to a slow twelve-bar blues) 'Oh darling, I really do have the blues, don't you know, oh yes, indubitably so. Oh yes, I most emphatically have the blues, baby, indeed I do, it is really such a ghastly feeling, you cannot possibly imagine just how awful I really feel, oh yes.' You get the idea.

Shirlie was good company for me and we had a great deal in common. We would talk for hours about religion, magic and philosophy. After a few shows I decided to try a psychic experiment, with Shirlie's help. Performers are subject to an incredible amount of focused energy from an audience during a show, and I thought that if we could harness that force in some way it could maybe be channelled or redirected, that I could transform emotional and psychic power into 'something else'.

I taught Shirlie a few techniques and after a couple of days we tried out our experiment during some shows. It was a practice based on a mental visualization technique where you draw energy into the body, fill it with light, and project it out again, as healing. After a few days things started to happen. We kept this a secret since we didn't want to freak anyone out or give any sceptics in our party the opportunity to create bad vibes, which would interfere with what we were doing. It was important to the experiment to 'have faith' that it would work. As with most magical actions, 'belief' forms a platform for success.

I won't go into details about what we did but during one show in Seattle something amazing happened. The show was going quite well but the house was only about half full and Ray was having difficulty getting the audience 'up'. Midway through the show Shirlie and I did our 'thing', and all of a sudden the crowd instantly came alive and Ray became more in control of the audience. It was an incredible feeling and the atmosphere in the hall was scintillating.

After the show neither Shirlie nor I said anything to anyone. The following morning we met for breakfast. Shirlie was reading a newspaper and when she saw me she looked up from it and said, 'Dave, you won't believe this, it's a review of last night's show.' With a shocked look on her face she handed me the paper. The reporter stated that the show was OK but that the Kinks had some difficulty getting the crowd going, since the house was less than half full. All of a sudden about half-way into the performance it seemed as if the place was suddenly full of people, as the show came alive with energy. People danced in the aisles, singing and shouting, transforming a good evening with classic rockers into a memorable one.

Unbeknown to every one in the band, Shirlie and I did our 'thing' night after night on that tour. Nobody knew what we were doing, but they all seemed happy with the results, so we decided to keep it our secret. One night Shirlie told me in private that it made her feel so good that she wouldn't have minded doing it for the rest of her life. It was an unbelievably fulfilling sensation.

I would have liked to have discussed it with Ray. It is one of my greatest regrets that he has tended to be so unreceptive to my ideas – musical and otherwise. He has always been so un-approachable, so cautious, always worrying that someone would steal his ideas or that something was going to be taken away from him. We've been close in some ways over the years, and yet at the same time so far apart. There is always 'power' when we are together. If only he'd listened to me more rather than sometimes thinking my ideas crazy, often preferring to be derisive or dismissive of them. I've never understood why he's treated me this way and it has always saddened me. One thing I've learned is that you can never argue with a Cancerian: they are always right. They prefer to teach rather than be taught. Ray's sometimes hard outer shell protects his soft insides. (He is a Gemini/Cancer cusp.)

The tour took us to Los Angeles, and on a day off Shirlie and I decided to go to the Whiskey to see Blondie. As I walked in and sat down I noticed a girl about twenty years old in the next booth. She had long, full dark brown hair down her back. I caught her glance and saw that she had the most beautiful brown eyes I had ever seen. I was so taken by her that as if in a trance I simply went up to her and said, 'My name is Dave, will you come to my hotel for a drink tomorrow?' She said her name was Nancy, and agreed. I told her when and where to meet me and that was that. It was as if I had no control over what was happening, as if it were all happening automatically. I left with Shirlie shortly after, but I knew I had met somebody very special that night.

As I lay in bed, all I could see in my mind were pictures of the lovely young woman that I had met in that dingy and noisy club. I mentally peered into those beautiful dark brown eyes of hers. Eyes that drew me closer and closer. Eyes so full of secrets, so full of mystery.

We were staying at the Hyatt on Sunset, a hotel renowned over the years for its rock star clientele. Anyone who is or has been anyone has stayed there. The stories you hear are legendary, from Johnny Cash insisting on making his bed up and sleeping in the elevator, to Mick Avory and John Bonham having a friendly brawl in the foyer, rolling around like a couple of sweating, angry apes. Or Keith Moon virtually throwing the whole contents of a room out of his window before throwing himself. The tales go on and on and become taller and longer and longer and taller with each telling. I love visiting the Hyatt still, sometimes just to buy a newspaper and sit and have coffee and reflect. They should have a miniaturized model version of it in the Rock 'n' Roll Hall of Fame.

The following day, Nancy showed up as planned and she, Shirlie and I sat in my room and chatted for what seemed like hours. Shirlie eventually left, leaving me and Nancy alone. Her voice had a velvet smooth tone, a lilt and sway that held an alluring charm. She seemed to have a 'natural wisdom' that belied her years. We kissed and it was beautiful – I was enchanted by her warmth, by her personality. We spent the evening getting to know one another. It was apparent that she was very knowledgeable about psychic matters, and we talked well into the night. The following day I left town with the band and wasn't to see her for another two months.

In June the Kinks were back in LA as part of another leg of the *Sleepwalker* tour. We had two days off after our show at Anaheim Stadium, where we appeared with Alice Cooper and the Tubes. I called Nancy and we spent virtually the whole time together, talking, walking, eating, enjoying each other's company to the full, kissing, and cuddling – but never making love. I decided that I wanted my relationship with her to be different from all my other relationships with women, most of which were centred around sex. I wanted this one to be special, purer.

One evening I was drinking in the Hyatt bar with Nancy when in popped Keith Moon. We sat and talked for a while. I hadn't had a proper conversation with him since the old days. He seemed strangely reflective, sentimental even. Through his silly jokes and false laughter I detected a terrible sadness. I never really knew him as a close friend but I had never seen him quite like this. We joked and reminisced, and through the almost pleading expression in his eyes I sensed someone deeply troubled. I was anxious to go off with Nancy because I was leaving LA the next day and I wanted to spend as much time with her as possible, so Nancy and I said our farewells and left. That was the last time I ever saw Moon. A few months later he was dead. My final image of him was of a sad and lonely guy sitting in the Hyatt bar. I sometimes wish I'd said something to him. It was as if his soul was crying out for help but he didn't know how to ask for it. That was the impression I got at the time. There must have been something more I could have said.

It reminded me of when my father died in the summer of 1975. One Sunday afternoon he came around the house for a visit. He had been unwell for a while but he was up and around doing his gardening jobs and whatever; nobody thought he was more seriously ill. On that day Dad looked strangely pensive. We talked about a number of things but somehow I knew that soon he was going to die. I could just feel it. It unnerved me and I became frightened. When working in the garden he would often do bird whistles; he did them really well. Outside the garden window that afternoon we could hear some birds singing and he immediately mimicked their whistles. He smiled at me and asked if I would like to go up the pub for a drink with him. I declined, saying I had a lot to do. In my heart I knew he was going to die and I was terrified – I didn't know what to do or say. A moment of cowardice on my part prevented me from sharing final precious moments with my dear father. I have never forgiven myself for that. The next day he went with my mother to Ray's house in Surrey, where a week later he was to die quite suddenly.

When my mother died some years after I made sure that I spent every available moment with her during her final weeks. It was stressful and draining but an experience I wouldn't have missed for anything. It's funny, isn't it? Every time I hear birdsong early in the morning, I think of my father. Maybe he's not so far away after all.

It was soon time for the Kinks to leave LA and continue our tour. As Nancy and I kissed goodbye in the foyer of the hotel, I couldn't bear the thought of leaving her, so I asked her to come with me. She rushed back to her flat and got a few things together and came to Detroit with me. We spent the remaining days of the tour together before I travelled back to England and she returned to Los Angeles.

When I arrived back in England, Nancy was in my every thought. I was besotted by her. Oh God, I thought, I already had a wife and family. What was I to do now?

12

In the late seventies in Britain, a complacent and limp music industry was lulled out of its sleepiness by the harsh and rebellious tones of Punk Rock. It was a crisp, sharp blast of fresh air – exciting, stimulating, biting and funny. Young musicians rose out of the depression of the dole queues, sparking an anger and bitterness directed at a society that continually massaged the wallets of the wealthy while ignoring the cries and plight of the ordinary person and the poor. Spitting contemptuously at a vain and uncaring world.

Although its combined venom and aggressiveness was more pronounced than that expressed by an earlier youth in the sixties, there was a familiar ring to it. Its rallying call echoed the similar frustrations and resentments of an earlier generation, one that I had been a part of; kids trying to break out of the oppression of a government that neglects its young and offers them little or no hope for the future.

Although the Punk rebellion was short-lived, it did in some way help to highlight the problems of growing up in what was quickly becoming a purely materialistic society. Thatcher's improvident solution later in the eighties was to delude the young by waving money in their faces, eliciting a wave of self-interest that produced an all-consuming greed and promoted the cult of the yuppie.

I liked the Sex Pistols, and the fact that their act was contrived made it even better, funnier, giving their music a tenacious irony. Someone had to contrive something. It was as much of a relief as anything else to hear bands like the Pistols, the Damned, X-Ray Specs, the Clash, Generation X and the Jam on the radio.

Paul Weller was obviously inspired by the Kinks. I initially met Paul during the recording of my first solo album at Konk in the early part of 1980. He came to the studio to wish me luck, which I thought was really nice. He also had with him an old 45 of my sixties single 'Suzanah's Still Alive', which he asked me to sign. He came across as a really serious and intense guy at first. I know the feeling because I'm like that sometimes, but I liked him. Over the years he has lightened up a great deal. Whenever we bump into each other we keep promising we'll make a record together one day. Who knows? It could still happen.

By September 1977 we had started recording an album that was later to become *Misfits*. We also released a single in England that winter called 'Father Christmas', which didn't do particularly well – which I suppose is not entirely surprising as it was really an anti-Christmas song in many ways. It was about street kids asking Father Christmas to stop messing with toys, preferring that he simply gave them the money instead, or gave their father a job because he was out of work. I loved that record, but it wasn't very well received. People didn't want to be reminded of life's problems at Christmas time. I think the general public was happier listening to the usual sentimental seasonal escapist slop.

The Kinks performed a special Christmas show at the Rainbow in London. It was a lot of fun; we dressed up in silly costumes and played many of our early hits. Earlier in the day we had rehearsed 'Father Christmas' as an encore. Ray was to come on stage dressed in the full Santa outfit and we would then promptly go into the song. From the wings I watched Ray change into his costume on the other side of the stage, and at that moment I decided to play a little trick on him. In those days we would usually finish our encores with 'You Really Got Me'. There are not many songs that can follow that. So as we mounted the stage for our last encore, I went into 'You Really Got Me'. It was wonderful to see Ray's expression as he came on stage in full Father Christmas regalia, having to sing 'You Really Got Me'. Every so often he would look over at me, snarling and sneering through his long white beard. It was perfect. Hilarious. The audience probably thought it was just a seasonal gesture on our part but it was really funny. Backstage afterwards Ray called me every name under the sun, finishing his disgruntled outburst by throwing his beard at me in a ferocious fit of temper. I've never had a Santa Claus call me a fucking cunt before.

The band was again going through changes. Andy Pyle was starting to lure Baptist away. Gosling had seemed a bit unhappy for some time and Andy, the consummate 'muso', always seemed as if he had his own private agenda anyway and was just looking for an opportunity to form his own band. Some people are so predictable – they sit there sucking up to you all the time, thinking that you don't know what's really going on in their mind, when in reality you know exactly what they are thinking. Pyle did us a favour in the end since he saved us from having to sack Baptist, who was obviously unhappy – though very loyal – and probably would never have left of his own volition. Everyone seemed surprised to see them both go, but I wasn't and, inwardly, I was relieved, even though they left us on the spot midway through the *Misfit* sessions. This held up the album a great deal and I think Ray felt betrayed, particularly by Baptist. Pyle was a good musician but a hired hand, but Baptist had been a great asset to the band and it was sad to see him go. But he had had his time and he left on good terms. I remember the last thing he said to me in the bar at Konk: 'Dave, you're not going to do anything, are you? You know, cast a spell on me or anything?' He was wondering why I was taking his leaving so well, especially considering how close we had been over the years. I turned to him and laughed and said, 'No, don't be silly, you're my friend, John. Besides, Andy has already done that, hasn't he?' I will always hold fond memories of Baptist. I loved him. But I was starting to get really fed up with having keyboards in the band, and although Baptist was talented I came to realize that his playing style was starting to sound a little over the top, a bit flowery. This was probably due to his personal frustration. It was time for him to move on.

Ray was himself an accomplished keyboardist who showed Baptist most of the major moves anyway, and I felt that his playing style suited the music better. The personal touches, the inflections, style, and particular emotional emphasis on certain passages in a song, belong to the song just as much as to the performance of it and can sometimes make or break a piece of music. Because Ray wrote a great deal of his songs on keyboard, I always preferred him playing keys in the studio. It was easier to get a hook, feel, or vibe of the song. Technique means nothing in the end. It's the personality, the soul, the essence of an individual's 'feeling' underlying the music that is more important to me. Nobody can play piano like Little Richard, who has such a distinctive style that you know who it is straight away. There are so many guitarists who are great players, but sometimes it is hard to tell one from the other. Pete Townshend has a great style. So do James Burton, Albert Lee, Robbie Robertson, Jeff Beck, B.B. King, Neil Young, Les Paul, Hendrix, Tal Farlow in particular, so brilliant, so 'him'.

Later in the nineties there was a show on MTV called *The Headbangers Ball* that I loved to watch. It was really entertaining but with a few exceptions you could take a musician from one band, juggle him around with another band, and it probably wouldn't sound much different. But I do like bands that mould their playing to fit in with the songs, the music, the compositions. Like Metallica – they write good songs and their playing complements what they are trying to say. The secret of any successful band, in my opinion, is that it sounds unified, as if everyone is pulling together. Sometimes the simplest guitar line or part in a song can have great emotional impact on the listener if it is embellished by a great sound and riffs. I love riffs. They're like pieces of magic that seem to come out of the air.

Bands like Living Colour, Soundgarden, Pearl Jam, Stone Temple Pilots, Nirvana and British bands like Oasis, Blur and Suede are really exciting to listen to. Their music 'fills' you up inside. That's the only way I can describe it. An attitude, a cohesion, a unity, a mixture of emotions, intangible feelings.

A journalist recently asked me if I found it funny that we are surrounded yet again by a generation of guitar bands as if everything has gone full circle, what with the Kinks probably being one of the first so-called Garage Bands. 'It has all been done before,' he said, 'there is nothing new happening.' He's right and wrong, but nothing new ever happens, we are all banging our heads against one wall or another. These young bands are continuing the legacy that bands like the Kinks instigated. With every generation there seems to be those same unanswered questions gnawing away at our consciousness. And until there are any real changes in people's attitudes in consciousness or any real answers to these questions, rock music will always sound fresh to me. It's like a hunger that's never satisfied, a rage that continues to go unheard.

I've always thought it would be interesting if we could sample all the shouts and cries, the noises and sounds of the planet, mixing screams of torture with the gushings of waterfalls, traffic noises, babies being born, guns exploding, birds singing, yer missus givin' yer gyp for staying late up the pub, the whole cacophony of mankind's sound, plug it into a ten zillion gigawatt amp, and then play it as a chord. This combination of human joy and misery ringing out into the universe would probably be heard by some far distant civilization as a mere chirrup of 'help' from the depths of the galaxy.

After Baptist's and Pyle's departure, Ray and I tried out a few session players, like Zaine Griff on bass. Even Mick wasn't cutting it in the studio so we tried out Nick Trevisick and Clem Cattini on drums. Clem, who is a great rock drummer and fellow Arsenal supporter, played on a track called 'Live Life'. We had recorded it a few times with various musicians but with little success. The only bit of the original that was worth keeping was, thankfully, my main guitar part. In those days we never bothered with drum machines very much. So Ray and I asked Clem if he could lay his drum part in with only my solitary guitar track as a guide. He said he'd give it a go. After a couple of run-throughs he had it. To be honest we never thought it would work, but Clem was brilliant and he helped us salvage a great little track. It really kicks along, thanks to his instinctive drumming.

Eventually we finished the *Misfits* album but we were still missing a regular bass player. One day Jim Rodford, ex-Argent/ Phoenix, turned up in the studio. Ray and I had first met Jim on our second-ever tour of the UK in 1965. He played bass with the Mike Cotton Sound, who at the time were Gene Pitney's back-up band. Jim and I chatted and joked about the old days and, at the end of the conversation, Jim said, 'Well, if you guys still want to do it and are still up for it, then I'm with you.' That was that. Jim joined the band and has been an important and integral part of the Kinks ever since.

Misfits could quite easily have been the Kinks' last album and, although it had been difficult to make, in the end it contained some wonderful songs and signalled a new beginning for us as a live band. With Jim's rock 'n' roll suss and sound musical instincts he was able to help Mick's sometimes wayward drumming style, and together they became a formidable rhythm section. With the addition of stage keyboard player Gordon Edwards, I felt for the first time in a while that we had at last a cohesive and unified rock band.

Both Gordon and Jim had good singing voices so this was a chance to dispense with the back-up singers. Gordon was a versatile musician, and although he was sometimes unreliable, he did have a natural rock feel which Baptist had always lacked.

At the start of our Misfits tour of the States in May '78 we had trimmed the band down to a five-piece unit plus Nick Newell on alto and tenor, who also played some percussion. Nick was a great guy and a 'cool' player. The band sounded better than ever. Things were starting to look good. Nancy travelled with me on the road and we were inseparable. We wanted to spend every available moment together. We were very much in love. Obviously, Lisbet knew nothing of this.

Tom Petty and Blondie opened for us on some of the dates, as did the Cars and Cheap Trick. Tom Petty always seemed so aloof and a bit wary of everyone, but I liked his band's minimalist approach. The Blondie band were nice people and Debbie Harry was relaxed and friendly. Cheap Trick were funny and good company and seemed a sincere lot until they started having hits.

I always like to spend as little time at a gig as possible. Quick sound checks, get out, back to the hotel. Sleep. Arrive back at the gig just half an hour before the show, leave straight afterwards, back to the hotel, or just go out.

One of my favourite songs from the *Misfits* album was 'Rock and Roll Fantasy'. It's a lovely song about being disillusioned with the rock business and wanting to give it up, and meeting a fan who reminds you of the reasons why you wanted to do it in the first place and rekindles the urge to keep going. You never know what may be waiting just around the corner. Elvis was dead, but Rock wasn't. After another year of hiccups and personnel changes the Kinks, thankfully, were very much alive and well. I always felt that if we had not been named the Kinks, then the name 'Misfits' would have served equally well.

Ray had remarried by this time, to a pretty blonde woman from south London called Yvonne. She seemed a nice girl at first. One night Ray invited me and Lisbet to dinner with him near his home in Surrey to introduce us to his new wife. After we had exchanged the initial pleasantries and poured a few glasses of wine, it became clear to me during the course of the evening that she and I had very conflicting views about almost everything, from politics to religion, you name it. We had a stinking row and I stormed out of the restaurant. I thought she was just some stuck-up spoilt middle-class kid from the suburbs who had stumbled on to a good thing – namely my brother. Anyway, after both our tempers had subsided we did eventually get on all right. Let me put it this way: we tolerated each other. Soon after they married, Ray bought an apartment in New York and he and Yvonne moved there temporarily.

13

Probably the silliest period in popular music history was the disco explosion in the late seventies and early eighties. I simply hated it; it was horrible. The Bee Gees are so talented, they write such beautiful songs. What happened? Frank Zappa's 'Dancing Fool' was hysterical, however; it was just 'too good', with that odd time-shift stuck in the middle just to trick the dancer, bless him. And John Travolta's classic dance scene in *Saturday Night Fever* was a peak in an otherwise musically impotent period. No wonder Travolta became a Scientologist – any involvement with reality would surely have spelt out the end for him after that. He did redeem himself perfectly with his wonderful performance in *Pulp Fiction* in the nineties. Now that dance scene with Uma Thurman was 'C-o-o-l'.

It just goes to show you never can tell. 'Beam me up Sooty, please.' 'I'm a gnu, a gnother gnu, yes I'm a gnu a gnaughty gnu.' What a period. Barry Manilow. Anyone who can perform a song called 'I Write the Songs that Make the Whole World Sing' has definitely got some kind of dodgy ego problem. Off to the shrink with you, dear boy, and no stopping at the bookshop for a copy of Hubbard's *Dianetics* on the way.

By the way, who invented Musak? I never did find out. What do they call Musak to throw up by? Musick.

Towards the end of 1978 Ray came up with a song called 'Superman', which was obviously inspired by the success of Chris Reeve's first *Superman* movie. The song was really about how feeble human beings are. How we are weak, clumsy, awkward creatures that muddle on from one day to the next. It actually has some very funny lyrics. At first I didn't like the idea of it. It seemed a bit corny to me. Ray was looking for a kind of disco-ish drum sound. I suggested putting a heavy guitar riff over the basic rhythm track to veer it away from that dance vibe, making it more of a rock 'n' roll record.

We had hired a new engineer at Konk named John Rollo. Rollo was a real rocker and he had a good feel for crunchy guitars and rock-solid drum sounds. He proved to be a great asset. We took Rollo with us to New York, where we spent a couple of weeks recording the basics for the *Low Budget* album. We stayed at a crummy hotel called the Wellington, at 7th Avenue and 55th Street. It was very cheap, not to say 'Low Budget'.

The *Misfits* album was a good record, but it took us far too long to make. This time around we wanted a more straight-ahead, more spontaneous type of record. I think it paid off in the end to record it in New York instead of at Konk. The trouble with working in your own studio is that you tend to take more time than you actually need. When you work to a deadline you can be more focused.

Gordon, our keyboardist, didn't turn up for the New York session and so we sacked him, silly sod, and rehearsed without a keyboard player. It was a shame about Gordon – he was a good laugh, and was definitely out for a good time. His girlfriend Maudie was the same, a little rich Chelsea girl who probably spent most of her allowance on drink and drugs. They were really funny together. I think Gordon was upset that he had missed out on the sixties bandwagon and wanted to make up for it in every way possible. He was desperate to become a 'Rock Star'. I was upset to see Gordon fuck himself up with the band. Maybe he just didn't know how to 'fit' in. I remember one time before a sound check seeing him go into the dressing-room, do a few lines, then down a half-bottle of Scotch before going on stage. For a sound check! I never said anything, as he only fell over a few times during the course of the day.

But by the end of a tour he would develop a true 'rock stagger' *á la* Spinal Tap. You know, head rolling side to side, legs buckling up under him as he heads side-on toward a taxi, scuffling his shoes along the pavement in a feeble attempt to keep upright. And then once in the taxi, slumping in the back seat, swearing and cursing at anything and everything in sight. 'Fucking cabs, fucking yanks, fucking city, look at it. How far's the hotel, driver, what?' The driver, responding in a broad Brooklyn accent, 'Hey, you guys from Australia?' Slurring reply, 'No, I fuckin' ain't. I'm fuckin' English, in I, just drive will yer. Is it far? I think I'm gonna throw up.'

Gordon was funny. He would carry a pillow-case around with him, full of all kinds of items he'd stolen from hotel rooms. Lamps, lampshades, brass light-switches, ashtrays, telephones, you name it. Silly bugger. He would often be found walking around in the hotel corridor in the middle of the night, stoned, dressed in a very smart silk paisley dressing-gown, looking for his room because he had forgotten where it was. He'd be shouting at the top of his voice. 'Maudie, where are yer, where's my fucking pizza?' In one hand he would be holding a joint, in his mouth would hang a Marlboro, and in his other hand he would grip a Heineken. It was inevitable that he'd fuck up. He would often call me up at four in the morning, totally out of it, just to talk about music, about his feelings, how much he loved me and that we should write some songs together, etc., etc. I was very fond of him. He was a good all-round musician, but too over-the-top, particularly at a time when we really needed to apply ourselves and focus on the future. I didn't find out what happened to him until much later. I understand he's still involved in music, I'm glad to say.

Our apartment at the Wellington was scruffy, but it was quite big and it afforded Nancy and me the opportunity to spend valuable time together, so we didn't mind. She flew in from Los Angeles and together we bought candles and tablecloths to make the place more presentable. But it was still a dump. Recently I was in New York and noticed, to my delight, that it had been refurbished. I stayed at the Warwick.

Nancy and I shared many unusual psychic experiences in the early years of our relationship and it was a time of great personal growth for us both. It is strange how sometimes you are inexplicably drawn to certain people in your life by forces almost outside of your control. That's how it was for me and Nancy: two strangers mysteriously thrown together who were on a similar path and who shared the same spiritual goals.

We recorded the *Low Budget* sessions at the Power Station and Blue Rock. The vibe was great and it was really starting to sound good. I was excited, since I had always preferred working in the studio as a four- or three-piece anyway. When I got back to the Wellington at night, Nancy and I would make food, meditate, make love, drink wine, talk long into the night. It was beautiful. A time I will truly never forget.

After my earlier experiences with drugs I wouldn't ever take anything, not even grass. I started to develop an aversion to drugs of all kinds, and was very wary of others who were users, though I must admit that the occasional odd bottle of Rémy Martin never went amiss.

That hotel really was a shithouse. Cracks in the walls and mouldings, fresh paint over rotting plaster and wallpaper, sleazy bent-over drunks leering at you in dingy hallways, cockroaches and other unnameable insects scuttering underfoot. All kinds of shit. A typical shopping list would include red wine, incense, take-away veggie Indian food, orange juice, books, apple pie, cockroach repellent, insect and fly spray. But we didn't care.

One morning at around seven there was a knock on the door. I got up and tentatively walked towards it, my senses full of that brittle early-morning feeling. A deep croaking voice belted out in a heavy Brooklyn drone, 'Hey, open up, this is the exterminator.' I thought, shit, what the hell does he mean? In my half-sleep, visions ran through my head of a heavy-set scar-faced mafioso type standing outside the room with a large gun at the ready. Nervously, I stuttered out, 'Um, well, um, not today, thank you.' By then it had dawned on me that this was the pest-control service, whose visits are a feature of New York apartment life, but it freaked me to think that it might have been The Exterminator. Fortunately he went away, and Nancy and I laughed about it. The truth is, we could have used his services. You have to be really tough to handle those bugs. New York – what a place. There really is nowhere like it.

While we were in New York a woman named Brenda worked for us. She had been secretly in love with Ray for years and was a real lush, but she was good, at least for a while, at organizing meetings, running errands, and stuff like that. Could she drink! Vodka by the bottle, any time of the day, anywhere. For any reason. She was thirty-five or so and a bit tarty-looking, with a longish face, peroxide blonde hair, and a thin, drawn look. Working in close proximity with Ray had probably prematurely aged her. Only joking, Ray! Of course her substance abuse had nothing to do with it. At shows she would always be chatting up young musicians and roadies from the support bands. Her one claim to fame was that she had fucked Waylon Jennings. Big deal. This often brought a derisive echo of laughter from our dressing-room when mentioned. There were few budding young guitarists who missed her lustful glance. She was a bit of a whore but had a heart of gold.

(God, have I been dying to use that phrase. It reminds me of some great classic cockney phrases that I love: 'Better out than in', 'I fucked her rigid', 'Like flies round shit'. Other selected phrases from the Male Chauvinist Dictionary include such lyrical proclamations as 'Don't swear when there's cunt about', or one of my favourites, an oldie but one that still hits the spot: 'You like it, don't yer?' One of Colin the Scrap's more home-grown yet memorable quotations: 'Give her one up the dirt-box and she'll never leave yer.' One of my own self-penned phrases and the original working title of this book: 'If You Don't Fuck, What Yer Doing 'Ere?' Dear me, Oscar, I digress.)

But Brenda really did love the band and the music, as much as other things. She was a genuine rock 'n' roll moll. She was also good to have around the studio, a good vibe. We have never really liked people hovering in and around the studio while we worked, particularly record company people. Clive only appeared on the odd occasion, maybe to hear a mix or two in the final stages. He had the savvy to stay away. It is so weird how people can have an odd effect on what's happening in a highly charged creative atmosphere. I remember a maintenance engineer who worked at Konk named John Tims. He was a really slow and methodical worker who looked like a bit of a psycho, with cropped spiky hair and a Norman Bates stare. He must have spent half the time with his hand stuck to his chin, as he would be continually stroking it. Whenever he came into the control room to fix something while the music was playing I would swear that the tape machines slowed down. It used to drive me crazy. I'd have to walk out while he fixed the problem.

There's nothing worse than when you invite someone to visit who is not used to the studio environment, and you keep playing the same song over and over and out of the corner of your eye you see them looking really fidgety and nervous. It's best to keep it simple, with as few people as possible, but every now and then it's great to have a 'vibe' person who has a genuine enthusiasm for the music and an ocean of patience.

Ray can sometimes be extremely funny in the studio. I remember one time he was getting really frustrated with Mick. For some reason Mick couldn't get a particular part right without the timing getting screwed. Ray was standing next to me as we watched from the other side of the control-room window. We stared at Mick, who was practising and really suffering, trying his best to get it together. Ray turned to me and said, 'I wonder how long it takes for a thought to travel from Mick's brain all the way down his arm and into his hands?'

Mick could sometimes be very frustrating, very slow, especially when he was nervous. Not that he was stupid in any way, it was just that it would sometimes take him a long time to deliberate over the easiest things. It used to really annoy me at times. But Mick was a very funny guy, very dry. Expert at stating the obvious, as if it was some kind of revelation.

Life was never easy in the studio for any of us. There was always so much tension, yet at times it was electrifying, exhilarating. We actually recorded the backtrack of the title track 'Low Budget' at Konk before we left for New York. I think we used the second take, live guitars, live drums. It was almost throwaway, as if it didn't matter. You always have to be positive when you're working with Ray or he will stay in the studio for an eternity trying this, trying that, until all of a sudden he has disappeared up his own arse. Sometimes Ray would be so intimidating that musicians who started out relaxed and confident could easily after some hours almost forget how to play. God, it happened such a lot. Get in there, get a good feeling, do it, and do it quickly before he gets the chance to change his mind. The times we have spent working a song backwards and forwards, inside and out, up and down, round and round, and then in the end choose the very first arrangement or performance. Nightmare. It's like being in a porno film where nobody ever 'arrives'.

I remember one awful argument Ray and I had during the latter stages of mixing an album – I think it was *UK Jive*. We had already had a minor fist fight on the roof of the studio which left our engineer running out of the building in fear, and our ever-faithful but ever-crafty tour manager Ken Jones in tears. I had been away for a few days while Ray was mixing. When I came back he had edited three of my songs down, cutting out important guitar solos, placing choruses in different places, etc. Without consulting me, of course. Blood was spilt and it was a sad and terrible scene.

As I turned to leave the building, I said to Ray, 'How the fuck could you do this to me, did you think I'd never find out?'

Ray replied, 'I did it because it was the best thing to do for the album.'

'You did it,' I said, 'because I was taking up too much space on the record and you didn't like it. If anyone did that to you, you would be hysterical with anger. You're just a selfish bastard.'

Ray said, in that oh-so-irritating quietly superior way of his, with a calm and fake upper-class whine, 'Dave, I'm a perfectionist, I'm a genius.'

I was so infuriated that I left the building shouting, 'You're not a genius, you're an arsehole. There's a distinct difference. And you're getting the word "perfectionist" mixed up with the word "wanker". Fuck you, I'm out of here.'

Oh well, we should have saved our energy. As it turned out, the experience of marketing the record was difficult enough without us going into a self-destruct mode beforehand.

Compared to some albums, *Low Budget* was a joy to make. It was mastered by June and dates were already in place for the summer tours. Back in London prior to these tours we auditioned keyboard players for the live shows and hired Ian Gibbons, a really down-to-earth and likeable guy with a cheeky sense of humour. Humour, of course, was a prerequisite for playing in the Kinks. Ian was obviously a good musician, but it is sometimes rare to find both in the same body. In the end it all comes down to personality. Musical ability is really secondary; there are a lot of good players around but not many who have the right personality combined with the right musical instincts.

The Kinks were about to embark on one of the most exciting and successful periods of our careers. *Low Budget* was released and we toured the States through October. It was one of our biggest albums in the US and, as was so typical of the Kinks, it became a hit during a recession. Songs like 'Gallon of Gas' underscored the financial problems America was facing then, what with the oil crisis and everything.

Ian Hunter, Herman Brood, and Johnny Cougar opened for us on some of the shows. The shows were great and the audiences fantastic. By November we had also filmed live footage from our US tour for an up-and-coming *Time-Life* video which was to be released to coincide with a live album, *One for the Road*, which eventually came out in the spring of 1980. It became one of our most successful albums. We finished off the year touring Germany and Europe with *Low Budget* and at last, after all the strife and rebuilding, things were really starting to look up.

Nancy flew to London in January and stayed temporarily in a small house in Highgate, where I would visit her. There was a lot of tension between me and Lisbet. We still shared a beautiful house in Southgate, north London, and by now I had four lovely boys by her whom I loved desperately (our son Russell had been born in May 1979). But I was in love with Nancy and wanted to spend all my time with her. Inside I was so torn; my emotions were being pulled in different directions. I felt so bad about what was happening, yet I just couldn't help myself.

In my mind I thought that the only solution would be for us all to live together. I actually believed it would be possible. I arranged a dinner in Muswell Hill with Nancy, Lisbet and the kids to feel my way with it. To my surprise neither Nancy nor Lisbet objected to meeting each other. They were checking each other out. We met at the restaurant; both Nancy and Lisbet behaved like sophisticated adults and in an uncomfortable sense it went OK. But when I talked to Lisbet that evening about the possibilities of us all getting along somehow, she was extremely upset by the idea.

By this time my family – my sisters in particular – were beginning to interfere. Gwen and Joyce were very angry and upset at my behaviour, saying that they just could not believe it was going on. They, as well as everybody else, thought that Lisbet, the kids, and I were the perfect family. Ray, to his credit, kept out of it, although he did say that he had never sensed more love in a house than in mine. Gwen thought it was black magic.

'Is Nancy part of a cult from California?' she asked. 'You know, Scientologists or whatever?'

If you can call falling in love brainwashing then I suppose I was brainwashed good and proper. They just didn't get it. But I guess being the youngest caused my sisters to be more than just a little over-protective.

196

Dolly had since moved out of London so I didn't see her very much. And my mother had developed an impartial view, or so it seemed. She was really only concerned about my personal happiness, although she tried to remind me in no uncertain terms about 'my responsibilities'.

One day Peg called me up and asked me to go round to her place. She insisted I come on my own and bring a picture of Nancy with me. Peg had a reputation in the family for being a bit of a witch, but she wasn't the only one interested in the supernatural. Gwen has always been interested in spiritualism. Also, when I was little, Rose, Joyce, Peg and Rene would often hold seances. I remember being very frightened by them.

People would make fun of Peg but it was obvious that she was unusual and very psychic. I sat in her parlour and we drank tea and reminisced about family stuff. Eventually the conversation led to a discussion about my relationship with Nancy.

I should preface this by relating a few incidents that had occurred a while back. Some years before, Peg and he n usband Mike had lived in Welwyn Garden City, about fifteen miles north of London. They lived next door to a woman called Mrs Pisani, a large, buxom woman who had a big mouth and a very noisy family. One day Peg got so pissed off with Mrs Pisani's antics that she made a Plasticine doll of her and stuck a pin in its head. In the middle of the night the noise of ambulances woke up the neighbourhood as Mrs Pisani was carried off quite unexpectedly to hospital. She had suffered a minor stroke. After some months she was apparently fine, but also a lot quieter.

There was another incident with Mike, Peg's old man. He was working the night shift and Peg felt that he wasn't giving her enough attention, that he didn't care for her any more. She finally got so pissed off that she made another doll, this time of Mike, and stuck a pin in its stomach. Yes, you guessed it, a few days later Mike developed terrible stomach pains. He went to the hospital and was diagnosed with a stomach ulcer. He stopped working nights.

As I sat listening to Peg in her front room I thought, oh shit, these were only the incidents I knew about. At least I didn't notice any Plasticine lying around. Although a lot of people were wary of Peg and thought her odd, I always loved her and had complete trust in her. She asked if I had a picture of Nancy. I said yes and showed it to her. As she looked at the photo she said, 'My God, doesn't she look like Sue! David, you really love this girl, don't you?' She went on, 'Certain family members asked me to put a spell on this girl, to get rid of her. There's no way that I am going to do that. Things sometimes happen for a reason and I think this girl is good for you. By the way, I saw Sue a couple of months ago around the Broadway. She's put on a bit of weight but she still looks good. I didn't speak to her.'

Whenever someone in my family told me about seeing Sue, I felt the inclination to try to contact her again, but on second thoughts I figured so much time had passed that I decided it wasn't such a good idea after all.

I continued to see Nancy while I lived at home with Lisbet and the boys. It was a tough time emotionally, but I felt inspired creatively. At last I felt more confident about my writing, and finally I got my songs together and went into the studio to record my first solo album.

Elliot Abbott hooked me up with a guy called Ed De Joy who worked at RCA in New York. Ed liked the songs, we struck up a good friendship, and we made a deal. Eddie was a really nice guy and was a great help to me; he made suggestions without interfering too much, unlike some of the typical ego-focused A & R people who were around at the time. Many of them were the scourge of the record business. Why couldn't these arseholes just leave the music alone? It was usually better to bypass the middle people and try to work directly with the presidents or heads of companies. But as the record companies merged and became larger conglomerates it became increasingly difficult for this to happen. The work load of the big company bosses demanded that they delegate to their various departments, and after the initial signings they usually ended up having little or nothing to do with the finished product.

But what the hell is A & R anyway? Generally, A & R, which stands for Artists and Repertoire, are the department that takes care of the creative needs of the artists. They're supposed to encourage the development of their work. Producers and A & R people have become far too self-important. Certain A & R people and producers tend to impose their own personal viewpoint on to a performer's personal vision, and that's what I take exception to. It should be an honour to be involved at this level, yet so many abuse their position. The fact that it still goes on is ridiculous. A good band and a good engineer can make records without all the interference, all the wankers chipping in. A producer's role should be to guide, not interfere – to gently stimulate, compliment and inspire musicians and especially composers to fulfil their potential without fucking around with it so much that it ceases to be their own any more.

If a record becomes successful, everybody down to the tea-lady takes the credit, but if it's a flop it's always the artist who bears the brunt of it regardless of what anyone says. The public isn't interested in what goes on behind the scenes, and why should they be? The personality conflicts, the games people play, record company politics – all the public cares about is whether or not they like the music. But inside, everybody's looking over their shoulders, too scared to be the one to make a bad decision or a wrong move or any decision at all in case they might lose their bullshit position.

Thankfully there are sensitive people involved in the business. Ed De Joy was a gentleman, Clive a class act, Mo Ostin from Warner Brothers an ambassador. When the Kinks were inducted into the Rock 'n' Roll Hall of Fame in 1990, the first person to come and congratulate me was Mo Ostin. I hadn't seen him for years. That really meant a lot to me.

For my first album I decided to play everything and 'produce' it on my own with the more than capable help of Rollo at the console. It was an exhilarating, uplifting and freeing experience. *AFLI-3603* (named after the actual sales bar code number) was a chance for me to do everything. I played drums, bass, keyboards, sang, and mixed it. It was great fun. It was also a chance for me to exorcize a lot of pent-up and suppressed feelings. On reflection I suppose I may have tried a bit too hard, but it was a necessary experience for me. The song 'Visionary Dreamer' had been in lyric form for some years. It was a love song to someone who has always been very close to me and always will be. 'Nothing More to Lose' was inspired by Eddie Cochran, with lyrics about the necessity for change in a world where all the systems and 'isms' have failed us.

'The World is Changing Hands' is about how young people have a stronger and broader spiritual potential than people now in power. 'Imagination's Real' is about how if everything around us is a product of our imagination, we can imagine the world being whatever we want it to be. 'In You I Believe' is a song about encouragement, about the fact that without belief we are nothing. All we need is reassurance so that we can achieve greater things. One of Ray's better qualities is that he has the power to 'believe'. To believe even in adversity. I have always admired that in him. But it was Nancy who helped me to believe in myself and to reinforce my inner view of the world.

14

By June 1980 Ray was supervising final cuts of the Kinks Time-Life video, which was going to be released consecutively with *One for the Road*, the live album. I went to New York to finalize details on the release of my own album. It was mastered at Masterdisk. Bob Ludwig, the head cutting engineer, had previously worked on various Kink albums and I was eager to work with him on my own tapes. Bob was a great guy, always listening, always trying to think of ways to enhance and improve the cut. He exuded a quiet confidence and had good judgement. I always thought of him as a kind of an 'engineer yogi'.

In Europe the Kinks did a few festivals in France and Belgium. Curiously, Ray had invited along someone he had met in London, Chrissie Hynde. He wanted to keep it very low-profile. They were clearly closer than mere friends and they appeared happy together. I was a bit wary of her. It was really good to see Ray smiling and joking around and having a good time. He seemed to be coming out of his shell a bit. Although Ray appears on stage to be quite an eccentric performer and extrovert, in private he can often be relatively quiet and introverted, but always thinking. Sometimes it is as if there are invisible signs up around him saying, 'Private Property, Keep Out'. He can make you feel very uncomfortable. The closer you try to get, the bigger the signs become. 'Enter at your Own Peril', 'Strictly No Admittance'. Joking apart, I know what it is like. The world, or rather people, will eat away at your soul if you let them. Sometimes you're left standing there feeling totally empty yet people still expect something from you.

In July I went back to New York again. Barbara Pepe was head of RCA's publicity at the time, and had put a promotional tour in place to coincide with the release of my album. Barbara and I got on amazingly well. At first she seemed quite hard, but as I got to know her I realized that it was just a hard outer coating, that tough 'New York' edge. We both loved sleazy bars and clubs, so when we finished our press stuff we would hang out. Barbara and I were quite a formidable team at the pool table. Nancy was now my constant companion, and the three of us spent two weeks together touring radio stations all over the country. I did countless interviews and was having a great time.

Nancy was pregnant as well. I felt a bit uncomfortable at first because my son Russell by Lisbet was still a baby, but Nancy really wanted to have a child and I was overjoyed when she had our son Daniel. We were very much in love and I could deny her nothing.

My solo album was really well received and got good critical reviews. It charted well and I felt on top of the world. By August Arista had planned the release of *One for the Road*. Elliot planned a fall tour and we played to packed and enthusiastic audiences everywhere, from Cobo Hall in Detroit, to the Nassau Coliseum in New York, to the Spectrum in Philly to the Sports Arena in San Diego. Johnny Cougar opened for us on most of the shows. We were enjoying a phenomenal resurgence and at last were savouring the fruits of all the hard work we had put in, the hard slog of the previous eight years or so. *One for the Road* charted high and became a hit album.

Back home the situation with me and Lisbet was getting much worse. I had hurt her terribly but I didn't know what to do. I was continuing to live with her at our family home with the children but I knew that at some point I was going to have to leave. The band continued to tour extensively throughout the rest of 1980, and by December Nancy had had the baby, our son Daniel, and was living in a small flat near St Johns Wood in north London. In January I started recording my second album for RCA. Sadly, Ed De Joy left the company to go into his own business. I was upset, since I thought things were going well with us. Ed suggested that maybe he could be involved with me on a management level, but after giving it serious thought I decided to pass. Elliot seemed to be doing a fine job and I was worried it would be a case of 'too many cooks'. Flashbacks of Robert, Grenville and Larry popped into my head. Oh no! Not that again! But I really missed Ed's involvement with my second record.

Ray was working on a project at Stratford in London, so it gave me time to work on the *Glamour* album. Prior to the recording of it, I did a session with drummer Bob Henrit, who had worked with our bass player Jim for some time. Jim and Bob were the original rhythm section for Argent. I had always wanted to work with Bob, as I liked his drumming style. I decided to use him on the sessions.

In between the *Glamour* sessions the Kinks also recorded another album for Arista, *Give the People What They Want*. So it was an extremely creative and productive period for both Ray and me.

Behind the scenes, Ray's marriage to Yvonne seemed to be falling apart. Chrissie was now Ray's constant companion. I didn't like her at first and, in fact, I called her a Virgo slut when we initially met. I thought I sensed something of the vampire in her and I always felt drained when I talked to her. She expected your full attention when she spoke, but seemed distracted when being spoken to. It irritated me. I thought she was very rude. Maybe she and Ray were well suited, the pair of them.

In the early stages of their relationship, I was concerned that she might be a negative influence on Ray and the band. At one gig, when she got on stage and expected to sing, I was really pissed off. In my anger I took a swipe at her. Ray quickly defused a potentially explosive situation. Eventually, Chrissie and I did become friends.

Years later, after Chrissie and Ray had split, I got to know her much better. I felt she changed a great deal after she had children – she became warmer, more giving, less aggressive to people and more aggressive towards the injustices in the world. I saw her once with her daughter Natalie (her child by Ray) in a café in Marylebone in the late eighties. Natalie reminded me so much of my brother when he was little – withdrawn, quiet, easily hurt. It seemed really strange. Ray evidently had shown little desire to participate in Natalie's upbringing. Perhaps it was too painful, and he apparently tried to cut the whole episode out of his life entirely. While perhaps it's in some ways understandable, I could never have done it. Chrissie told me that although she had gone through a marriage (to Jim Kerr of Simple Minds) and had a new boyfriend, she was still in love with Ray and thought she always would be.

But there were destructive forces around them in the end. I remember that they used to have terrible rows, smashing furniture, often wrecking their apartment. I really think they both got off on it. It was a relationship doomed for disaster from the outset, since they both had selfish and manipulative tendencies, even though I believe they truly loved one another.

One day Ray invited me and my sister Peg to the house, since they were both concerned that it might be haunted. Apparently there was a strange presence in an upstairs room. After we arrived Peg took a discerning look around. Ray and Chrissie had said that there was something, some force, that tried to push them both down the stairs. I personally didn't sense anything. I thought it was just some kind of strange energy field that had been created by the two of them simply being together. They actually split up soon after that. It was an emotionally traumatic period for Ray and had a devastating effect on all of us who cared about him.

Right before I started recording *Glamour*, a new guy had taken over at RCA in New York. He was polite and sympathetic but that all-important feeling of empathy was missing. He lacked Ed De Joy's spirit and enthusiasm for my work. But I had a brilliant time recording *Glamour*. It was the Reagan/Thatcher era, and the idea behind the album was that you can't always believe what you see with your eyes and hear with your ears. It is what's going on behind the scenes that controls the outer appearances of things. Its essential themes are Vanity, Megalomania, Illusion, Control. Some critics called *Glamour* a 'hot potato', and generally it was not well received. A number of media people found it 'unpalatable'. On reflection it my have been a bit raw, too gritty, but perhaps its point of view was too out of synch with the sensibilities of the time. People were more interested in 'buying' and 'selling' than in questioning the ethics of any one particular regime or system. The album charted briefly then vanished. It wasn't until the nineties that similar ideas and notions came to the forefront, when the strain of political deception started to pull at the seams of government, unravelling the pin-striped suit. The world in the nineties is now faced with problems of an undeniable apocalytpic nature and it is irrelevant whether we find it 'distasteful' or not to make our feelings known.

I wanted to do a short film based on the record, about a forties film star, a Cary-Grant-meets-Ronald-Reagan type, who gets elected president. He looks so dashing, smart, clever, he's a publicist's dream. A man concerned only with his self-image, consumed with himself. In the background, in old-fashioned black-and-white, are scenes depicting a modern-day holocaust. He, of course, is oblivious, going to meetings, making TV appearances, attending functions, making speeches, continually failing to notice the awful misery and carnage around him. At one point a strange, alien hand appears as if from nowhere, breaking in through the ethers from another world, its forefinger stretched in a desperate attempt to lure the President's gaze away from the 'immediate' and into the future. Alas, the 'star' doesn't see it, being blind to all but himself. He looks on out towards the horizon as the sun sets. He prepares for his 'big close-up' in the final scene of this awful tragedy but his concerns are only for the 'present' with himself, not about what he is doing. Or rather not doing.

Glamour today, oh I believe it's true, always it's fooling you . . .
Glamour today, destroy it with your mind and let the truth
unwind . . .
Look at all the people . . . who get caught in the trap, strain their
eyes to see somebody else's fantasy, can it be . . .
It's what you feel, what's inside . . . that's reality . . .
Glamour today, although you can't cut it with a knife, it will rule
your life . . .

The promotion and marketing people thought it was too serious, too heavy. Yeah, sure. We spent a lot of time on the artwork and there is a lot more information there than at first meets the eye. 'Eastern Eyes' is a love song about finding enlightenment. The East is depicted as a material cripple and the West as a spiritual cripple. Love presents itself as understanding and becomes the active ingredient that pulls the two together.

Eastern Eyes, they smile over all our western trials,
Egypt calls me back, but I must change the past in me.
Peace let there be, I know now I love you, oh let it be
Please leave us be, we are seeds of heaven . . . Eternity . . .

'World of Our Own' is a song of hope. When the world's tyrants have had their fill and become exhausted by their 'mad and evil cravings, people will still be here, long after they have gone, we will build a world of our own. All that's true never dies, in a world of our own, each child a star for his own.' Another track, called 'Telepathy', got some half-decent air-play, but overall the album sadly bombed.

Meanwhile the Kinks were still riding high. Ray wrote some great songs for *Give the People What They Want*, which was released that summer and became a hit. But I still wasn't satisfied. I liked the album but I felt it didn't go far enough for me. The title cut is a great song and a particular favourite of mine, which we occasionally still play live. Ray is a lyrical genius and this song has a wit and fervour that perfectly express his more aggressive writing style. 'Better Things' is a very special song, typically Kinks, beautiful, full of melancholy yet bursting with hope and pride. The feelings expressed in it often remind me of 'Days'. It always has a deep emotional effect on me. I felt that in a way Ray was trying to say that he would gladly love to see the back of me, yet at the same time he just couldn't let go. *Here's hoping all the verses rhyme, and all the very best of choruses too . . . I hope tomorrow you'll find better things . . .* But there was still much unfinished business at hand.

The Kinks were a huge success. Again we toured the States to large audiences. On a couple of the shows our support band was the Pretenders, and in Denver I met the band for the first time. They seemed all right, but a couple of them were caught up in that 'rock star' posey drug thing. I always liked their drummer, Martin, who was the most down-to-earth of any of them.

Nancy and I hung out with Ray and Chrissie during days off on the tour. It had been some time since Ray and I had really socialized. We became closer for a while. It was nice. Chrissie was very funny, she had a good sense of humour and she and Nancy got on really well. Although things weren't going too well with me at RCA it was nonetheless a fairly happy period. But Chrissie and Ray's relationship was destined to end, since each needed and demanded constant energy and attention from the other, like two magnets of the same polarity trying to suck at each other's life force, which in the end only served to repel.

I had moved out of my family home and in with Nancy. The day I left was dreadful, having to tell my boys that I was going. I was in such pain and hurting inside, seeing how brave and understanding they were. It really affected me, but I just couldn't see how I could do it any other way. I was beginning to feel like an emotional ping-pong ball and I had to do something. Many years later my son Simon said to me, 'Dave, it wasn't really quite so bad because we saw more of you after you left than we did before.' I must admit I spent as much time with them as I could whenever I could. Now most of my sons are grown up and they have become my closest and dearest friends. They are a great joy and inspiration to me and I love them more than my life. Lisbet has always been a good and loyal friend and I feel extremely fortunate to have had such love around me. Even in the darkest times I have always known that I was loved and its effect on me has been immeasurable.

Love like that makes things happen. It sustains, guides, and protects you. Regardless of my many faults, I have always had the capacity to love in many different ways. It first came to me from growing up in a big family, where love virtually oozed out of the walls of the house. When I think back, it was my mother and my sisters, Dolly in particular, who taught me about kindness, about 'sensitivity mixed with determination', and above all about unconditional love.

As 1981 drew to a close the Kinks were very much in top gear, and although success in the UK still eluded us, we were bigger than ever in the States. Disappointed with my lack of success with *Glamour*, I left RCA and Elliot Abbott hooked me up with Warner Brothers.

During November Nancy and I spent some time away in North Devon with our little boy, Daniel. I loved to roam the North Devon countryside, especially Exmoor, allowing nature to fill my soul with its secret power and beauty. Yet after some days of reflection, I became extremely depressed. The Kinks had been my life, but I needed something of my own. It was vital for me creatively and emotionally to get away from Ray, if not totally, then at least to find some success of my own, some creative independence. I was starting to feel disillusioned and empty. The Kinks were doing well, but inside I thought I would never be free of Ray, of his demands, and at the same time I realized that he needed to explore his own creative instincts too. I felt confused. Special, creative people need space and encouragement and I didn't want to get in his way, yet deep down I sensed a surge of energy that was clawing at my insides for expression. Nancy was great; she helped me through this difficult time, as always supportive, wise, and comforting to me.

We cancelled a tour of Europe due to my depression, but by the end of the year we had organized a January tour of the States. I was reluctant to go but Elliot persuaded me to do it. He felt that it was not a good time to upset promoters as well as disappoint fans. I liked Elliot, and although feelings were riding high by the time we parted company prior to the end of our Arista period in late 1984, he was good for Ray and always seemed to have our interests at heart, despite our occasional differences of opinion. In the end I think that maybe he took on too much. He eventually became distracted by other acts he wanted to manage. In this business it is so important to be focused. One minute you're up, then you're down. You must keep your eyes open at all times. It can be a fickle and false existence.

15

Nineteen-eighty-two proved to be one of the most extraordinary years of my life. What follows is an account of an episode that totally changed me in every way. The events that I will endeavour to recount to the best of my ability are – whether believed or not – absolutely true. All that I can expect of the reader is to try to keep an open mind and not be too eager to judge or jump to any erroneous conclusions. What I am about to describe left a deep and profound impression on my soul, the implications of which I am still – some fourteen or more years later – trying to come to terms with.

It was 13 January. The tour was barely two or three days old. We had already performed at the Syracuse War Memorial and the Meadowlands in New Jersey. The aircraft lunged to a halt, nudging me from my drowsiness, then taxied and bumped its way along the tarmac towards the arrival gate. We had arrived at Richmond Airport, Virginia. I had felt strange all morning, distant, detached, as if observing my surroundings from afar. Nancy and I picked up our bags as cheery flight attendants escorted us from the plane. I wondered if I was feeling odd because I was still suffering from jet-lag from the flight over from England, and thought no more of it.

After we had checked into the Sheraton Hotel in Hampton Row we had three or four hours to relax before the sound check. We were to play that night at the Coliseum. The suitcases promptly arrived and Nancy and I started to unpack. As I began sorting through my things the most astonishing thing happened. It was around 1.30 p.m. I looked up, startled by a sudden pressure in and around my head. It felt as if an invisible metal band or something had suddenly attached itself to my forehead and was pressing in on me. After a few moments it subsided, giving way to the strangest sensation that my whole head was expanding. Then it started again. It was as if some kind of psychic switch had somehow been turned on inside my head. Momentarily dazed, I tried to collect myself.

All of a sudden I began hearing these strange voices talking to me, in clear and unmistakable tones. Their voices were authoritative but warm and strangely comforting, which lessened my initial alarm. This was unlike anything I had experienced before. They felt as if they were a little distance above my head; that's how I perceived it at the time. For all I knew they could have been operating from thousands of miles away. I couldn't see them but I could hear them and, more importantly, I could feel them and smell them. There were five distinct intelligences and each one gave off his or its own particular odour. It felt as if they were all male, but it is possible they may not all have been. The smells were very stimulating and deep, extremely pleasant and uplifting, and after a while I was able to distinguish one entity from another by its smell. Smells that I cannot begin to describe, like exotic flowers, jasmine, but deeper, magnolia, but so full it was as if you could taste them, touch them.

After my initial shock had subsided, I became acutely aware of my surroundings. Everything looked slightly different, as if there was a fine and delicate layer or web of matter over everything in the room. I could feel my thoughts and senses reorienting so that I could more easily determine what 'they' were saying and doing. These intelligences communicated by pure energy and, most interestingly of all, by smell and sound. They used the vibration of 'scent' or smell as a vehicle to convey various types of energy, of information. In between thought as we know it there is other information that is not readily assimilated by the conscious mind, but more through feeling. They were gently gaining control over my consciousness, but without actually tampering with my own ideas or thoughts.

I looked over at Nancy. She looked back and smiled as if everything was normal. Obviously she didn't know what was going on. I tried to explain to her what was happening, but the intelligences would only let me explain a little part of it. To my great relief she readily accepted everything I told her. Her unswaying faith and trust became of paramount importance over the days that followed. 'They' showed me many things.

Sometimes they projected an energy into my head that translated into words via a centre in my brain, similar to radio waves, sometimes the information seemed to come at me at such an incredible speed it was difficult to absorb.

I was now enveloped in some kind of mysterious telepathic rapture with these beings. I became agitated and started to panic. I called to Nancy to come and sit near me on the end of the bed.

'What's going on?' I said. 'How am I going to be able to function, do shows? What the hell do I tell people? Oh God, now I really am going mad.'

I held her hand and said that under no circumstances should she leave me alone. Just as I thought I would fall into an uncontrollable panic, a warm and comforting fragrance enveloped me, calmed me. I felt renewed, confident, clear, and emotionally full. I was overcome with an incomprehensible joy. I was so happy.

Nancy could neither see nor hear what was happening. She told me that although I seemed the same outwardly, she could feel an unmistakable presence that convinced her that what was happening was real. If she hadn't been there, I don't know what I would have done.

The intelligences took complete control of my being. They showed me a hidden side of life, a view of a world within a world. My lower abdomen became numb and although I was able to walk around normally, I seemed to lack sensation there. They told me that I was not to have sex, the reason being that part of what was happening to me was due to the fact that they were manipulating latent forces in my body. In other words, they were transmuting sexual energy on to a higher vibrational level, enhancing consciousness.

The intelligences did not tell me who they were, but two of them said they had always been my spirit guides, and two others were entities that were not of this earth but were involved in missions here as watchers and nurturers of our race. The other intelligence was the projected consciousness of a man living in a physical body on earth. They communicated many things to me, most of which I have only just begun to assimilate now.

They showed me the 'World of Ethers', irrefutable knowledge of the 'Etheric Planes', and its interaction with the physical, emotional and mental levels. They stated to me in no uncertain terms that the study and understanding of this energy field would play a vital part in the next stage of our planetary development.

They demonstrated to me how to manipulate this energy. At their prompting I turned on the television. There was a commercial on for cake mix. I was soon to find that these intelligences were not without a sense of humour. I thought it really funny that there I was, a rock musician in a hotel room in Hampton, Virginia, communicating with discarnate beings who had gained control of my consciousness, watching in bewilderment a Betty Crocker cake mix commercial. Who on earth would believe such a thing?

As I watched I started to notice a bluish-grey substance appear around the screen. At first it looked like some kind of gaseous smoke. The 'stuff' began to mould and congeal into various forms and shapes, some taking on the appearance of weird yet strangely alluring creatures.

The intelligences told me that these types of lower astral malevolents operate on and affect the consciousness of the watcher via a kind of magnetic transference. This energy field is active all the time, and by practising certain psychic disciplines we can enhance our ability to affect this substance to a greater or lesser degree. The substance is extremely malleable and is highly susceptible to thought and feeling. It works on an individual's aura through a kind of psychic absorption.

Etheric magnetism, they told me, operates on a sub-atomic level and interpenetrates all levels of physical matter as we know it. We live in a sea of mind energy that is full of thought and feeling. We are like mental fish, swimming around unaware of the water or fluid that surrounds us. Certain psychic healing methods can have a strong effect on this substance, which I call 'neotuotonic'. In other words, it's an effect which adds to the nourishment and growth of a magnetic particle of 'ether'.

As I continued to observe the events that were taking place in the room, in my mind, the intelligences injected what seemed like a brilliant white beam of light, a ray of force, into my head, and directed it out through my fingertips and towards the 'etheric forms'. When the force hit them they were transformed and diffused into the atmosphere. I was amazed. Things that I had previously believed possible only in theory had now become reality.

The telephone rang. It was our road manager telling me that the sound check had been delayed due to the late arrival of the equipment trucks. What a relief; now I had some more time to try to figure out what I was to do. The intelligences informed me that I would be able to go about my daily business as usual.

Nancy ordered room service and when it arrived I saw a greyish substance emanate from the food. I waved my hand over the plate as instructed by the intelligences, and the matter that surrounded the food was transmuted. They told me to ask Nancy to bless all my food and drink beforehand to purify its vibrations, which she willingly did.

I finally had to leave for the sound check. I drove to the gig with my manager and tour manager. They seemed to notice something 'different', but neither of them said anything. I looked at the tour manager and thought how strange he seemed. It was as if he was only partly there, as if he was an actor in a play showing only a part of himself. As we drove up to the Coliseum, one of them said, 'Wow, it looks like a giant crown.' The other said, 'No, it looks more like an enormous cake.' I interjected by saying that I thought it looked more like a giant spacecraft. We all laughed.

Once inside the arena I glanced again at our tour manager. One of the intelligences spoke: 'He carries "one" precious stone. One jewel is not enough to make a crown, but this stone is more precious than he knows. It is greater than the whole crown he seeks. The crown of power. The jewel he possesses is the gem of loyalty.' They were telling me I should be looking for certain qualities in people, that everyone has something in them – like a gem – which has spiritual value. I felt really warm inside and went over to him, placed my hand on his shoulder, and asked him if he was all right.

I noticed that the intelligences were also sifting and gathering information about my surroundings and the people in it. Every time I looked at my colleagues I seemed to be able to see right through them, to see their motives and their inner feelings. Having access to certain knowledge in a way is a burden, because by karmic law we can only express certain kinds of knowledge or truth to others that they are 'allowed' to know. It is a difficult concept to get across. Karmic law is a cosmic law that binds us to a set of predestined conditions, conditions that have been inherited from our past, created by our use of free will. The sum total of all previous thought and action reacts upon us in this life, and how we deal with it affects future conditions in a similar way. These forces act and react upon us at various levels: personal, group, national, racial, and global. Certain kinds of 'knowledge' can only be 'known', not 'taught' or shown by another. We can push each other along in this direction or that, help each other this way and that, but we cannot 'know' for somebody else. That is why the language of symbols and dreams is so important to us.

I believe that things like astrology are just as important as the more physical sciences such as astronomy, if not more so. Like the tarot, the symbolic language helps us to develop our intuitive knowledge of things. It is like working out, flexing and expanding our psychic muscles. 'They' explained to me that before we can travel to the stars we have to 'get our own back yard in order first. People are our first priority.'

The intelligences also told me that certain spacecraft periodically orbit earth, and that they contain crystal computers that house information down to the minutest detail regarding all the thoughts and actions of every single person living or who has ever lived on earth. A complete karmic profile, like a karmic photofit, the ability to see all conditions that contribute to a person's make-up. What he or she really 'is'. All events that brought a particular soul to a specific point in time, all that has been experienced to date. Details of how and why these forces have shaped and formed character. This staggered me. I tried to make a pathetic joke. 'I guess I had better be careful what I say in the future, hadn't I?'

'It's a pity you were not so careful in the past,' they answered. They showed me many revelations about myself and where I had been and what I had done in various past lives, information which is too personal to go into here. Except to say that certain aspects of what I was shown were very painful indeed.

As the sound check started I looked over at my brother. God, I thought, how could two people be so different and still be brothers? The music picked up momentum and I felt alive, exhilarated. I felt so at home on that stage. 'They' showed me how music can be a potent vehicle for producing spiritual effects on the physical realm. Yes, even rock music. Probably more so. It was as if the vibrations, the harshness of the sound, the clanging guitars and banging drums were shaking up and breaking down layers of dark psychic mire that had built up in the ethers.

After the sound check I walked towards the exit, full of emotion, and out of the corner of my eye noticed Ray entering a dressing-room. He looked lonely and sad, with that crooked smile just like when he was a boy. We were just two scruffy, clumsy kids with nothing in common other than our love for one another and our music. I wanted to cry. I always felt like Ray's older brother. He always seemed so fragile, so sensitive.

As he disappeared through the doorway I left the building and went back to the hotel. A wonderful fragrance enveloped me. A fragrance that touched my soul. I closed my eyes. 'They' showed me a vivid picture of my brother. He was standing still in front of me. His body was like the trunk of a large and thick rose bush. Growing out from the main body of it were branches that reached in all different directions. At the ends of the branches were hundreds of different kinds of flowers. The perfume was lovely, rich. It was a very elevating feeling. As I drew closer to the bush my feelings became scratched and torn on the many thorns. I became extremely upset.

When the car reached the hotel I ran up to my room, grabbed hold of Nancy, and cried. 'That bastard,' I said, 'he's used me all his life, taken advantage of me, hurt me.' All of a sudden it seemed to me as if I had spent most of my life trying to help him nurture and protect those beautiful flowers. Through my tears and anguish and realization of this bittersweet karma, I could still smell those flowers. Their fragrance took away the anger and resentment I felt towards him. In that moment I forgave him everything.

I wrote a poem about that experience that I have never shown anyone before, not even my brother. Here is an excerpt from it:

I had a dream while the world took a sleep,
I saw people around me who roamed like sheep,
but not you. You were alone, apart. But so sad.
How can you not measure the beauty contained
within each thought, that crystallizes on your glad imagination.
Is it that the world has starved the child of his unborn secrets,
of your soul's true quest.

It is not strange of you to tell me that you wish only to
be a gardener.
For in my vision when I looked at you, I saw only flowers.
In the same vision, rhymes became memories, music reason.
My sight became true.
Each loving caring thought you have created in the magical web of
music has become an everlasting flower
That lives in the real yet hidden world.
Flowers in a garden that will stand forever
in proud and eternal beauty.
For those who care to see, to come and see.
In the midst of this picture I saw the loveliest of all flowers.
Belief. Its petals so tender, but stalk so strong.
Its fragrance passed through me so freely
that neither of us even knew.

Later that first night, at the show, I could see in the surrounding
ethers mischievous demon-like creatures impinging themselves
on the auric bodies of the unsuspecting crowd, impressing them
with negative images and thoughts. Confronted by this bad
energy, the intelligences poured a brilliant beam of white light
through my forehead and out to the crowd. The results were
startling. The same people suddenly looked more pleasant. The
negative energies had vanished.

Every time I would see one or more of those weird forms I
would do a mental practice and project light and they would
become transmuted or diffuse into the ethers. God, I thought to
myself, this is like *Star Wars* meets *Poltergeist*. But it was very real.

During the show I felt this amazing upsurge of energy within
me. Light beams pulsated in through the top of my head and
projected out towards the audience. This light travelled at great
speed, hit the back wall of the auditorium and circumnavigated
its way around the entire crowd. All of a sudden it felt as if
everyone in the building was part of a family. I was overcome
with an incredible feeling of unity. It was ecstasy. Throughout
the show the intelligences demonstrated to me other forms of
psychic phenomena.

After the show everyone was full of excitement. There was a
tension, an energy in the air that I have never felt at a show
before. Soon Nancy and I went back to the hotel to relax. As I

entered the room I felt a thud in my heart like a deep drum. My mind was suddenly swamped in a terrible sadness. I fell to my knees.

Nancy came to my aid. My soul and my whole being were drawn towards the man Jesus. In a gasp of breath I suddenly understood what he was and what he did. It hit me like a sledgehammer. I cried aloud, 'Those bastards, those bastards, look what they've done to our children.' I was overwhelmed by an incredible force that seemed to rush through the very pores of my skin. I closed my eyes and then opened my arms. In my mind I felt as if I was reaching out to embrace the whole planet. I deeply sensed how as a race we have been manipulated, mistreated and abused as if dragged from one civilization to the next like slaves, tricked by horrific forces. We are referred to as children by these intelligences. They see us like stumbling children, limping from one life to the next, lost to our own devices.

The intelligences showed me the images of terrible suffering in the world. I was overwhelmed, completely awestruck. They were manipulating forces in my body to bring about these astonishing visual and mystical effects. They told me that it was man's purpose on earth to awaken and control these forces.

This energy that these beings had somehow stirred within me transformed my consciousness into a state of spiritual expansion where I seemed to touch a universal consciousness. I experienced a tremendous surge of emotion inside, an intensity that realized profound feelings of universal love and compassion for all life, for all mankind on this sad little planet of ours. My body shuddered as if I were being shaken by a large invisible hand. An incredible energy forced itself into my throat centre, making me reel.

I became acutely aware of the presence of Jesus. I became completely overshadowed by Christ's power. I was given glimpses into the unique magic behind Jesus's mission to earth and I was shown many things about the man and the truths contained within his simple teachings. I felt profoundly ashamed and embarrassed that I should be shown these things when there was so much in my life, in my character, that was lacking. I had so much anger, so many weaknesses. Yet I was embraced by an inexplicable flood of love and joy.

The Master Jesus, I believe, was and is a great magician, a

manipulator of great forces, the nature of which we are only now beginning to understand. Of all the spiritual masters who have been on earth, none was more misunderstood, I feel, than the Master Jesus. He was a being of great knowledge, power, and influence.

There is so much we do not understand about our planet, about ourselves and each other. 'This is now changing,' I was told. 'All that was previously held secret will now be revealed.' They impressed upon me that there would come a time when we would all have to come face to face with this Christ 'force' and with what it is and what he, Jesus, did. They told me that Christ consciousness had descended many times to earth, through Krishna, Buddha, and other great masters and prophets. In modern times this impulse has influenced wonderful teachers such as Gandhi, Yogananda, Vivikeneda, Ramakrishna and many others, some of whom have chosen to work in secret.

Jesus said, 'I am the way, the truth and the life; none shall come to the father save by me.' In this I believe he meant that the awakening and control of the phenomenal force of Kundalini is the only way back to the Godhead. At least for 'us'. In the spiritual process of Jesus we find the essentials of the ancient yogas. The Upanishads, the teachings of the *Bhagavadgita*, Taoism and Buddhism. 'I am the way' – the 'I' being the enlightened soul touched by supreme consciousness, the 'way' is the method of awakening this latent force, Kundalini, demonstrated by 'his' example. The 'truth' is the revelation brought about by the rise of this force. And the 'life' is the soul transformed. Living the complete spiritual life. 'None shall come unto the father save by me' indicates that the only way back to the Father or Supreme consciousness/Godhead is by the understanding and activation of this divine force, Kundalini. When aroused, this latent force opens up such a vast area of consciousness that it is impossible to grasp by intellectual means alone.

The intellectual process is part of the conscious mind and the conscious mind is only a part of total consciousness. It is when we get outside the control of the intellect that we can make strides towards real spiritual knowledge and progress. Somehow we need to control 'it' and not have 'it' control us. The intellect is all wrapped up in the 'little man' that is represented in

the symbolic figure of Shiva dancing. This is a graphic illustra-
tion, as Gopi Krishna explains, 'of the amazing transformation
brought about by the arousal of Kundalini – Serpent Power.
Shiva's arms pull and extract subtle etheric nectar from the cells
and tissues of the organic frame in Kundalini's ascent. Trampled
underfoot in Shiva's cosmic dance of spiritual emancipation is
depicted the diminutive figure of the man of little understanding. The lower self, who being deceived by the ego, thinks
too highly of his own narrow self and in this way denies himself
the mighty vision of his own immortal nature.' The power of
Kundalini ascends to the Brahma chakra (an etheric centre at the
top of the head) and finds union with the Father or Supreme
consciousness. It is in this super-vitalized state that the Holy
Spirit is manifest. The eye of Shiva opens (often referred to as the
all-seeing eye, the third eye, the eye of Horus). The soul becomes
fully active on the etheric plane. The 'eye' directs and controls
etheric energy and becomes an instrument of Pure Spirit of
supreme will and the sign of the White Magician.

A representation of Shiva dancing. Photo: Davies

According to Eastern mysticism and certain Western occult traditions it is believed that this force, Kundalini or Serpent Power, is latent within all people. It resides at the base of the spine in the subtle body or aura and is normally in a dormant state. When activated it has a profound effect on the subtle nervous system. It rises through the chakras, or energy vortices, in the aura that are situated in the sex centre, the solar plexus, the heart centre, the throat, the forehead (called the Christ centre) and finally at the top of the head, traditionally referred to as the Brahma chakra. When awakened in part it can bring about great inspirations, ideas, heightened awareness and knowledge. In certain individuals it can produce greatly inspired writings, poetry, music, expressions in art of all kinds. Its subtle activity has surely stimulated the minds of great philosophers and teachers throughout the ages, unbeknown to them. Many I am sure stumbled on to this power quite by accident. Imagine the awful confusion experienced by such a great artist as Van Gogh, who I am convinced innocently stumbled upon aspects of this force and was sadly so ill-equipped to deal with its incredible unyielding fire, being thrown into alternating states of intense euphoria and deep despair which resulted in dreadful depressions that took him to the brink of madness and eventual suicide.

When this force is fully aroused and understood, it can bring about phenomenal changes in consciousness, resulting in stunning psychic, mental, and spiritual revelations, producing outstanding attributes within the individual. It is believed that the mystery and power of this force lies at the root of all religious and spiritual thought on this planet, that awakening and controlling the force of Kundalini is the only way back to the Godhead.

There are many ways to bring about its awakening, some of which can be dangerous. Some require rigorous yogic disciplines. But each must find his or her own path to enlightenment. For me, the study and practice of Buddhism is a perfect and safe path. It is a wonderful concept for living in the modern world. The studies and disciplines of karma yoga, kriya yoga bhakti, jnana, and indeed all the yogas, in particular, raja yoga, are positive and scientific ways to realization, I feel. But in the end it is the 'getting there' that is more important than 'how' we get there.

Understanding and awakening this amazing force and learning how it works is, I believe, the way to the truth and the life. I don't understand why knowledge of this energy still remains a mystery. Perhaps people are just not interested. Or perhaps information is deliberately being concealed from us, particularly when dealing with an energy that is also potentially very dangerous. Like everything, there is always a dark side of which we must be aware and extremely cautious.

The influence of Kundalini is and has always been active in the world and is intrinsically linked to the earth itself. It is my view that the origin of all the spiritual teachings on earth, whatever they are and from wherever they have come, was inspired by this strange mystical force. I believe the whole mystical and spiritual experience is related to and wrapped up in this force.

The effects of Kundalini allow us the ability to see and understand more fully the workings of the etheric world: how it functions, how we can 'use' its energy, how we can do something about the world from the inside out.

In order to understand more of what Jesus did and how the power of Christ operates, we need to find out more about the etheric plane and its magnetic and magical properties. I talk about Christ not Christianity. In my opinion there is a universe of difference. The awakening of the Christ within is a personally transforming experience and has little to do with manmade religions. Modern Christianity has been remodelled by man to suit his own ends. While dishing out half-truths here and a little bit there we are discovering that this doctrine and others like it have become mere instruments of control in the world. The church that was supposedly built on 'rock' was relocated without us knowing about it and placed on 'sand'. For example they had removed the all-important concept of karma and reincarnation.

Yet Jesus spoke openly about karma when he said, 'Cast your bread upon the waters so that it may be returned to you,' and 'As you sow, so shall you reap'. The Lord Buddha also stated, 'Action and reaction are opposite and equal.' All this hell and damnation stuff is the weapon of tyrants, of jealous, bitter and miserable old men trying desperately to hang on to power at all costs. The Christ impulse postulates total freedom in the spiritual life.

Christians talk about Jesus being the only Son of God, but I think that we are all potential sons and daughters of God, that we all have 'Christ' potential within us. I believe we are all spiritual beings, whether we know we are or not. My mother was a very practical yet a very spiritual person. She had what I call 'spiritual common sense', yet she believed neither in God nor in religion.

We are all so busy believing in the evil in people that we forget to look for the 'gems' of goodness that are there also. The world is full of 'magic' and we are all magicians asserting our craft, our influence upon it and everyone in it, be it however slight or however great. Our free will gives us the privilege of choice. It is up to us individually to decide what part we want to play, what kind of action we wish to take, if any. I firmly believe we can change the world by changing the way we think about the world. There is a vast storehouse of energy sitting out there – in here! – waiting for us to tap into it. A world of energy with which we are already interacting whether we like it or not. In spite of all the pain and confusion in the world I believe that now in the nineties there are more opportunities to create real change than at any other time in our recent history. I feel we must take charge of these opportunities in every way.

We are being helped by these intelligences, who prompt us along whenever they can, but there is only so much they can do. At the end of the day we really do have to help ourselves, we have enough resources and knowledge at our fingertips to do something about world conditions. We just need to get our priorities in order. The dreadful fanaticism that exists in the world of finance is so awful, so destructive to our spiritual well-being, that something must be done or this trance-like quest for greed will drag us all down into a bottomless pit. The longer it goes on, the harder it will be for us to get back. Religious fanaticism is just as damaging to the soul and to the prospects of any real spiritual salvation. We have to stand on our own two feet and somehow work it out together, using everything at our disposal. It is time to stop blaming God for everything. We must take the onus off God and place it firmly and squarely on our own shoulders.

What could be a greater insult to God than to kill another human being in his name? That is not spirituality, it is tyranny and murder. To harm another human being in the name of God is the Devil's work. Fanaticism is a product of man's fear, not of

God's wrath. It would be better for God not to exist at all.

The days that followed were full of lessons and meaning for me. My telepathic contact with these beings lasted some six days. After the intelligences left I temporarily lapsed into a deep depression. The tour was nearly over, fortunately, and I could look forward to a few days of recuperation. God, did I need it. I tried to tell Ray about my experience but the barrier immediately came down. Curiously though, just before going on stage in Charlotte, North Carolina, the following night of the tour, Ray came up to me and said, 'Dave, whatever you did last night do it tonight.'

Soon I met a gentleman who helped me to understand the nature and meaning of my 'telepathic' contact, my awakening, Sir George King. A man of exemplary character who possesses great knowledge, he is a mystic, a medium, a master among men who has written many books on metaphysics. One in particular that had a tremendous impact on me was *The Nine Freedoms*, published by the Aetherius Society. He explained much to me about my experience and about the intelligences involved. It was an experience that truly changed me in every way and one that I will never forget.

I'd like to leave these borrowed words that may be of help to the reader:

The etheric or energy body of every human being is an integral part of the planet itself and consequently the solar system. Through this medium every human being is basically related to every other expression of the Divine Life, minute or great. The function of the etheric body is to receive energy impulses and to be swept into activity by these impulses or streams of force, emanating from some originating source or other. The Etheric Body is naught but energy, held in relation to the emotional and mental bodies and to the soul by their coordinating effect. These streams of energy, in their turn, have an effect on the physical body and swing it into activity of some kind or another, according to the nature and power of whatever type of energy may be dominating the etheric body at any particular time. (*Telepathy and the Etheric Vehicle* by Alice Bailey, Lucis Publishing Company, New York, p.2)

The Hindus teach that the Human Soul is a portion of an immutable principle, the Soul of the World. The Anima Mundi, the all pervading Ether (Akasa) of space. This ether is simply the conductor of certain types of energy and serves as the inter-relating medium between 'essential' spirit and tangible matter. Pythagoras, who did so much in his day to link the Eastern and Western philosophies, gave this same teaching. (*The Light of the Soul* by Alice Bailey, Lucis Publishing Company, New York, p.75)

The mystical life is the centre of all that I do and all that I think and all that I write. It holds to my worth the same relation that the philosophy of Godwin holds to the work of Shelley and I have always considered myself a voice of what I believe to be a greater renaissance – the revolt of the soul against the intellect – now beginning in the world. (William Butler Yeats, from *Yeats: The Man and the Mask* by Richard Ellman, W. W. Norton & Company, New York)

We toured Australia and Japan in February of 1982. I thoroughly enjoyed playing Japan. They're very respectful of artists and treat you really well, even if the occasional interviewer tries his best to dissect your brain. When we got back to England in April I started plans for recording my third solo album. Most of the songs were inspired by my experiences in early January.

We returned briefly to the States in August to play a few selected shows. One of them was the US Festival. It was a phenomenal event; there must have been between 150,000 and 200,000 people there. Before the show we crossed swords with Bill Graham, who was promoting the event. Bill had in the past always been pretty good to us, but this time there were some terrible vibes floating around. (That reminds me again of *Phantom of the Paradise* and my favourite character, 'Beef', the campy glam rock star. Beef is waiting anxiously backstage, twittering to go on, when he says in a very affected voice, 'Hey, baby, the karma in here is so bad, you can almost cut it with a knife.' Great film!)

The US Festival was being held that year in Glen Helen regional park, San Bernardino, California. We wanted to play the dusk spot. We thought that it had already been agreed upon but evidently not, according to Graham. It was the prime spot, going on stage just as the sun was setting so that we could take full advantage of the lighting rig. But Graham insisted otherwise and wanted us on much earlier. I don't know why, except that perhaps he was being pressured by other acts on the bill, such as Tom Petty or Pat Benatar.

But we just took our time getting changed, wasting as much time as possible, knowing full well what we were doing. Graham was going insane, shouting and screaming, he was really losing it. We stood our ground throughout the mayhem, and in spite of Bill's screams, threats and ranting we mounted the stage just at the crucial time. The sun had just set.

It was a fantastic show, one of the best, and although Bill and I came close to exchanging blows, it turned out fine. After our final encore, Bill was really apologetic. He knew what a great show it had been.

I started to think that maybe the Kinks were invincible. I will never forget that day as long as I live. It was one of those shows when everything just went so right.

Soon we were back in England and I began mixing my album for Warner's, which I now named *Chosen People*. While I had been in the States earlier I had come across a book written by a Native American Indian called Black Elk. It was the story of his life and told of the ways of his people, the Lakota. I became immersed in his story, and it had a profound effect on me. In his tribe's philosophy it was written that they would one day meet a great white brother who would show them the ways of a new and different world. The great white prophet would join hands with the Indian and together they would walk towards the future, sharing each other's knowledge, eventually reaching the promised land. Well, it didn't work out that way, did it? The white man, apart from virtually annihilating an ancient race of people, also tragically destroyed a crucial psychological link they had with their 'magic'. With the spiritual side of life.

Chosen People was inspired by Black Elk.

Warriors all are we, Worship the Sun, Great Spirit . . .
Born of the Mother Earth . . . Seek for the true white brother.
We are the chosen people, give back our sacred land, we are
the four grandfathers, a destiny for man.

It is written in our prophecy that we shall find the true white brother and we will join together to help build humanity . . . There is a place for everyone . . . We are the chosen people, give back our holy land . . . we are the air, the forest, we are Great Spirit's hand . . .

The song 'Freedom Lies' is very close to my heart. We are brought up to believe that we live in a free country, yet certain ways of thinking are still very much taboo. Freedom lies. You are allowed to say what you think as long as it falls in line with 'normal acceptable social parameters and modes of thinking'. It is a paradox.

'Take One More Chance' is a song about love, personal on one level yet at the same time a plea to the people of the world to make one last concerted effort to change in order to bring about harmony. The girl represents scepticism and fear of change. The singer tries to seduce the girl on the dance floor, pleading with her to dance with him. To take one more chance, for this is the last dance. 'What have you got to lose?'

I always loved Jo Stafford's voice from the late forties/fifties, especially when she sang 'No Other Love', which is a rip-off of Chopin's Étude in E. It is such a delicious melody; it always drives me crazy. I wanted 'Take One More Chance' to sound like the sort of song a crooner would sing but with a rock back-beat. I would have loved someone like Tony Bennett to have recorded it.

'True Story' is about my telepathic contact. After I sat down and listened to the record, I thought, yeah, great, now everyone and his brother is going to think I've lost it for sure. But it didn't matter, really, and besides, what could I do, pretend it didn't happen?

On the lighter side, I remember that Zappa recording: 'I'm the slime oozing out of your TV set.' I'm a great fan of fifties and sixties sci-fi – *Outer Limits, Star Trek.* I am positive that Gene Roddenberry was influenced by these 'beings'. A couple of years back I was invited to attend a Kinks Convention in London. I mingled with the crowd and after a while I was pleasantly surprised to find that most of these Kinks fans were also Trekkies. I don't think I'll bother trying to draw any conclusions from this, but I learned, too, that William Shatner is a big Kinks fan, as is Leonard Nimoy. I remember once in 1978 Leonard Nimoy got up on stage in Milwaukee and introduced the band. It was a wonderful moment, one of my greatest thrills. The audience was stunned.

I also loved the Coneheads. Ray and I were invited by the *Saturday Night Live* crowd to participate in the very first Coneheads sketch. At the time our management thought it was bad for our image. Shit, I'm so pissed that we didn't do it. It falls under the heading of 'my greatest regrets' list, along with never meeting Elvis Presley face to face even though I watched him perform at the Forum in LA with the Supremes as back-up band (of course my seat was so far back it could have been Weird Al for all I knew); never hearing Ray Charles sing 'Ducks on the Wall' (maybe that could still happen); never meeting Eddie Cochran; never sleeping with Natalie Wood and Gene Tierney, two of the most beautiful women that ever lived; never meeting Orson Welles, and the list goes on.

During a rehearsal at Konk, Ray came up with a quirky little idea for a song that eventually became 'Come Dancing'. We recorded it in a few days and within a month started shooting the video, with Julien Temple directing. Julien was such a posey sod, walking around in a fur coat like he was Orson Welles, even though he was only doing a promo video. You can see where they got the inspiration for the Patrick Church character in the Comic Strip's TV movie *The Yob*. 'Yeah, it's gonna cost 75 grand, but we're gonna make it look cheap.' Classic. It always brings a smile to my face. I love Keith Allen. He is such an under-rated actor.

Watching the 'Come Dancing' video also makes me smile. Ray looks so much like my mum's brother Uncle Frank it's uncanny. Frank was a real Jack the Lad, always up to some mischief or the other. He spoke with a very broad cockney accent. He told great stories and was loud and lively, funny and rude, yet sentimental and caring. What a wonderful character. In family circles it is said that Ray looks like my mother's side of the family and I look more like my father's. Well, I don't know; some people even think that Ray and I look alike, would you believe!

We planned a UK tour around the release of the 'Come Dancing' single, but the record didn't chart. I thought the record was great fun; it harked back to our youth when our sisters went to the Palais every Saturday night to dance. But the same old story was emerging. Whereas in the States we could get virtual blanket air-play, in our home country we couldn't persuade the poor old BBC to play it. Lost in a mire of short-sighted and fickle programming policy whatever we did, we just couldn't get it on the air, the boring bastards. But luckily the last laugh would be on us. The record became a hit on re-release in 1983.

By the end of 1982 I was excited about the prospects of working with Warner's on my next solo album, and the Kinks were working full steam ahead on songs that would make up our next album for Arista, *State of Confusion*. While '82 had been one of the most extraordinary years of my life, '83, in spite of having our first top five hit in Britain in years, became one of the most disappointing, disillusioning and confusing for me personally.

228

16

Early in 1983 we finished recording and mixing *Confusion*, which was to be a summer release. *Chosen People* had been scheduled for release around September. I made plans to do a promotional tour for it directly after the Kinks tour of the States was completed.

'Come Dancing' was the lead cut from *Confusion* and was a hit in the States. 'Heart of Gold' was a lovely song. I believe Ray wrote it about Princess Anne.

Prior to the recording of *State of Confusion* Ray invited me to his house to go over arrangements and help him sort out some of the songs. I helped arrange songs like 'Don't Forget to Dance', 'Bernardette', 'Property' (a song probably about his problems relating to his divorce from Yvonne), and 'Clichés of the World', which I particularly liked. Knowing how Ray had been reluctant in the past to give me credit for my creative input, I tried to make sure that I would do better this time. I discussed it with Elliot beforehand, and he promised me that he would get it straight with Ray. He agreed with me that it was only right and fair that I should receive some credit other than just that of performer. I was really worried that Ray would go back on his word. Elliot promised he would also talk to Arista about it.

When the liner notes were finally finished there was no mention of my name as either co-producer, co-writer or arranger, nothing. I couldn't believe it. I was flabbergasted. I called Elliot and went ape-shit over the phone.

He told me he couldn't believe it either, since he had spoken to Arista personally and dictated the label credit and liner notes to them directly. I contacted Arista, but the wheels had already been set in motion and there was nothing I could do. I found out that Ray had called their offices the night before the liner notes were to be printed and changed them. What a fucking arsehole.

He'd done it again. After all these years, after all we'd been through, Ray was still using me. Sometimes it seems it just never ends.

Elliot tried his best to pacify me and convinced me to do the *State of Confusion* tour in spite of much protest on my part. Cancelling would have been tantamount to cutting off my nose to spite my face. He assured me that this would never happen again. Yeah, right. Elliot was well-meaning, but Ray is such a manipulative sod that he will stop at nothing to get what he wants. Fuck it, I thought, what a fool I am. I fall for it every time.

Recently I bumped into someone who had met Ray for the first time. 'He's so interesting, so sensitive, charming and delightful,' she said.

'Darling, he is, but he is also a self-centred, manipulative, ruthless jerk.'

She laughed and said, 'No, I can't believe it.'

I continued. 'Well, be thankful that you don't have to work with him, and be thankful that you don't love him. Because he'll use you.'

'God, Dave, you sound really bitter.'

'Yeah,' I replied, 'I'm not really, just saddened. All my life I've helped him, supported him emotionally, musically and have given him so much for so little in return, and I am still not free of him. He is financially secure, yet I still have to work to pay my way. Always struggling. Yeah, I suppose I'm a little bitter. But what the hell does it matter in the end? It's the work that will outlast all of us. Work and love, that's all there is.'

State of Confusion did pretty well for us. In August 'Come Dancing' was re-released in the UK and became a top five hit. The BBC finally started to play it because it was a hit in America: how curious. Jonathan King hosted a TV show in England at that time, and would play hits from the US charts. If it's on the telly, then it must be good. Thanks, Jonathan.

I struggled with Warner's to get some money to pay for a promo video for my album but had no luck, so I took the plunge and financed it myself. I shot it in London one afternoon during breaks in the Kinks' rehearsals for *Top of the Pops*. The track was 'Mean Disposition'. It is a song about a man who starts off his life with great ideals and ambitions but sees his dreams slowly dissolve as he grows older. In the end it leaves him embittered

230

and cruel; we must never allow the world to steal our dreams. The video is a slapstick piece. It depicts a bully who goes through life throwing his weight around and who finally gets his comeuppance when a kid drops a pot of paint on his head, humiliating him. The video actually turned out OK.

At the beginning of September I went back to Los Angeles to start my promo tour for *People*. I hired a friend of mine who worked in marketing and promotion, Shelly Heber, to help give the album a push. The initial meeting with the people at Warner's seemed OK so I started doing press and radio stuff.

Back in England Ray had started work on his *Return to Waterloo* project. I didn't feel that it was something I could really get my teeth into, so I suggested to Ray that he record it using the other band members. But there was one song on it, 'Sold Me Out', which I loved. We eventually ended up recording it for our last Arista album, *Word of Mouth*.

Back in LA I was having a difficult time with a number of interviewers. People seemed strangely wary of me, uncomfortable. I thought, what the hell's going on? Just because I was talking about metaphysics and spiritual matters in general, people made me feel like I had some highly contagious disease. During one interview, when I started talking about extra-terrestrials and stuff, the engineer walked out. The guy was actually shaking with fear, he couldn't handle it. He left muttering nervously under his breath about having to take his dog to the vet, or something. It was pathetic. I laughed in disbelief. What the fuck was the matter with these people?

I felt like a bloody alien myself. The record was doing badly and I was confused. Shelly then heard that the deal I had with Warner's may have been just a tax write-off for them. An 'out of the box failure', as she called it. I believe that Elliot must have asked favours of friends he had there to try to appease me, as he knew how much I wanted to make the record. Shelly was just as upset as I was. But in spite of my determination the album virtually never saw the light of day. Why do record companies do such shit? Elliot of course denied that this was the case. But I felt he let me down. I really liked Elliot, but to be fair he was by this time already firmly in Ray's pocket and knew on which side his bread was buttered.

What the hell was going on with everyone? Every time I

231

mentioned aliens, telepathy, spirituality, a huge portcullis came crashing down in front of me. Nobody wanted to know. After an interview with a newspaper I overheard the reporter talking to her editor on the phone when she thought I wasn't listening. 'Yeah, it's going fine,' she said. 'God, he's really out there . . .' I thought, what does she mean? I've never felt saner in my whole life. I felt that Warner's had fucked me over and the media thought I was crazy. Perfect. I was dumbfounded. Every time I talked to anyone about you know those um, things . . . well . . . ah . . . I felt like a fucking Klingon and I was so angry that I probably looked like one as well.

Shelly also told me that the Warner's people didn't like the title *Chosen People*. 'Ooh, he's not one of those, is he?' someone at their office asked. One of what? A Jew? A Martian? A Mexican? What, for Chrissake? However, I persisted in trying to get the album off the ground. I flew to New York and completed my press stuff. During one interview I was taken into a basement and virtually interrogated by these weird guys. They looked like FBI to me. 'Were you abducted?' they asked. 'Did they operate on your brain? Did they examine your sex organs, do you have any implants?' I wanted to implant my fist in their faces for asking all that shit. I told them that when I was a boy I often had vivid dreams of strange little green men that would come in the night and stick these weird tubes in my arms. I was so terrified that I didn't tell anyone, not even my mother. They just lapped it up. It was great.

What in God's name was the matter with everyone? One day during an interview I clumsily blurted out in my frustration that it was ridiculous that thousands and thousands of people believed without question the doctrine of some weird guy in a white robe who lived thousands of years ago and who talked to a burning bush, yet everyone thought I might be crazy. I was unhappy, but shouting at people wasn't the answer. I was disillusioned and hurt. I needed a new strategy. I was becoming a little too belligerent.

There was a cut called 'Love Gets You', which was released as a single from *Chosen People*. They wouldn't play it on top 40 radio because they didn't like the way I sang the words, 'D'you wannit . . . Love gets you anyway, D'you wannit, any way it can.' They thought it was too suggestive, as in 'D'you wannit

darlin'? Know what I mean, nudge, nudge . . . wink, wink . . .'
Stupid. Stupid, you earthlings are all so stupid. Help me,
somebody, please.

I went back to England to lick my wounds and ponder what
had gone wrong. Ray was well into his film and another Kinks
tour of the States was looming. I felt hurt and totally let down.
Against my better judgement I cancelled the whole tour. Ray and
Elliot were in an uproar. It was an important tour and on
reflection I should have mustered up the strength to do it. I don't
know. I was confused and felt totally disillusioned. I didn't think
anybody cared or understood what was going on inside me,
except for Nancy, of course.

Articles from New York newspapers made their way to the
office. KINKS CANCEL NATIONWIDE TOUR. DAVE DAVIES
COMMITTED TO INSANE ASYLUM. Stuff like that. Fans were
calling the studio asking for the hospital address so they could
send me cards! Life is so weird. Back in the seventies when I
thought I was really losing my mind, nobody seemed to give a
shit. Now, when I felt that I had truly found myself and my path
in life, everybody was saying that I was mad.

I met a guy in London named Richard Lawrence, a leading
psychic practitioner and a researcher and author. Over the
years we have become great friends. He instantly understood a
great deal of what I was going through and was helpful and
supportive to me. Let people think what they want, I knew I
wasn't going crazy. I was going sane. Saner than I had ever
been.

By December the Kinks finally regrouped and we did some
shows in the New York and Massachusetts area. We played the
Roseland Ballroom on New Year's Eve in NY. It was a wonderful
evening and just what we needed. Cyndi Lauper opened the
show for us. I really liked her, she had a good sense of humour
and was really funny. During the show she squawked at the
monitor guy, saying, 'What are you doing with my voice, it
sounds really squeaky.' Some guy shouted back from the
audience in typical New York fashion, 'Hey, babe, it's not the
equipment, it's your voice.'

Fortunately for her, she went on to do great things. But she had
a difficult time that night. Kinks audiences in those days could be
a little hostile to support acts. But she did well. In the end, we all

had a great time, but from my point of view 1983 was more like out with the new and in with the old.

'Don't Forget to Dance' was the follow-up single to 'Come Dancing' and it did reasonably well in England and the States. I always felt that the song was, in a way, Ray's ode of love to Chrissie. In January of 1984 we went back to America to make good some dates that had previously been cancelled. In between touring Ray was editing and putting the final touches to his film *Return to Waterloo*. Even though I didn't want anything to do with it, I watched the rough cut and really liked it. Ray does have an incredible depth of talent that I feel we've only seen a part of. As he grows older his work will continue to surprise us.

Ray and Chrissie were going through some 'domestic strife', to put it mildly. Later that year, Chrissie, on tour in America with the Pretenders, out of the blue married Jim Kerr from Simple Minds. Ray was devastated. But I think for Chrissie it was the only way out. All just a part of life's rich tapestry . . .

I always felt that if he'd been less emotionally distracted, the film would have turned out even better. During the US 'make up' tours, Mick and I were really bumping heads. There was always one problem or another. I felt his playing was getting sloppy, his manner too nonchalant. I was also becoming more and more frustrated with him as a person. Mick could be a lot of fun on the road but I was starting to tire of his attitude. He was always acting like a buffoon. He was becoming particularly abrasive, even arrogant. I still don't really know what was going on in his mind at the time. Maybe it was me. Maybe we had just become two totally different people who had simply grown apart.

After one show Mick lost it and in a fit of temper he went for me. Luckily there were people around who intervened to prevent a fully-fledged punch-up. I remember looking over at Mick after the outburst and thinking to myself, 'That's it, Mick, it's over.'

I had worked really well with Bob Henrit on my solo stuff and thought that his playing might give us the added kick and tightness that I felt had been missing for a while. Ray and Mick were very close and Ray was a little surprised by my suggestion to try Henrit out on a few sessions. I love Mick, he has always been like a brother to me, but sometimes even brothers can be thoughtless, insensitive, difficult to work with. Mick, more than anyone else, understood the situation between me and Ray. He always seemed sympathetic to my side of the story, but when things got a little rough he always ended up playing on Ray's team. Some time after he left we became good friends again. That made me happy.

We still owed one more album to Arista and Elliot began talks with Clive with the idea of renegotiating a new contract with them. Neither party wanted to terminate the relationship, as things were going pretty well, but Elliot intimated that maybe we could get a better deal with a bigger company. Within weeks there was an offer on the table from MCA's Richard Palmese. We had known Richard from our early Arista days, and Ray and Elliot liked him. Talks continued, but we still had to make an album to fulfil our Arista commitment.

Then, however, a touch of paranoia set in. If we left Arista in favour of an MCA deal, maybe they wouldn't work the album properly. Like a lover spurned, they might turn bitch and leave us in the lurch. But if the deal with MCA was right and the money good, this might be a move that could help further our careers.

What a mistake we made in choosing MCA. I don't know exactly what happened in the end, but I think Arista couldn't or didn't want to match MCA's deal so we went for the bigger offer. What's that saying? 'If it ain't broke, don't fix it'? I believe Ray thought at the time that Elliot fucked up the deal with Arista to the extent where it just couldn't be repaired. But I honestly think it was much simpler than that. Elliot thought we could make a killing.

In the end, after Elliot's departure, it would be MCA who would try to do the killing, with the Kinks the would-be victims. I remember one night on stage at the Universal Amphitheater towards the end of our tour to promote *Think Visual*, our first MCA album. Ray shouted into the microphone, 'MCA, you're gonna have to shoot us.'

The MCA years were a very difficult period for the Kinks. I am still bewildered by it all. In my opinion we made some of our best albums with MCA, a big company that was supposed to have every facility at its fingertips, the machinery to promote and market a product nationwide. Yet they could not sell records – Kinks records, at any rate. It just didn't make sense.

I should have guessed it the first time I met their head of

promotion. It was all I could do to get him to make eye contact. I immediately felt uncomfortable in their offices. There was something in the air, like the smell of fear. Weird. Maybe it was just the aftershave. I don't know for sure. At the meeting I looked anxiously around the room. I pulled down the blinds and reached nervously for a cigarette. In the back room I could hear disco music, Donna Summer I think. The sweat started to pour from my brow. I felt like a cat in a musk factory. God, I've got to get out of here. God, no, it was ABBA!

If I left without a word they'd know something was up. I had to stay cool. *It's OK, Dave, you'll be fine, I tried to reassure myself. I took a long hard pull on my cigarette. Dick entered the room. Dick Easy, they called him. 'Don't know why, there's no stars up in the sky, stormy weather,' came into my head. No, singing out loud will only make me look suspicious. 'There must be some way out of here said the joker to the priest.'*

If I don't make my move now, it will be too late, I'll never get out alive. It's either him or me. I pulled out a .45 and let him have it there and then. Straight between the eyes. As he lay there I kept thinking over and over those words my mama told me: 'Remember honey, life is like a box of chocolates, you never know what you're gonna get.' Shit, I gonna kill that silly bitch when I see her. There was something rotten in the state of Denmark and it wasn't the chocolate truffle.

Warner's had earlier delivered me a mere flesh wound. But now there were other forces at work that wanted our creative blood. The moral of this story is: find people that genuinely care about your work and don't be misled by the lure of the dollar. I suppose the truth of the matter was simply that certain people did not do their job when it mattered the most. In the beginning, I'm sure everyone's intention was to make a go of it, but they didn't understand how to promote a British rock 'n' roll act. It was an unfortunate episode for everybody.

During the recording of *Word of Mouth*, which sadly became our last album for Arista, Mick left the band and Bob replaced him. I wrote two songs that ended up on the album. One was called 'Guilty' and the other was 'Living on a Thin Line'. I wrote a bass riff that formed the foundation of the whole song. I thought that it would be great to write a song for Ray to sing. After pondering over the Kinks' up and down career and trying to make sense of it all, the phrase 'walking the tightrope' popped in my head. I laughed to myself and an image came to mind of Ray and me as jugglers on a tightrope under a big top. We were on opposite ends, walking towards each other. Every time one of us dropped a juggler's club we both had to start again. Funny, I thought, well at least I wasn't juggling with giant thorns.

I also started to think about how artful governments were, always sucking up to the rich and playing down the real problems. All those poor sods living on the breadline and nobody really giving a shit. I have always had an aversion to politicians in general, with some exceptions. Churchill, for instance, was an exceptionally gifted man; it is unusual to find such courage, artistic flair, cleverness and natural born wisdom all in the same body. And I have a fondness for Michael Foot, whom I sense to be a genuinely good man deep down. John Kennedy was a revolutionary, a figurehead for a generation that had never before been represented. And then there's Gandhi, a truly great man. Great Soul.

Thinking about me and Ray and people being on the breadline gave me the idea for 'Living on a Thin Line'. After I played Ray a demo of it I mentioned that I had written it for him to sing, but he didn't seem particularly interested, so I recorded it myself. It has become an extremely popular song with our fans over the years.

> All the stories have been told of Kings in days of old, but there's no England, now . . .
> All the wars that were won or lost somehow don't seem to matter very much any more . . .
> All the lies we were told . . .
> all the lives of the people running 'round, their castles are burned.
> Our eyes see change, but inside we're the same as we ever were . . .
> Living on a thin line . . . tell me now, what are we supposed to do . . .
> Living this way each day's a dream . . . tell me now what are we supposed to do . . .

'Do It Again' was a great track from that album. It was selected as the first single and we filmed the video in Brighton and on the London Underground. The shoot was great fun and I achieved a lifetime ambition of driving an underground Tube train. Well, for a few hundred yards at any rate. Ray insisted on Mick playing a small part in it. He and Ray played buskers on a platform. Mick got up, looked around, seemed fed up, then walked away. Ray shook his head as if to say, 'Ah, well,' and began strumming his guitar again. Ray, you sentimental bastard, you.

The second single was 'Summer's Gone'. Fine, a good track. But I was starting to wonder why 'Thin Line', which was getting all the air-play and showed up at number 4 on the FM radio charts, wasn't released as a single. I spoke to Elliot about it.

'Yeah, I'm ecstatic about the idea,' he said, and he pushed to get the cut out as a single. But then Elliot finally told me that there was a little problem. It seemed that Ray's deal with our music publisher, Carlin Music, stated that the first three singles off the album had to be written by Ray Davies. (Sorry, 'Davis'. For some reason, Ray likes to spell our name without the 'e'. I don't know why.) I don't know how much Ray got for the deal. But I was fuming. I just couldn't believe it. Elliot and I tried to persuade everyone, including Ray, to push for its release, but after the dust settled it was too late. Or that was what I was told. 'Thin Line''s momentum had waned by now and we had missed the window of opportunity for its release. What a load of bollocks. I was not only deprived of the possibility of a long-awaited hit as a writer, but the Kinks were deprived of a potential hit single.

We toured yet again in the States promoting *Word of Mouth* in 1985. Our new drummer, Bob, took a while to fit in. I started to feel more comfortable on stage again, but I was growing increasingly more disillusioned with Elliot. Maybe he didn't want to work with us any more. I don't know. After all that stuff with 'Thin Line', it had left a bad taste in my mouth. I started to feel that he was really only Ray's manager and not the Kinks'.

In June we turned down a ridiculous amount of money to play Sun City in South Africa. But to play would have been tantamount to supporting apartheid and it would have weighed heavily on my conscience. Definitely not on. After we cancelled, I found out that Cliff Richard and Queen played there and cleaned up. That's funny.

In July we toured for the last time with Elliot as our manager. We worked right through September, then returned to London. In November a premature announcement by MCA's publicity department bumped Arista out of the race to sign the Kinks. It was announced on MTV that the Kinks had signed with MCA when in fact we hadn't. Arista were pissed off and backed out.

But it wasn't long before we did sign with MCA. We now had no
US management, but prospects of a fruitful union with our new
record company looked promising, at least at the outset.

17

We signed the MCA contract in January of 1986 and started recording preliminary tracks for the forthcoming album. The MCA deal covered only the US and Canada, and in the UK we signed with London Records for the UK and the rest of the world. I had obtained my own lawyer, Michael Eaton of Eaton and Burley, who helped negotiate the new record deal.

Nancy was expecting our second child in late February and was having a difficult pregnancy. She had developed toxaemia and the doctors were becoming concerned.

Ray and I formed a new company, Kinks 85. I thought that now was a good time to resolve once and for all the ownership rights to the actual name 'The Kinks'. After some initial disagreement with Ray we finally came to a written agreement that the name was to be jointly owned by both of us and that the name 'The Kinks' could only be used with each other's consent.

Ray was having a miserable time after the break-up with Chrissie. We went into the studio to rehearse and throw ideas around nonetheless, but the vibe wasn't good. I went home thinking, 'Shit, we've hit another slump, now what?' We had a potentially great record deal and there didn't seem to be any enthusiasm for it. Ray was going through hell and couldn't write. He was staying in his country house in Surrey part of the time with his daughter and her boyfriend, and was having second thoughts about Mick, about Elliot, about MCA, about even the shirt he was wearing. Everything. I had seen Ray through some bad patches, but this time I just couldn't get close. I knew he was deeply hurt and upset, but I felt that he was lashing out at me as if in some way it was my fault. But in his pain he was probably just lashing out at everyone, at the world. I felt bad for him but there was nothing I could do.

I developed an obsessive desire to write screenplays. While at home in London I started work on two of them, one loosely based on my childhood. I had always been a tremendous movie fan and by this time I had made a number of friends in the Hollywood film community.

I also purchased a small cottage in Devon, realizing a lifetime dream. I had always adored the Devon countryside and felt that it would be an ideal place to write and maybe one day to live permanently. It was a quiet little place tucked away at the edge of National Trust woodland in a small valley not far from the sea. The house had a magical charm. It was a place where, apart from work, I could take my children. Where I could paint, meditate, listen to music, cook, and think.

Lana was born towards the end of February. She was gorgeous, absolutely beautiful. I was overjoyed. After all these years I had finally got the little girl I so dearly wanted. Inside it seemed as if an emotional space had been filled. A space that had been created all those years ago by another girl, a baby girl who had been taken from me in my youth. This was 'it', I thought. I felt complete. To have my wonderful boys and now a beautiful little girl as well.

I thoroughly enjoyed the little free time I had. I bought and refurbished an old Citroën H-van, converting it into a camper. I built a platform on the roof and purchased a small electronic telescope. I went UFO-spotting, travelling all over North Devon and North Wales in it. On Holdstone Down, at the edge of Exmoor, overlooking the Bristol Channel, I saw on various occasions what I believed to be UFOs. No, not weather balloons or satellites. Besides, satellites do not zig-zag across the sky at extremely high speeds. These things moved so fast that the telescope became useless. It was easier to track them with the naked eye, that's how close they seemed. They looked high in the sky, like small balls of light. One minute they were stationary, then they would move off quite suddenly at incredible speed. I was so excited by the sightings that I wrote to the Ministry of Defence about the phenomenon. But I never heard back.

My son Christian shared my enthusiasm for Citroëns, and though he was too young to drive I would take him camping and to car rallies, together with other family members. Apart from the Citroën DS, which I was head-over-heels in love with, the

2CV was a favourite of ours. It has such a special feeling about it – the design, the shape, has a particular aesthetic appeal. When you look at it you feel cosy, peaceful. It has such modesty, yet it is fun. It sounds like a sewing-machine. It is quirky, odd, and I just love that gear shift. For a time I owned a late forties Citroën Light 15, a beautiful car. But the DS was my favourite. The DS is a goddess. It is sexual, sleek and elegant. So stylish. It is superior, sophisticated, yet humorous. It is fifties sci-fi. When you have driven one you will never want to drive anything else.

I had never been into cars, not since my youth, but I always liked the older styles. I have a close friend, an artist, who was into fifties American cars. We would discuss for hours the artistic merits of particular models. We could clear a whole restaurant in under an hour. We could freeze 'golf bores' dead in their tracks at ten paces.

Around 1973, when computer design really started to kick in, that's when it all started to go wrong, I feel. That's when styles began to look and feel cold, soulless, mean, arrogant, horrible. Before that, a car was more a work of art rather than a hunk of meaningless metal flying around like a giant, angry phallus.

The November night skies in Devon are for some reason magnificent. When I look back, the times that I have spent with my children and the time I spent in Devon are the most special, most wonderful times in all my life. Listening to the Dvorak Serenade in D while sipping wine and looking up at the stars. Watching my children being born and seeing the room light up as a new soul is thrown into existence. Excitedly catching the precise moment of birth so that I could later ponder their astrological charts. Watching my children grow, sharing their innocence, seeing the world through their eyes. Seeing them become men, arguing the toss over politics, philosophy, religion, cricket and football. Listening to Mahler's Fifth and Ninth, Samuel Barber, César Franck, Sibelius, Berlioz's *Symphonie Fantastique*, Bach's Magnificat in D, Wagner, Beethoven's Pastoral Symphony. Driving through the countryside in my old Citroën DS. Buying a Paddington Bear hat for Lana at Paddington Station.

I love train stations, especially Paddington. I love the atmosphere, the intensity, the rush, the anticipation. The thrill of watching excited holiday-makers. I could sit with a pint of

Guinness and watch each train leave and arrive, arrive and leave, for hours or until the beer ran out. Stern-faced businessmen trying to look important as they buy their evening paper, but really only looking like animated versions of the Faller's platform people I used to have on my model train set. Snotty-nosed toddlers with socks around their ankles looking bemused as they are dragged from this place to that. Lovers locked in a kiss, occasionally looking up to see that cold, heartless clock ticking away. The awful pull of separation. And the moments of nervous impatience waiting for a lover's return.

In May and June we eventually got going on the album and gave ourselves plenty of time to rehearse and record it. Every time you set out to make an album you hope that it will be the best, but this time we really wanted to make sure it was special. We worked extremely hard and by the end of August it was finished. The title was *Think Visual*. Ray and I were very excited and we jointly decided to share the workload of press and radio interviews in order to cover as much ground as possible. We felt very optimistic.

'Rock 'n' Roll Cities', a song I wrote, was the first single after a lot of debate and to-ing and fro-ing with Palmese, Ray, and the promotion people. Although we all thought that the beautiful song 'Lost and Found' was the obvious hit single, it was decided that 'Cities' would be good as a primer to build the AOR base. It did get a great deal of air-play in the beginning. 'Cities' was like a commercial for touring, for the album. While making a demo of my own of it at Konk, I had my drum-kit set up but just couldn't lock into the thing. It was just a straight ahead rock backbeat. The Avory body was upstairs doing some business in the office, so I dragged him down to play on it. It worked really well in the end. We ended up using the demo version with just a few overdubs.

The title track 'Think Visual' is tremendous. It really slots into a style all of its own with a quirky little rock/vaudeville link section. 'Lost and Found' is one of my favourite Kinks tracks. Even before we recorded it I knew it was one of those special songs. 'Repetition' is an unusual song about the predictability of life. Both amusing and depressing.

Think Visual was a very underrated album in my opinion. Most of our albums with Arista had been hits, with the exception of *Word of Mouth*. All of a sudden things seemed to be going terribly wrong. We toured the States, and Ray and I did every interview in sight, but after a while it started to feel as if we were simply wasting our time and energy. Like trying to swim up Niagara Falls doing the backstroke. By July 1987 we started to realize that it just wasn't going to happen. After sixteen weeks on the *Billboard* charts, *Think Visual* had only reached number 81.

In addition to 'Cities', I wrote another song for the album called 'When You Were a Child' – a song about how people grow old and lose touch with the inner child, becoming bitter and resentful of the way life has treated them. Ray's song 'Killing Time' is a great rock 'n' roll track. I liked the relaxed dirge-like droning vibe. Classic rock with wonderfully poignant lyrics. Very Kinks.

'Natural Gift' should have been a single. 'What the hell's the matter with everyone?' I thought to myself when I arrived back home after the tour. I don't think MCA knew what they had. They just didn't understand what the Kinks 'meant'. It was a baffling time, to be coming off a string of successful albums and tours and for it all suddenly to fall flat. 'Working in the Factory' is one of my favourite cuts from the album. There is a lot of truth in the song. Music did come along and set us free, but in a way it seemed as if we were just working in a factory.

By this time Ray had met and married a dancer named Pat Crosby. She seemed really nice, quiet and sensitive. Pat eventually ended up dancing on some of our later stage productions of 'It' and 'Aggravation'. My son Simon, who was now in his teens, had a band which played at the wedding reception, with Ray's daughter Victoria on vocals. It was really special. I felt extremely happy for Ray. Maybe now at last he could find some real, lasting happiness.

I got a call from my sister Gwen, telling me that Mum was in hospital under observation after complaining of bad stomach pains. She sounded really nervous and anxious. Eventually the doctors decided to operate. I rushed out of the house and drove to the Whittington Hospital, arriving just as they were rolling Mum into the lift that would take her to the operating theatre. She was in typical form, putting on a brave face, hiding her real fears, joking and laughing.

'Don't worry, David, I'll be all right,' she said. 'There was no need to come all the way down here.' I gave her a big hug and kiss and tried to reassure her as best I could as she disappeared into the lift.

Gwen had been at Mum's side most of the time and she had a bad feeling about the operation. I tried to comfort her and then we went back to her house. She was living in Ray's old house in Fortis Green, the one he had lived in when he was married to Rasa. Ray was in New York on business.

In the morning, Gwen and I returned to the hospital. Peg arrived just as Mum was coming out of the anaesthetic. The doctor took Gwen, Peg, and me to one side and told us that Mum was fairly comfortable at the moment but that she had had a serious operation. The cancer was much worse than they had at first realized, and it was unlikely, he said, that she would live more than three or four weeks.

Gwen, Lisbet and I took turns sitting with her. My sisters and their families rallied round. Gwen was great; in fact, everyone was. But Gwen and her husband Brian bore the emotional brunt of it.

Over the weeks that followed and after my fear had subsided, I started to realize just how privileged I was to share such treasured moments with my dear mother. There were many periods of fear, anxiety, pain and sadness, but there was also much laughter. I would not swap those memories for the world.

Mum would often ask where Raymond was. I said he was in the States on business. Peg and Gwen were really angry at Ray for not coming home once he had heard of her condition. One morning I called Ray from Mum's room and put her on the phone with him. 'Hang in there,' he told her. 'Everything will be all right.' After she put the phone down I could see that she was upset, but she never said anything, she just kept looking out of that bloody window.

During one bad spell, I was asleep in an armchair next to her when she suddenly awoke.

'David,' she said, 'who are those people?'

'What people, Mum?'

'Those,' she said, pointing to empty space.

'Tell me what they look like,' I said. She described these imaginary people to me. I asked her whether she liked them or not. 'I don't know,' she said, and started to get upset. I suggested that maybe they were there to help her, to take care of her. She said she wasn't ready to go with them as they were beckoning to her.

'Go away,' I said to them politely, even though I couldn't sense them. But they were very real to her. If she said they were there, then they were. That was that as far as I was concerned.

These spirits or angels or imaginary visitors came to her a few times during her last days. She started to get used to them and in the end I believe she felt quite comfortable with them. Her health was deteriorating rapidly and the stress and strain were showing on Gwen and me. I really don't know what I would have done without Gwen. Lisbet was very close to Mum and was wonderful throughout.

I learned a lot about Mum and about myself during that time. One day, much to my surprise, she said to me that Raymond (as she always called him) would never help me and that I had to find something of my own. She went on to say that although she loved him equally and more than her own life, this was simply the truth. That it was not in his nature to be otherwise.

One morning Mum received a letter from Ray. I watched as she opened it and read it. She was so happy. She cried and smiled and laughed. I read the letter and it was very moving. Ray told her how he would never have written a single word had it not been for her. That she was at the heart of his inspiration. The letter meant so much to her, more than Ray could have ever imagined. But I could have killed him for not coming home to see her before she went. I never understood it. Maybe he was afraid.

One evening I was feeling really whacked, and Mum insisted that I go home and get some sleep. Reluctantly I did, but before I had even reached my front door, she had died. It was her way of telling me that I had done enough. She didn't want me to see her die.

Ray finally made his entrance at her funeral, on cue and as usual, always spectacular. Gwen and I were weary and drained with the stress, toil and pressures of the preceding weeks. In the small chapel where the service was held, Ray got up, walked to the lectern and gave an extremely moving and insightful dedication to this wonderful woman whom we all loved and adored. As I sat there touched by the beauty of his words, I silently smiled to myself. How typical of Ray. All the hard work had already been done and then he waltzes in for the spoils. But it was a wonderful tribute and I am sure it delighted my mother, who I believe was very much present, albeit invisibly, observing the event with her usual patience and gracious good humour. In my mind I could imagine her standing proudly with arms folded and with a slightly twisted yet wry smile on her face.

After the funeral I drove to Devon and spent a few days in contemplation. I started writing a play about Mum which I later turned into a film script about her life. It was an important exercise for me, a way for me to come to terms with my grief. I felt her close to me while I was writing. It was definitely a collaboration. My mother was my best friend, my guru, and my teacher, and when she died a part of me died as well. But after a while I started to realize, as with my father, that in some subtle way she could communicate more freely now that she was released from life and her physical constrictions. Her death gave me an inner strength.

By the end of the eighties a series of bad business moves coupled with bad advice started to put pressure on my financial resources. I'd changed accountants and started getting bills for unpaid back taxes out of nowhere. I had a difficult time trying to sort out my business affairs. I spent more money on accountant's bills than anything else during the period that followed. The more work they did, the more they got paid. The old Catch-22. You need someone to help you sort out the paperwork, someone who understands the bureaucracy, and then it becomes time-consuming and complicated. Complication means more work. More work means more money. You become dependent on them. You don't have the time to deal with it yourself because you are working to try and make a living. The more work they do the more they get paid. It's a joke. They are supposed to provide a service yet they end up being in control if you don't watch out. They are there to protect your interests while at the same time they are draining your resources.

If they mess up, it's your fault and they are free from all responsibility. You just have to hope that the people you hire are reputable and trustworthy. At the end of the day you have to be philosophical. But it was obvious that someone had it in for me.

And to this day I don't know why they wanted to screw things up for me. Probably the usual jealousy mixed with greed.

Eventually I met an accountant named Lionel Martin who seemed a smart, affable, genuine guy and I hired him to help sort things out. With a pile of paperwork and tax bills that seemed to fall out of the sky, I was in for a bit of a rollercoaster ride, ending up with me having to sell most of my property. Since I had signed my first cheque at the age of sixteen I had never had a problem with my accounts, or with the revenue service. I had always paid my taxes and had never had any trouble. What the hell happened?

There is an awful lot of jealousy and spitefulness in this business. Some people are so resentful and envious of your achievements it is pitiful, pathetic. Everybody wants a bit of you. Everybody wants to be your friend, yet some are so twisted that they just can't wait to stab you in the back at the first available opportunity. What they don't realize is that in the end it all comes back on us all. It's like bad voodoo. It may work in the beginning but eventually we all have to pay the price. I forgive you, you stupid, stupid earthlings. I firmly believe that we all have to 'account' for everything we do.

In 1988 the Kinks recorded a live album which we called *The Road*. It reached number 110 in the charts. It was a fantastic record but the dice were loaded against us yet again. By mid 1989 I was becoming more disillusioned generally. In England the political climate was getting cold, with heavy showers expected. Thatcher had made her killing and was on her way out, leaving in her wake a wave of misery unprecedented this side of the war. The awful and incredible political deception of the eighties was starting to take its toll on a gullible nation that had neither the stomach for nor the natural inclination to handle such a concept as 'consummate greed'. Power corrupts. Rule Britannia.

Being 'true' Englishmen to the core, eternally optimistic, stiff-upper-lipped and all that, we went back into the studio in true bulldog spirit to record what was to become, after some litigation, our final album with MCA, *UK Jive*. We met a guy in New York called Kenny Laguna who was really keen to manage the band. He was familiar with the MCA set-up and thought that he could help with the record. Kenny was a nice guy with a big heart. He was very supportive of us and I'll always remember his kindness. (Although he did have a tendency to wear lime-green luminescent socks!)

We thought we'd give Kenny a try but, to be fair to him, the rot had already set in and there was little he could do. We had to face the fact that we simply had to get away from MCA before they buried us completely.

I wrote two songs for *UK Jive*, 'Dear Margaret', and 'Perfect Strangers'. I felt that the latter was one of the best songs I had ever written. During time spent in New York searching for management, I also met Gene Harvey, a successful entrepreneur who had worked with Whitney Houston, and we discussed his possible involvement as our manager. He played the album and thought that 'Perfect Strangers' should be the single from it.

'Some smart radio promotion guy could get hold of this and make a hit out of it,' he told me. I didn't want to tell him at the time that I had had a fist fight with Ray just to get the bloody thing on the CD. It wasn't actually on the album as such, since vinyl albums didn't have as much room on them as CDs. I think it might have put Gene off a bit. Oh well. Anyway, Gene and I had dinner and spent a pleasant evening together. New York has such great restaurants, but it wasn't always easy, especially in the old days, to get decent vegetarian food when travelling. On the road it was either pizza or nothing. I've always wondered about that, that quiet but still present discrimination against those of us who don't eat meat.

What is an ethic anyway? In one country it may be considered unethical to eat the meat of a cow because they believe the cow to be sacred. In another country people make money from selling hamburgers and nobody gives a shit – 'Fuck 'em, they can't talk, can't answer back, so we might as well eat 'em, that's what I say. I'm smarter than they are so I can do what I like. Nice juicy steak, mmmmm.'

Who is more right? I don't want to get into the 'veggie' argument here about wasting valuable land and using it for grazing McDonald's hamburgers with legs, or that the grain used for feeding the animals we breed for eating could and should be used to help feed the starving people of the planet. Let's not get into that, because in my view there is no argument. If we as human beings cannot cultivate a proper respect for all life on the planet, how can we expect other more advanced life to give a shit about us?

To some alien species we probably seem as little evolved as a dog – or a pig, more like. I like pigs. They grunt all day long, wallow around in their own shit and eat whatever you give them. A bit like human beings, aren't they? 'I am not a pig, I am a Human Being.' I love Patrick McGoohan in *The Prisoner*: 'I am not a number, I am a man.'

I prefer cats to dogs, but I love animals. I believe that we have a spiritual responsibility for everything we come into contact with, everything we interact with. We have committed unbelievable crimes, unspeakable atrocities against the planet in general as well as to each other throughout our history. How dare we assume even for an instant that we are any better than animals? Yummy, how about a nice, juicy 'human' burger? If we cannot demonstrate compassion, how can we expect compassion to be shown to us? It's only logical.

I don't believe we have any direct karma with animals but I do sincerely believe we create good karma for ourselves by respecting other forms of life. Maybe it's not just the cow that should be thought of as sacred, but all life. And possibly the most sacred form of life as we know it is the very 'being' beneath our feet, the planet earth.

Some people believe that the earth is a highly evolved life form. Many ancient cultures, including certain American Indian ones, treat it as such. We are sacred creatures and more important than animals, even though some of us might prefer animals to other human beings. Some people treat their animals better than humans yet they'll sit down and eat a nice 'juicy' lamb chop. Jesus Christ, tell me I'm crazy, please! A sheep is probably the most inoffensive of all creatures. It is self-sufficient, it requires only grass to live, if you call it a name or insult it it will run away, it doesn't support any dodgy football team, it has totally unbiased political views and it is generous enough to supply wool for us so that we may make clothes to protect ourselves from the cold in winter. 'Yeah, but they're stupid. So kill the bastards and eat them. Yeah, that's what I say.'

If we ate everything that we considered dumb or stupid, then we would be too busy eating one another to be bothered with a mere sheep. What would it feel like if you went to the butcher's and saw your pet dog hanging up in the window with its throat cut and its guts hanging out? 'Eat the bloody 'fing, yeah, get it down ya, son.'

To me it is a question of creating a new set of ethics that are based on spiritual impulses. 'Spirituality' is not a bunch of unisex fairies and angels prancing about in lace and chiffon in God's backyard, casting a thin membrane of magical dust over everyone and everything. Nor does it have anything to do with the confessional. I'm convinced that confession is good for the soul, but aren't we kidding ourselves if we think that as mere mortals we have the power really to forgive anyone anything? True forgiveness is a beautiful thing and a sign of strength. But priests playing God, encouraging their congregation to do virtually what they like as long as they 'stay' within the fold, I don't know about that. The buying off of sin, the emotional bribery just to appease the masses. Where does it say in the bible, 'Those who live by the sword shall receive three Hail Marys and a slap on the wrist'?

Spirituality is fundamentally about love and respect, the first two rungs on the ladder to our salvation. They're two of the hardest things in the world to understand, it seems, brothers and sisters. (Didn't you love Burt Lancaster in *Elmer Gantry*? 'Come on you sinners.' Brilliant.) But spirituality is also about using common sense. If there is dog shit on your path, you do not remove it with a bison or a feather or a custard pie or a machine-gun. A spade or a shovel will suffice. If you have neither you may just have to pick it up with your hands and move it or step over it and leave it for the next poor unsuspecting bastard who may come along. Mind you, there's always some silly sod who is going to step straight in it.

In reality the body can digest almost anything – wood, even shit if we want. I would hate for anyone to have to eat that. But we do always have a choice. Anyway I won't go into that, I really don't want to get into that 'Veggie' argument. I simply 'choose' not to eat meat. I have my reasons. But to get back to the point, who is more right? Leaving the 'veggie' argument out of it all together, neither is; yet both are. In the light of reason, each is 'right' in his own way according to his/her/its/them/err/this/err/thing's (shit, this politically correct crap is making me crazy) particular culture or tradition. That is why the question cannot be answered. We need to expand our views to draw ideas from the realms of 'spiritual' reason. Would we wage war against the one that was 'right' or the one that was 'right'? We are constantly waiting for physical proof of everything, making a line of demarcation here or drawing a line there, and all we are really doing is walking around in circles. By the time we reason out that the earth isn't flat after all, it might not be here, or rather we might not. All right! You keep that cow over on your side if you love it so bloody much. But watch out . . . if that fucking cow puts as much as one foot over that line, I'm gonna eat the bastard. You see if I don't.

18

In 1990 the Kinks were inducted into the Rock 'n' Roll Hall of Fame. Ray and I both felt a little uncomfortable with the idea at first, but it was a nice tribute, a show of respect for a body of work that has spanned some thirty years. The Kinks have influenced so many people in the music business. It was a gesture that was well appreciated. It was also quite a touching irony that Graham Nash was the one who inducted us, especially since all those years ago he had been such a staunch supporter of the band.

As much as I appreciated the recognition, I've always had my own ideas about how these particular ceremonies should be conducted. So I'd like to announce here the winners of the Dave Davies Special Achievement Awards. Two awards go to Ray Davis of the Kinks. First, a Lifetime Achievement award for 'The Most Exasperating and Impossible Creative Genius I Have Ever Worked With'. Second, 'The Most Important and Influential Rock Singer/Songwriter of Our Time'. Bruce Springsteen will get the award for 'Appearing at the Most Hall of Fame Awards Ceremonies'. Don't worry, Bruce, you'll get the proper award when it's your turn. Be patient. To Chuck Berry, for 'The Longest Running Cool Guitar Player Award'. Bruce, please, hang on, not yet, not yet. Jeez, some people.

Now, 'The Greatest Guitar Player in the History of the World Ever to Play in Clogs Award' goes to Brian May. 'Best Rock 'n' Roll Band in the History of Rock' goes to (shit, these envelopes, you can never open them when you want to) aah . . . um . . . to the Rolling . . . sorry, wrong envelope, that was for the 'Oldest Rock 'n' Roll Band Still Playing Live Award' and the 'Oldest Rock 'n' Roll Band Still Alive Award'. Oh, here it is. The award goes to the Kinks. Bruce, stop it, you're gonna get it in a minute . . . if you keep on the way you're going. Remember, Bruce, patience is a virtue.

Oh, all right. 'The Most Talented Singer/Songwriter, Guitarist, Performer, Rock Video Star, Humanitarian, Working Class Hero Award' goes to, shit, sorry Bruce . . . goes to Ray Davies. Never mind, Bruce, maybe next year, tell ya what, we can all get up on stage at the end and sing Chuck Berry songs. Or 'Born in the USA'. We could do 'Born to Run' as an encore. Or 'Born Near a Factory in the USA' or 'Seen Running from a Factory Some Years After Being Born in the USA'. I could sing 'Born in the UK Now Living in the USA'.

We'll have such a great time, it'll be such fun. We can all meet in a bar around the corner beforehand, get really pissed or drink loads of Perrier water, ha, ha, ha, and let Weird Al Yankovic 'do' all of us.

Recently we were invited to play at the opening of the Rock 'n' Roll Hall of Fame Museum in Cleveland. Bruce was there, as well as hosts of others. I thought it was fitting that Chuck Berry, who had inspired us and all the British Invasion bands, closed the show. It was great fun to spend a few days with all these music legends, although I did find it curious that the Kinks were the only British band on the bill.

After our induction into the Hall of Fame we were still tied to MCA, but in the end we were frustrated with them and asked for a release from our contract. We finally agreed that it would be of mutual benefit and we got out of the deal, to much relief. So we now needed to find ourselves a manager before embarking on any further fruitless adventures. Ray and I met an array of managers before we came across a guy called Nigel Thomas. I liked him straight away but I didn't tell him that. He seemed his own man. And he wasn't a member of AA, which was startling news considering that he was in the music business. Alcoholism is nothing to joke about, believe me. I have had many friends who have suffered terribly because of it, in some cases ruining their lives completely. But Nigel was a practising drinker, which was such a relief. A man with his own particular point of view, pompous, self-opinionated, a bit slippery when wet, but a charmer. He was also very funny and really good company. A delightful character.

Nigel spoke with an upper class accent. He started his career as a stand-up comic for the Krays and later got into management, handling such artists as Joe Cocker and Kiki Dee among others.

In his own way he was a bit of a rebel, and both Ray and I got along famously with him. He reminded me a little of Robert Wace at first. A sort of mixture between Wace and Terry-Thomas.

After the management contract was sorted out Ray, Nigel and I organized a trip to New York to meet with various record companies. I couldn't believe that after all these years we still had to schlep around town and face the daunting task of doing the record company run again. Maybe this time we would find our perfect creative home.

After meeting with various people we ended up in the offices of Columbia Records, who had now been taken over by Sony. They seemed enthusiastic. Great. Afterwards, Nigel, Ray and I had a protracted dinner and after much discussion we thought we would give them a shot. The contracts were prepared, lawyers were hired, and the thrashing out of the deal began. Eventually everybody's happy. There you have it – a few smiles and handshakes, enthusiastic meetings with hardened radio promotion people. Kid Leo, I liked him. A good guy. What else is there? Oh yes, cross your fingers, pray, work hard, and hope for the best.

Phobia took ages to make, more than a year. We spent several hundreds of thousands of dollars on it, and although I thought it was going well, I also felt that it was taking too long and costing too much money. I was getting frustrated creatively and was eager to pursue contacts I had made involving screenwriting and film scores.

Nancy and I decided to move to Los Angeles with the kids and we rented a place in Hollywood. Nancy was originally from LA and her family and friends still lived there. In early 1991 we released an EP as a teaser for radio, a limited-edition collector's EP. Things actually started to look up.

Nigel became a stabling influence on Ray, and I started to feel more confident about his involvement. Ray and I were getting on really well. After all the hard work, all the mixing, the creative discussions with Columbia, re-mixing, getting Bob Clear-mountain to mix some tracks, trying desperately to keep the boat on an even keel, we finally had an album at the end of 1992. Hurrah. Hallelujah.

The album included a track called 'Hatred'. The original deal was that Ray and I were going to write the song together. I don't know what happened there. We messed around with some riffs and stuff in the studio – I did a bit, he did a bit – then Ray went away and came up with this very funny lyric about our love-hate relationship. It was hilarious. We couldn't stop laughing during its recording. 'I hate you and you hate me, now I guess we understand each other.' Trust Ray to write a lyric like that. He really makes me smile sometimes. Not often. 'Wall of Fire' was a cool track. Ray, Nigel and I wanted it out as the first single but Columbia was uncertain. In the end we went with 'Hatred'. The album was scheduled for release in March 1993 in Europe and April in the US.

I wrote a song called 'Close to the Wire', which tells the story of a man whose life has fallen apart through bad business deals and investments. The yuppie falling victim to his own greed. In the bridge he reflects on better times. 'Whatever happened to all the dreams we shared together, a taste of wine, a moonlight song, that last for ever.' It also touches on a familiar Kinks theme of struggle and survival through adversity.

Another song, 'It's All Right', tells how modern society uses people up and throws them away. The protagonist says, 'Whatever you do to me, you will *never* destroy my spirit.' Let's hope that there is life on Mars so that we can evacuate our species there in the future. That is if there is intelligent life out there (which of course there is). We might end up needing their help.

Ray and I worked our balls off promoting the record, but it was great fun. We did some joint interviews, which had been virtually unheard of before. On the few occasions when we had, I could rarely get a word in. We appeared on *The Tonight Show with Jay Leno* and performed 'Hatred'. Billy Crystal was also on the show and he kept doing this silly gag with a pair of underpants he had been holding throughout the interview. I got fed up and snatched them away and pulled them over his head. It got a lot of laughs and Billy was a great sport about it.

In January 1993 I was with my family spending New Year in LA when I got a call from Nigel's office. Nigel had died in his sleep the night before. I just couldn't believe it. Don't get me wrong, but after the initial shock had dissipated I started laughing in disbelief. I just could not believe it, poor sod, just his bloody luck. I was confounded. I felt like – well, imagine Ben Hur having gone through so much shit and he was on the last lap of the chariot race and a wheel falls off his horse and cart. Shit, I thought, it must be God's year for doing irony. And just the day before, Nancy had announced to me that she was pregnant again. I was a little emotionally confused, to say the least.

I flew to London for Nigel's funeral. It was tragic, of course, but in a way it was a celebration, exactly what he would have liked – family, friends and business associates enjoying the benefits of his generosity. I'd known Nigel only for a comparatively short time, but I regarded him as a good friend. I often think about what might have been. I miss him. He, Ray and I had worked so hard to get the Columbia deal and the *Phobia* album together and then he suddenly kicked the bucket. He would have seen the humour of it all. I can see him shaking his head in his usual sardonic way. 'Sorry, chaps, bloody bad luck if you ask me. Another Armagnac?'

Ray was the last one at the graveside and he really made me laugh. He said he wanted to make sure Nigel was really dead. 'It wouldn't surprise me,' he said, 'if Nigel had staged the whole thing and was just waiting for everyone to leave so that he could get up, jump in a waiting car, and do a runner. Do a Reggie Perrin.'

We hired Gene Harvey to pick up where Nigel had left off. I liked Gene, he was a gentleman. I was still in London after Nigel's funeral and went to the office to go through the usual mail. It was the day I sold my Devon house and I was really depressed. I thought that nothing would ever go right for me again.

I opened a letter and to my shock and surprise it was from Sue. I read the letter with the excitement of a schoolboy. She explained that our daughter Tracey was to be thirty that March and that all her life she had wanted so much to see me, but had been terrified to contact me, perhaps out of fear of rejection or simply because she was concerned that she might be an imposition on my life. Sue left her work number and suggested that it would be better to speak to her first before arranging anything with Tracey.

I raced to the phone. It was so strange; while I was waiting for the phone to be picked up at the other end I felt a tingling feeling in my stomach, just like I used to get when I would turn the corner and see her house on the way to pick her up for a date all those years ago.

'Hello, is that Sue Sheehan?'

'Dave,' she said, sounding totally surprised. 'God, it's been so long.' I could sense the same excitement in her voice as I was feeling myself. After the usual exchange of pleasantries, Sue told me that Tracey was desperate to see me, that she couldn't wait any longer. Sue and I decided to meet first before telling Tracey. We arranged to meet that night at Hatfield Station at 7 p.m.

After I had put the telephone receiver down, I just couldn't sit still. I felt like an excited kid. I kept looking at the clock, thinking to myself, 'God, it's only four. Oh well, I'll go now anyway. The train will take at least half an hour and when I get there I can walk around or something.'

I actually arrived at Hatfield Station at 5.30. I had a little walk round and found a pub to take on board a bit of Dutch courage as I was so nervous. God, I thought, after all these years I wonder how much she's changed. During our telephone conversation Sue had told me that she was working, but living on her own. She had divorced her husband some years before.

Six-thirty arrived slowly. Time seemed to be deliberately dragging by. I walked around some more. I came back to the station at about ten to seven and all of a sudden I heard her call my name. I would have recognized that voice anywhere. I looked around and there she was.

'Sue,' I said excitedly. 'You look really well.' We joked and laughed about us meeting after all that time. Meeting now in our forties. Although we were obviously so much older, I had the strangest feeling inside that something was still the same.

We walked to Hatfield Old Town. For about 300 yards we said nothing. We just kept looking at each other with these silly grins stuck to our faces. Passers-by probably thought that we were a couple of mentally challenged patients from the local care centre. When we got to the bottom of the road, I turned to her and blurted out, 'Sue, you broke my heart, do you know that?'

The smiles instantly turned to tears. She said that I had broken her heart as well. We held on to each other in the middle of the street. Then we began to talk, venting many suppressed and pent-up feelings. We went to a local pub and talked for about two hours before we decided to call Tracey.

Sue showed me pictures of Tracey at her wedding. Pictures of Tracey's two little boys. They looked like really sweet kids and I was relieved to see that her husband looked like a decent guy. Shit, I was a grandfather.

I showed Sue pictures of Nancy and the kids. She cried when she saw Nancy. 'God, we could have been sisters, couldn't we?' she said. 'It's so strange.'

Tracey was to meet us at the pub and I waited for her in the car-park so that we could be alone. Soon she arrived. We sat in her car. I felt like a complete jerk, I just couldn't think of a damn thing to say to her. She started talking nervously about her work, about how she often thought about me, how she didn't want to interfere with my life. I thought to myself, 'God, she's got such beautiful eyes, so melancholy.'

She was bravely trying to put on a front. In my daze I turned to her and said, 'Tracey, I know this sounds strange as I don't know you, but I've really missed you.'

She turned and looked head on at me and said, 'I've really missed you, too.' With that we both suddenly started to cry uncontrollably, apologizing to one another, faking nervous laughter in between each wave of tears. We talked some more, then went back to the pub where the three of us sat until closing time, chatting like silly nervous children with really stupid grins on our faces.

Afterwards we went back to Sue's house and had tea. Sue played a record by Enya called *Caribbean Blue*. Tracey said, 'Oh Mum, take that bloody record off, I hate it.' But I insisted that she leave it. I wanted to hear what Sue liked. As I listened, it made me feel as if I was tuning into her real feelings.

We were all in a bit of a daze. It was so special, so beautiful. Soon it was time for Tracey to leave, as she was worried about her kids. But we arranged to meet a day or two later. We walked out to her car. The stars seemed particularly bright that night for some reason.

After Tracey had driven away, Sue and I went back into the house and we talked and cried, cried and talked until the early hours. All the time that bloody Enya record was playing. I sensed a deep sadness in Sue. She cried bitterly, telling me how her bloody mother had ruined her life. Of how her parents had told her that I hated her and that I never wanted to see her again. It was a day and a night of mixed feelings, to say the least.

I told Sue about the incident with the birthday scarf and we both cried. She remembered how terribly upset she had been when I didn't buy her anything for her birthday. But we laughed, thinking of my mum proudly wearing it and me being too shy and uncomfortable to say anything about it.

As I left I promised that I would phone the next day. I smiled as I looked up at the early morning sky. For a moment I felt the same as I had done when I was fifteen. I just couldn't believe it.

I visited Tracey and her family at their house and met Sue for a drink a few days later. Then I returned to LA and explained to Nancy what had happened. I told her that I wanted to spend some time with Sue, to talk things out. Nancy was really wonderful. She was so understanding. She said that she knew I had had a problem with Sue all my life, that she had often sensed it, and that maybe it was a good idea to spend some time together to get all those inner feelings out into the open once and for all.

I flew back to England. Sue met me at the airport and showed me some poems she had written. I had had no idea how talented she was. It was an important time for us both, a chance to work through all our repressed feelings and emotions. It was so wonderful to meet Tracey after all those years and to know that she had developed into such a wonderful person. Sue gave me a poem she had written for me.

FOR DAVID

You brought me springtime daffodils,
But they would not let you in,
You were not allowed to see me or our beautiful new-born child
They slammed that big door on you,
and you had to walk away.
The jailer's key turned in the lock and I knew we could not win.
Snow lay on the ground that day
But it must of felt so warm compared to some of the frozen
hearts, that surrounded the three of us.
Was what we did so very wrong that we could not share our joy.
When they sent you away that morning they sent away half my
soul.
If I gave you a springtime daffodil, for every time I've missed you
You'd find that you'd be swimming in a vast yellow sea of Love.

I presented Sue with a gift and before she even opened the box she knew what it was: a lovely dark purple-blue silk scarf. We held each other and cried. But Sue and I knew that the clock could not be turned back. Although we resolved many things, we realized that it could never be the same. We couldn't relive our youth, couldn't put back something that had been snatched from us so cruelly all those years ago. It just wasn't meant to be – we had to be content with that. Our lives had taken totally different paths and we were to say goodbye again, with a promise always to remain friends. But this time we would say goodbye to each other because it was our choice and not someone else's. Inside I felt that we had made things right, somehow. We gave something back to each other that had been missing in both of us for thirty years.

During this period I had been constantly travelling back and forth between London and Los Angeles, recording the *Phobia* album in London, working on scripts and film music with producers in LA, but the more time I spent there the more I missed England. It's interesting how when you live in another country the things you take totally for granted in your home country suddenly take on a new importance.

I must admit I've always loved England with a deep and distinct passion. I love that feeling I get when I've been away for a while and the plane comes in to land at Heathrow. It feels so great to look out of the window and see the English countryside. Then to go through Customs, where they look at you like you're an arch-criminal or drug trafficker. You get in a taxi and the driver is slagging off everyone in sight: 'Oh that bloody Major. I don't know, ruined the bleedin' country, ain't they. The Conservatives I mean. Look at the unemployment, da, da, da, da, da. Did you 'ear, Bruce Rioch's Arsenal's new manager. And yeah, it used to be really nice round here, before. Look what they've done, they sold it all off ain't they? Bit by bit they sold the bloody country off.'

The English, always complaining. Loath to give compliments, cynical, pessimistic, resenting success and loving failure, always one rule for the rich and one for the poor, regardless of government change. Championing the underdog. Sensible, unimpressed. Snobs, fish 'n' chips, Morris Minors, clotted cream, bitter, pint. Thatched cottages, policemen with funny hats, wonderful hedgerows, Ramsgate, cockles and whelks. The smell of the Devon countryside. Drunken conversations with old friends. Nostalgia, yearning for things past, concern about the future. The Criminal Justice bill. Urban decay. Fights in the pub. Arsenal, Arsenal, bloody Spurs supporters. Pakistani off-licences selling cheap Bulgarian wine. Lovely, proper English Indian high-street restaurants. Tandoori, kebabs. Match of the Day. Muswell Hill. Camden on a Friday night, chucking up, the air full of the smells of the city, of beer, homelessness, tragedy. 'I had a husband and family, he lost his job, we lost our home, I lost my children, I lost hope, I lost everything.' Her sad and dirty plaited hair hanging limply to one side, an old woman in her youth. Such despair. Hopeless drunks lying on the doorsteps in gutters next to empty cans of Special Brew. Wow, look there! A 'designer tramp'. Chippendale figure, cool shoulder-length hair, you know that two-tone hair dye that's grown out, tight leather pants, un-shaven, smelly, begging with a polystyrene cup in hand. Poor bastard probably begging for petrol money, living in the back of a BMW can be hell, especially if it's clamped and on a meter. Life sucks.

Next door a 'Brasserie' full of noise and impatience. Cheap plonk, sweating summer nights, young women stinking of Opium perfume and BO. Ah, nectar. Angry Mercedes owner, frustrated at being unable to park outside his favourite bistro, shouts arrogant abuse at the sky. A gorgeous old Citroën DS flashes by, snatching my attention away from student street musicians. God, that almost felt as good as fondling a perfectly formed pair of tits, you know, the kind that fit snugly into a 36D. Fashions of the nineties hang in shop windows, depicting the latest styles. Second-hand poverty is all the rage these days. The impoverished look. Modesty and humility with just a touch of flair. Everything has style. Attitude. It's cheaper than buying from Oxfam. Old rich bitch from Hadley Wood walks by, tries to blend in, her carefully chosen mountain boots propping up beige riding jodhpurs, stinking of . . . hey, what's that, embalming fluid? It smells expensive. Giorgio, that's it. There's nothing more boring than middle-aged women that work out. In some cultures it was considered a symbol of wealth to be 'fat'. All these strange alien creatures from outer space with breast implants, thin tight lips, gaunt expressions on their faces. The ultimate look of the 'superior', extremely wealthy, successful, and, of course, healthy woman. From the planet Guilt. Rich people like to look thin, maybe it is a subconscious suppression of the awful starvation there is in the world. Ah, ha, I can see that you are really fat on the inside. You need to go on an 'inner diet'. Greed is like saturated fat that builds up around the soul and can cause serious problems, like soul attacks. Better work out.

Some things are the same wherever you go, from Kensington High Street to Los Angeles. I walk down Rodeo Drive and see Gucci women with leather tans, skin cancer, and cool shades having a champagne brunch at the Beverly Wilshire Hotel. Century City, shopping malls with food from all over the world: burritos, noodles, spaghetti and sushi. Ben & Jerry's ice-cream. Mac software, books and toy stores.

Farmer's Market on Fairfax with *huevos rancheros* at Kokomo's, the best. Fruit and flowers. Struggling writers sipping coffee, staring at the table praying for inspiration, while an elderly Jewish woman with blue hair carefully counts out money in her frail shaky hand before deciding whether to buy a corned beef on rye. I want to hug her, but I bite my tongue. CBS employees from the studio next door, executive and producer eating meatballs and Cajun shrimp while passing tourists – eyes blanked in that 'jet-lag stupor' – stagger around as if being dragged by an invisible lead. Regulars propping up the bar, old carved faces, weary stories that place a smile in my ear. A Bud at ten, a cheap Chablis at lunch, vodka at six. Irresistible, sad but always beautiful.

Santa Monica and palm trees, getting mugged after dark on the beach. The 3rd Street Promenade, Portobello of LA. Bargains and rip-offs await.

I never venture downtown, it looks just like any other big city in the US. It could be New York or Chicago but never London or San Francisco. But I like Ventura Boulevard in the Valley: the Psychic Eye new age shop, and Jerry's Deli and the bowling alley next door. More ice-cream at Swensen's then back over the hill to Hollywood.

Hollywood Boulevard is great. Jazz on Vine Street, even Anita O'Day, she must be seventy – how cool at her age. Cheap diners, El Capitan, Mann's Chinese Theater, the pavestones impress.

Tourists and sleaze, hookers, cheap motels, excited children looking up at the lights, trashy T-shirts, two for six bucks. A faded print of Marilyn Monroe, an imitation Rolex from the guy in the shop doorway.

On to the Sunset Strip. Rock 'n' roll. The Lingerie, the Coconut Teaser. Further on down Sunset the House of Blues, the Viper Room, the Whiskey still stands as does the Roxy, both offering up distant muddled memories of nights misspent. Tower Records and Book Soup. The Rainbow Room seems never to change. I'm sure the same roadies hang out there that did in the seventies.

The news-stands are great in Hollywood. I love to sift through the magazines and newspapers from all over the world, everything on everything from classical cars to *Variety*, from *Architectural Digest* to *Hustler*.

Melrose, the King's Road of LA, for clothes, records, Doc Martens, and much more, stores and restaurants galore. The Bodhi Tree book shop, the Formosa Café on Santa Monica Boulevard near La Brea, where pictures of Hollywood stars new and old adorn the walls. They stare back at you as if issuing a silent warning.

Looks like I'll have to wait until I get back to London before I get a proper English Indian meal. Nobody understands why I like LA. It's too hot, there's gang violence, riots, mudslides, fires and earthquakes and it is such a hedonistic society. It's a young people's city but it has no heart or soul. The young people are trying to make it work with their music and art and coffee bars. I like movies, and Hollywood is where they make them. It's false and phoney but I don't care.

I miss the London pubs, noisy boozers and semi-pro bands with changy guitars ringing out into the busy street. Boots the chemist, Woolworths, Horlicks, HP Sauce, PG Tips, English hamburger joints that have never heard of a malted-milk shake. In England I make it with Horlicks, Haagen-Dasz vanilla ice-cream, semi-skimmed milk, fresh bananas, a lump of ice, blended to a thick mixture. Delicious. Oh, yes, second-hand record stores. Let me in there. Yes, yes, ooh mother, that smell of vinyl, ooh, ooh, more. I loved Ritzic from Sgt Bilko, I adored Bilko. Have you ever noticed that CDs don't smell? I am trying to persuade record companies to make vinyl-smelling CDs.

Twelve-inch ones recorded directly from analogue masters, complete with scratches sampled from old 78s. Do you think it will catch on?

Trafalgar Square, the Tower, Big Ben. The British Museum hasn't lost its charm. Japanese tourists queuing up at McDonalds. Soho – whatever happened to all the tarts and strippers? I took my American friend to a strip joint and we sat for an hour listening to Dire Straits and drinking Kaliber for which we paid four quid a go. And not a stripper in sight. The woman in charge recommended a place down the road that was much better. 'If you give me six quid each I'll call them and they'll let you in for free,' she said. Oh great. Where is it? Lead me there. I can't weight (that's a feeble attempt to convey a veiled message to 'fat', I mean rich, people). We left and drowned our sorrows in a nearby pub, which at least had women in it, even if they were only pretty and not tarts – well, as far as I could tell they weren't. The pub did have two distinct advantages over the strip joint. For one, they had Old Peculier, a really delicious but dangerous beer, and two, you guessed it, wow, are you quick, they didn't play any music by Dire Straits. Joy. Shit, that Old Peculier is really out there, man, it tastes like it was brewed by large stoned middle-aged Hell's Angels during a Satanic invocation to Mephistopheles.

I love that line from *The Voyage Home* when McCoy (De Forest Kelly) is talking to Spock shortly after his soul has been rejoined by some ancient Vulcan ritual to his physical body. 'Hey, Spock,' he says with a kind of wry glee, 'you really have been where no man has been before, haven't you?' Cool.

Go easy on that Old Peculier, there are not many people that know how to perform that 'Vulcan Ritual', not in London at any rate. Someone invited me to a Dire Straits concert at Wembley. I put on a brave face, but when we drove into the car-park I just couldn't go through with it. When I saw all those BMWs and Golf GTis it was more than I could bear. I made my apologies, walked to the nearest Indian and had a curry. They were playing Hari Prasa Chaurasia, 'The Musical Hour Glass'. If you speed up his flute-playing it sounds like Irish folk music. It's really cool.

After I had washed my egg vindaloo and malai kofta down with a delightful Châteauneuf du Pape (avoid 1993 for God's sake – pretentious, moi!), I wiped my mouth with the usual pink napkin, paid my bill, said a fond farewell to the proprietor, did a double-take on the chintz wallpaper, and decided to sample the local talent in the pub next door. There was a raunchy little band playing bad Status Quo covers, if that's possible. All right, guys, only joking. Great, this will do, I thought. I went to the bar and ordered a pint of Guinness. That's me sorted for the evening.

After a while my simple enjoyment was quashed as the band began to play Dire Straits songs. I left the pub, looked up at the night sky, and thought to myself, 'What on earth have I done to deserve this?'

Yes, it's always nice to be home. Shit, I'd better check on my air ticket, British Airways, of course. I hope my travel agent remembered that I wanted an open return.

19

I stare blankly out of yet another hotel room window at the start of a thirty-day tour of the UK. Yesterday Aberdeen, before that Dublin, tonight Manchester. Still struggling, still working, still searching. In front of me a computer screen stares back in the quiet of the early morning. The local church bells chime eight o'clock. Last night's empty Guinness cans lie strewn across the table. How I wish I was in my own bed sleeping instead of working.

Time flashes by with no thought for our place in it. In the morning I get up and write. At lunch or close to it I drive to the next town with my longtime friend and minder Terry, always ready with a joke if he sees me down, always ready to be silent when I need to talk, never missing a trick especially if there's a perk about. Bless him.

At four, a sound check; at nine, the show. At night I walk, think, write some more, sleep and hopefully dream of where I would really like to be. How I wish I was in a restaurant in Los Angeles with my dear friend John, drinking, laughing, talking about the world, philosophy, people, music, art, movies, yeah, especially movies. Or holding my little girl Lana in my arms, making her feel secure, lost in her innocence. Little baby Eddie, so soft, so sweetly sleeping. Watching old black-and-white movies late at night with Nancy. Walking in the Devon countryside, absorbing nature as it silently watches over me.

That beautiful old Devon cottage where I thought I would eventually grow old, when I was ready to be old. How I wish I was with my sons. Feeling their strength, intelligence and exuberance. The deep warmth of their friendship, their unspoken love. Joking with their mates, their girlfriends. In my heart being twenty-five.

It seems all I have ever done is work. Getting up on stage,

267

performing, it's like an addiction, there's nothing like it. It can be such a high, yet other times I think, God, I just can't face another day of it. But once I'm up there it's the greatest place in the world to be. It's like an insatiable mistress, a woman you have fallen so hopelessly in love with that you just don't know what to do. 'She never gives rest, always demanding to be pleased . . . But you just never can resist, even when you're brought to your knees . . .'

Always away from my family. Always hotel after hotel. Now it's night, another show over, and I am sitting alone in my room. Over the last few years it seems as if my relationship with Ray has become somewhat cold and emotionless, except for those magical moments on stage. Sadly, most of the time he seems very much like a stranger to me.

I am still totally frustrated and flabbergasted by Ray's detached and abusive attitude towards me – all the put-downs, the childish mind-games – when I know deep down that he loves me and that at heart he is a deeply compassionate person. Maybe I am just a glutton for punishment, but I never really understood it all. I firmly believed all these years that in the end everything would be all right, that love and our combined talents would see us through. But I believe that Ray has never understood the true spirit or concept of collaboration.

Once, in the early seventies, I received a call rather unexpectedly from Ray's psychiatrist. After some persuasion I reluctantly agreed on an appointment to meet with him. He explained to me that some of Ray's inner problems had to do with me. Or rather our relationship. To be honest, we all have problems, but I was quite taken aback to think that Ray's problems ran so deep. I realized much later how much our psyches overlapped and affected each other. One sentence reverberated through my head all the way home in the car, because I thought it seemed such a very strange thing for a psychiatrist to say. He said that if I didn't get away from my brother then he would eventually end up destroying me. Not consciously, but purely because he just couldn't help it. And many years later, my mother, on her deathbed, would say something very similar.

But in spite of it all, I love my brother. Maybe that's all that's necessary. That it was the love between us that helped to make it all happen – us against the world.

Who would have dreamt all those years ago, sitting in Mum's front room in Fortis Green, playing Johnny and the Hurricanes, and Chet Atkins records, that we would still be doing it, still be playing together? Ray has a unique and special talent and I know he will go on to achieve even greater things, but for now I believe the Kinks still have a way to go. In spite of all the problems, I love what the Kinks represent to our true fans.

I feel comfortable in the nineties, as if my whole life has been leading up to this point in time. I feel that rock has been an overwhelming force for good in spite of all that has been said to the contrary. Kinks music is people's music. It is simple, sad, poignant music for lovers, and especially lovers who have lost. It is music that makes you laugh and makes you cry, and also makes you think. It will lift you up and then it will show you just how terribly fragile human beings can be. Human frailty that yearns to be understood. That somehow seeks reconciliation with a harsh world. It is music about 'hope'. More than anything it says that tomorrow will actually turn out all right; somehow everything will be OK.

It is riding a number 41 bus to Holloway Road. It is dancing in a deserted ballroom. It is about being thrown into a situation with people you have absolutely nothing in common with and trying to make it work. It is about unfashion, about non-glamour, it is about genuine, honest fun. Whether it is Aunt Lil being wheeled home totally pissed in a wheelbarrow after a party down the Archway at four in the morning, with Uncle Frank effing and blinding, or whether it is Ray singing his heart out into a microphone that has no cord . . . It is about people looking up at the stars wondering what the hell they are doing in this strange alien place, it is about our feelings, our insecurities, our pain, and our joy. In all honesty, I believe rock can change the world, and nobody does it better than the Kinks.

Oh well, Birmingham tomorrow. Looking back, I feel that I have been really fortunate. I feel rich in experience. After everyone has had their say it will be the music that will speak louder than any of us. It will outlast us all.

It's getting late. Maybe I'll have one last look downstairs to see if there are any of the guys or crew around. I can't sleep anyway. Lift, lift, come, come, come . . . aah. I press the button for the lobby. Songs poppin' in my head. 'Lazy old sun, what have you

269

done to summertime?' Ricky Nelson's 'It's Late', Soundgarden, especially 'Black Hole Sun'. Ding . . . Lobby . . . Doors open. Aren't many people around, wonder if there's anyone in the bar . . . in the bar . . . no one. So I'll walk to the bar next door where there's a CD juke-box. At the juke-box sits a girl with long black hair. She seems lost in the music. After a while the music stops. She looks up, puts more money in the juke-box. In between selections I go to the bar and buy a beer. In the background 'Maybe Baby' by Buddy Holly and the Crickets starts up. I shake my head and smile, quietly thinking to myself, it's funny, I always did love that record. Mmmm . . . Manchester girls, they always were the prettiest.

I pick up my beer and find a quiet corner. In my mind I think back and imagine myself in my forty-ninth year standing in front of that funny little house in Denmark Terrace where I was born, where I grew up. My life has taken me all over the world and I have met a strange assortment of people from all walks of life. How things have changed. All my old friends now gone, my family dispersed. I see myself as a little boy, running mischievously into the sweet shop, arse hanging out of my trousers, a scruffy, cheeky little kid looking for adventure. There is a part of that little boy that has remained with me. He has always been my best friend. That part of me has never changed. He's always there to remind me of the endless possibilities that exist in the world, all that life has to offer. We can be anything or anyone we want to be, but we can never escape our real selves. Maybe I just never grew up. That ageless child, always looking, always inquisitively lost in the joy of the moment. I wonder where he will take me tomorrow. Climbing on the back of a truck, chasing a ball, looking up a young girl's skirt, seeking out old friends that he's yet to meet.

ETERNAL

Memories remembered, access to the past obtained.
Dissolving images leave my mind emotionally freed.
Ties of tomorrow stretch their sinuous arms towards me.
I glance at today, with the benevolence of a father,
Yet with the innocence of a child.
I move my Will, surely, securely
towards the Future . . . Towards the Eternal . . . .

Courtesy of Doug Hinman, author of *You Really Got Me: An Illustrated World Discography of the Kinks, 1964-1993* (1994, with Jason Brabazon). Only original releases are listed.

UK Singles
Pye

7N 15611	**Long Tall Sally/I Took my Baby Home** *Feb 1964*
7N 15639	**You Still Want Me/You Do Something to Me** *Apr 1964*
7N 15673	**You Really Got Me/It's Alright** *Aug 1964*
7N 15714	**All Day and All of the Night/I Gotta Move** *Oct 1964*
7N 15759	**Tired of Waiting for You/Come on Now** *Jan 1965*
7N 15813	**Ev'rybody's Gonna be Happy/Who'll be the Next in Line** *Mar 1965*
7N 15854	**Set Me Free/I Need You** *May 1965*
7N 15919	**See My Friends/Never Met a Girl like You Before** *Jul 1965*
7N 15981	**Till the End of the Day/Where Have All the Good Times Gone** *Nov 1965*
7N 17064	**Dedicated Follower of Fashion/Sittin' on my Sofa** *Feb 1966*
7N 17100	**A Well Respected Man/Milk Cow Blues (Export only)** *Apr 1966*
7N 17125	**Sunny Afternoon/I'm not Like Everybody Else** *Jun 1966*
7N 17222	**Dead End Street/Big Black Smoke** *Nov 1966*
7N 17314	**Mr Pleasant/This is Where I Belong (Export only)** *Apr 1967*
7N 17321	**Waterloo Sunset/Act Nice and Gentle** *May 1967*
7N 17356	**Death of a Clown/Love Me till the Sun Shines (Dave Davies)** *Jul 1967*
7N 17400	**Autumn Almanac/Mr Pleasant** *Oct 1967*
7N 17405	**Autumn Almanac/David Watts (Export only)** *Oct 1967*
7N 17429	**Suzanah's Still Alive/Funny Face (Dave Davies)** *Nov 1967*
7N 17468	**Wonderboy/Pretty Polly** *Apr 1968*
7N 17514	**Lincoln County/There is no Life Without Love (Dave Davies)** *Aug 1968*
7N 17573	**Days/She's Got Everything** *Jun 1968*

7N 17678	**Hold My Hand/Creeping Jean (Dave Davies)** *Jan 1969*
7N 17724	**Plastic Man/King Kong** *Mar 1969*
7N 17776	**Drivin'/Mindless Child of Motherhood** *Jun 1969*
7N 17812	**Shangrila/This Man He Weeps Tonight** *Sep 1969*
7N 17865	**Victoria/Mr Churchill Says** *Dec 1969*
7N 17961	**Lola/Berkeley Mews** *Jun 1970*
7N 45016	**Apeman/Rats** *Nov 1970*

RCA (Victor)

RCA 2211	**Supersonic Rocket Ship/You Don't Know My Name** *May 1972*
RCA 2299	**Celluloid Heroes/Hot Potatoes** *Nov 1972*
RCA 2387	**Sitting in the Midday Sun/One of the Survivors** *Jun 1973*
RCA 2418	**Sweet Lady Genevieve/Sitting in my Hotel** *Sep 1973*
LPBO 5015	**Mirror of Love/Cricket (French import)** *Apr 1974*
LPBO 5042	**Mirror of Love/He's Evil** *Jul 1974*
RCA 2478	**Holiday Romance/Shepherds of the Nation** *Oct 1974*
RCA 2546	**Ducks on the Wall/Rush Hour Blues** *Apr 1975*
RCA 2567	**You Can't Stop the Music/Have another Drink** *May 1975*
RCM 1	**No More Looking Back/Jack, the Idiot/The Hard Way** *Jan 1976*
PB 9620	**Doing the Best for You/Wild Man (Dave Davies)** *Dec 1980*

Arista

ARISTA 97	**Sleepwalker/Full Moon** *Mar 1977*
ARISTA 114	**Juke Box Music/Sleepless Night** *Jun 1977*
ARISTA 153	**Father Christmas/Prince of the Punks** *Dec 1977*
ARIST 189	**Rock 'n' Roll Fantasy/Artificial Light** *May 1978*
ARIST 199	**Live Life/In a Foreign Land** *Jul 1978*
ARIST 210	**Black Messiah/Misfits** *Sep 1978*

ARIST 240	(Wish I Could Fly Like) Superman/Low Budget *Jan 1979*
ARIST 12240	(Wish I Could Fly Like) Superman/Low Budget (12") *Jan 1979*
ARIST 12240	(Wish I Could Fly Like) Superman/Low Budget (12") (remix) *March 1979*
ARIST 300	Moving Pictures/In a Space *Sep 1979*
ARIST 321	Pressure/National Health *Nov 1979*
ARIST 415	Better Things/Massive Reductions (with KINKS 1) *Jun 1981*
KINKS 1	Lola/David Watts *Jun 1981*
ARIST 415	Better Things/Massive Reductions *Jul 1981*
ARIST 502	Come Dancing/Noise *Nov 1982*
ARIST 12502	Come Dancing/Noise (12") *Nov 1982*
ARIST 524	Don't Forget to Dance/ Bernadette *Jun 1983*
ARIST 12524	Don't Forget to Dance/ Bernadette (12") *Sep 1983*
ARIST 560	State of Confusion/Heart of Gold/Lola/20th Century Man *Mar 1984*
ARIST 12560	State of Confusion/Heart of Gold/Lola/20th Century Man (12") *Mar 1984*

Konk (Arista)

ARIST 426	Predictable/Back to Front *Oct 1981*
ARIPD 426	Predictable/Back to Front *Oct 1981* (picture disc)

Arista

ARIST 577	Good Day/Too Hot *Aug 1984*
ARIST 12577	Good Day/Too Hot/Don't Forget to Dance (12") *Aug 1984*
ARIST 617	Do It Again/Guilty *Apr 1985*
ARIST 12617	Do It Again/Guilty; Summer's Gone (12") *Apr 1985*

London

LON119	How Are You/Killing Time *Dec 1986*
LONX119	How Are You/Killing Time; Welcome To Sleazy Town (12") *Dec 1986*
LON132	Lost And Found/Killing Time *Feb 1987*
LONX132	Lost And Found/Killing Time; The Ray Davies Interview (12") *Feb 1987*

LON165	The Road/Art Lover (live) *May 1988*
LONX165	The Road/Art Lover (live); Come Dancing (live) (12") *May 1988*
LON239	Down All The Days (Till 1992)/ You Really Got Me (live) *Sep 1989*
LONX239	Down All The Days (Till 1992)/ You Really Got Me (live); Entertainment (12") *Sep 1989*
LONCD239	Down All The Days (Till 1992)/ You Really Got Me (live)/ Entertainment (CD single) *Sep 1989*
LON250	How Do I Get Close/Down All The Days (Till 1992) *Feb 1990*
LONX250	How Do I Get Close/Down All The Days (Till 1992); War Is Over (12") *Feb 1990*
LONCD250	How Do I Get Close/War Is Over (CD single) *Feb 1990*

Columbia

6589922	Scattered/Hatred (A Duet)/ Days (CD single) *Jul 1993*
6599227	Only A Dream/Somebody Stole My Car *Nov 1993*
6599222	Only A Dream/Somebody Stole My Car; Babies (CD single) *Nov 1993*

US Singles

Cameo

C308	Long Tall Sally/I Took My Baby Home *Apr 1964*
C345	Long Tall Sally/I Took My Baby Home (reissued) *Dec 1964*

Reprise

0306	You Really Got Me/It's Alright *Aug 1964*
0334	All Day and All of the Night/I Gotta Move *Oct 1964*
0337	Tired of Waiting for You/Come on Now *Feb 1965*
0379	Set Me Free/I Need You *May 1965*
0366	Who'll be the Next in Line/ Everybody's Gonna be Happy *Jul 1965*
0409	See My Friends/Never Met a Girl Like You Before *Sep 1965*
0420	A Well Respected Man/Such a Shame *Nov 1965*
0454	Till the End of the Day/Where Have All the Good Times Gone *Mar 1966*

0471	Dedicated Follower of Fashion/ Sittin' on my Sofa *May 1966*
0497	Sunny Afternoon/I'm not Like Everybody Else *Jul 1966*
0540	Dead End Street/Big Black Smoke *Dec 1966*
0587	Mr Pleasant/Harry Rag *Jun 1967*
0612	Waterloo Sunset/Two Sisters *Aug 1967*
0614	Death of a Clown/Love Me till the Sun Shines (Dave Davies) *Aug 1967*
0647	Autumn Almanac/David Watts *Nov 1967*
0660	Suzanah's Still Alive/Funny Face (Dave Davies) *Feb 1968*
0691	Wonderboy/Polly *May 1968*
0762	Days/She's Got Everything *Aug 1968*
0806	Starstruck/Picture Book *Feb 1969*
0847	Village Green Preservation Society/Do You Remember Walter? *Aug 1969*
0863	Victoria/Brainwashed *Dec 1969*
0930	Lola/Mindless Child of Motherhood *Jul 1970*
0979	Apeman/Rats *Dec 1970*
1017	God's Children/The Way Love Used to Be *Jul 1971*
1094	King Kong/Waterloo Sunset *May 1972*

Warner Brothers

7-29509	Love Gets You/One Night with You (Dave Davies) *Sep 1983*
7-29425	Mean Disposition/Cold Winter (Dave Davies) *Nov 1983*

RCA (Victor)

74-0620	20th Century Man/Skin and Bone *Dec 1971*
74-0807	Supersonic Rocketship/You Don't Know My Name *Jul 1972*
74-0852	Celluloid Heroes/Hot Potatoes *Oct 1972*
74-0940	One of the Survivors/ Scrapheap City *May 1973*
LPBO 5001	Sitting in the Midday Sun/ Sweet Lady Genevieve *Aug 1973*
APBO 0275	Money Talks/Here Comes Flash *May 1974*
PB 10019	Mirror of Love/He's Evil *Aug 1974*
PB 10121	Preservation/Salvation Road *Dec 1974*
PB 10251	Starmaker/Ordinary People *May 1975*

PB 10551	I'm in Disgrace/The Hard Way *Dec 1975*
PB 12089	Imagination's Real/Wild Man (Dave Davies) *Sep 1980*
PB 12147	Doing the Best for You/ Nothing More to Lose (Dave Davies) *Nov 1980*

Arista

AS 0240	Sleepwalker/Full Moon *Mar 1977*
AS 0247	Jukebox Music/Life Goes On *May 1977*
AS 0290	Father Christmas/Prince of the Punks *Dec 1977*
AS 0342	A Rock 'n' Roll Fantasy/Live Life *Jun 1978*
AS 0342	A Rock 'n' Roll Fantasy/Get Up *Oct 1978*
AS 0372	Live Life/Black Messiah *Oct 1978*
AS 0409	(Wish I Could Fly Like) Superman/Low Budget *Mar 1979*
CP 700	(Wish I Could Fly Like) Superman/Low Budget (12") *Mar 1979*
AS 0448	A Gallon of Gas/Low Budget *Aug 1979*
AS 0458	Catch Me Now I'm Falling/ Low Budget *Sep 1979*
AS 0541	Celluloid Heroes/Lola *Aug 1980*
AS 0577	You Really Got Me/Attitude *Nov 1980*
AS 0619	Destroyer/Back to Front *Oct 1981*
AS 0649	Better Things/Yo-Yo *Nov 1981*
AS 1049	Come Dancing/Noise *Apr 1983*
AS1-9075	Don't Forget to Dance/Young Conservatives *Aug 1983*
AS1-9309	Do It Again/Guilty *Nov 1984*
AS1-9334	Summer's Gone/Going Solo *Mar 1985*

MCA

MCA-52960	Rock and Roll Cities/Welcome To Sleazy Town *Nov 1986*
MCA-53015	Lost And Found/Killing Time *Feb 1987*
MCA-53093	How Are You/Working At The Factory *Jun 1987*
MCA-53699	How Do I Get Close/War Is Over *Nov 1989*

UK EPs
Pye

NEP 24200	*Kinksize Session:* I've Gotta Go Now/I've Got that Feeling/

Things are Getting Better/
Louie Louie *Nov 1964*

NEP 24203 *Kinksize Hits:* You Really Got
Me/It's Alright/All Day and All
of the Night/I Gotta Move *Jan
1965*

NEP 24214 *The Hitmakers* (various): You
Really Got Me *Jun 1965*

NEP 24221 *Kwyet Kinks:* Wait Till the
Summer/Such a Shame/A Well
Respected Man/Don't You Fret
Sep 1965

NEP 24242 *The Hitmakers* (various): Tired
of Waiting *Feb 1966*

NEP 24243 *The Hitmakers* (various): All Day
and All of the Night *Feb 1966*

NEP 24258 *Dedicated Kinks:* Dedicated
Follower of Fashion/Till the
End of the Day/See My
Friends/Set Me Free *Jul 1966*

NEP 24289 *Dave Davies Hits:* Death of a
Clown/Love Me till the Sun
Shines/Susannah's Still Alive/
Funny Face *Apr 1968*

NEP 24296 *The Kinks:* David Watts/Two
Sisters/Lazy Old Sun/Situation
Vacant *Apr 1968*

7NX 8001 God's Children/The Way Love
Used to Be/Moments/Dreams
(stereo) *Apr 1971*

PRT
KD 1 You Really Got Me/All Day
and All of the Night/Misty
Water *Sep 1983*

KDL 1 You Really Got Me/All Day
and All of the Night/Misty
Water (12") *Sep 1983*

KPD 1 You Really Got Me/ All Day
and All of the Night/ Misty
Water (pic. disc) *Sep 1983*

Konk/Grapevine
KNKD 2 *Waterloo Sunset '94 :* Waterloo
Sunset/You Really Got
Me/Elevator Man/On The
Outside *Oct 1993*

UK LPs
Pye (All the original LPs excepting reissues and
compilations have been reissued on CD by
Castle Communications.)
NPL 18096 **The Kinks** *Sep 1964*
NPL 18108 **Hitmakers** (various) *Dec 1964*
NPL 18112 **Kinda Kinks** *Mar 1965*
NPL 18115 **Hitmakers Vol. 2** (various) *Mar
1965*
NPL 18127 **Hitmakers Vol. 3** (various) *Nov
1965*

NPL 18131 **The Kinks Kontroversy** *Dec 1965*
NPL 18144 **Hitmakers Vol. 4** (various) *Mar
1966*
MAL 612 **Well Respected Kinks** *Sep 1966*
NSPL 18149 **Face to Face** *Oct 1966*
NSPL 18193 **Something Else by the Kinks**
Sep 1967
MAL 716 **Sunny Afternoon** *Nov 1967*
NSPL 18191 **Live at the Kelvin Hall** *Jan 1968*
NSPL 18233 **Village Green Preservation
Society** *Nov 1968*
MAL(S) 1100 **Kinda Kinks** *Nov 1968*
NSPL 18317 **Arthur** *Oct 1969*
NPL 18326 **The Kinks (2LP)** *Feb 1970*
NSPL 18359 **Lola vs Powerman and the
Moneygoround: part one** *Nov
1970*
NSPL 18365 **Percy** *Mar 1971*

RCA
SF 8243 **Muswell Hillbillies** *Nov 1971*
DPS 2035 **Everybody's in Showbiz** *Sep
1972*
SF 8392 **Preservation** *Nov 1973*
LPL2 5040 **Preservation Act 2** *Aug 1974*
SF 8411 **Soap Opera** *May 1975*
RS 1028 **Schoolboys in Disgrace** *Jan 1976*
RS 1059 **Celluloid Heroes** *Jun 1976*
PL 13603 **Dave Davies** *Sep 1980*
RCALP 6005 **Glamour (Dave Davies)** *Oct
1981*

Dave Davies' two LPs on RCA were later
reissued together in 1992 on a single CD as
**Dave Davies and Glamour (Mau Mau
MAUCD 617)** with the omission of the track
'Move Over'.

Arista
SPARTY 1002 **Sleepwalker** *Mar 1977*
SPART 1055 **Misfits** *May 1978*
SPART 1099 **Low Budget** *Sep 1979*
DARTY 6 **One for the Road (2LP)** *Jul 1980*
SPART 1171 **Give the People What They
Want** *Jan 1982*

PRT
KINK 1 **The Kinks Greatest Hits**
(withdrawn January 1984,
included previously unissued
material) *Dec 1983*
PYL 6012 **The Album That Never Was**
(Dave Davies) *Oct 1987*
(This compilation of Dave's 60's recordings was
also reissued on CD).

Arista
405275 **State of Confusion (German
import)** *Jun 1983*

206685	**Word of Mouth** *Nov 1984*
302778	**Come Dancing with the Kinks/ The Best of the Kinks 1977- 1986** *Oct 1986*

London

LONLP 27	**Think Visual** *Nov 1986*
LONCD 27	**Think Visual (CD)** *Nov 1986*
LONLP 49	**The Road (The Kinks Live)** *May 1987*
LONCD 49	**The Road (The Kinks Live) (CD)** *May 1987*
828.165-1	**UK Jive** *Oct 1989*
828.165-1	**UK Jive (CD)** *Oct 1989*

Columbia

4724892	**Phobia (CD only)** *Apr 1993*

Konk/Grapevine

KNKLP 1	**To The Bone** *Oct 1994*
KNKCD 1	**To The Bone (CD)** *Oct 1994*

US LPs

Reprise (The first 4 LPs have been reconfigured and reissued on CD by Rhino Records. Reprise has reissued *The Live Kinks* through *The Kink Kronikles* on CD.)

RS 6143	**You Really Got Me** *Nov 1964*
RS 6158	**Kinks-Size** *Mar 1965*
RS 6173	**Kinda Kinks** *Aug 1965*
RS 6184	**Kinkdom** *Nov 1965*
RS 6197	**The Kinks Kontroversy** *Mar 1966*
RS 6217	**The Kinks Greatest Hits** *Aug 1966*
RS 6228	**Face to Face** *Dec 1966*
RS 6260	**The Live Kinks** *Aug 1967*
RS 6279	**Something Else by the Kinks** *Jan 1968*
RS 6327	**Village Green Preservation Soviety** *Jan 1969*
RS 6366	**Arthur** *Oct 1969*
RS 6423	**Lola vs Powerman and the Moneygoround: Part One** *Dec 1970*
2XS 6454	**The Kink Kronikles (2LP)** *Mar 1972*
MS 2127	**The Great Lost Kinks Album** *Jan 1973*

RCA (All original RCA LPs through *Schoolboys in Disgrace* have been reissued on CD by Rhino Records.)

LSP 4644	**Muswell Hillbillies** *Nov 1971*
VSP 6065	**Everybody's in Showbiz (2LP)** *Aug 1972*
LPL1-5002	**Preservation** *Nov 1973*
CPL2-5040	**Preservation Act II (2LP)** *May 1974*

LPL1-5081	**Soap Opera** *Apr 1975*
LPL1-5102	**Schoolboys in Disgrace** *Nov 1975*
APL1-1743	**Greatest – Celluloid Heroes** *May 1976*
AFL1-3603	**Dave Davies** *Jul 1980*
AFL1-3520	**Second Time Around** *Aug 1980*
AFL1-4036	**Glamour (Dave Davies)** *Jul 1981*

Arista

AL 4106	**Sleepwalker** *Feb 1977*
AL 4167	**Misfits** *May 1978*
AB 4240	**Low Budget** *Jul 1979*
A2L-8401	**One for the Road (2LP)** *Jun 1980*
A2L-8609	**One for the Road (2LP)** *Mar 1982*
AL 9567	**Give the People What They Want** *Aug 1981*
AL 9617	**State of Confusion** *May 1983*

Warner Brothers

23917-1	**Chosen People (Dave Davies)** *Aug 1983*

Arista

AL8-8264	**Word of Mouth** *Nov 1984*
AL11-8428	**Come Dancing with the Kinks/ The Best of the Kinks 1977- 1986** *Jun 1986*

London

MCA-5822	**Think Visual** *Nov 1986*
MCAD-5822	**Think Visual (CD)** *Nov 1986*
MCA-42107	**The Road** *Jan 1988*
MCAD-42107	**The Road (CD)** *Jan 1988*
MCA-6337	**UK Jive** *Nov 1989*
MCAD-6337	**UK Jive (CD)** *Nov 1989*
MCAD-10338	**Lost and Found (1986-89) (CD only)** *Aug 1991*

Columbia

44K-74050	**Did Ya (CD only)** *Oct 1991*
CK 48724	**Phobia (CD only)** *Apr 1993*

Note: DD in the index stands for Dave Davies; RD for Ray Davies; K for the Kinks